FROM ALIENATION TO FORMS OF LIFE

T0326751

From Alienation to Forms of Life

The Critical Theory of Rahel Jaeggi

EDITED BY AMY ALLEN AND EDUARDO MENDIETA

The Pennsylvania State University Press
University Park, Pennsylvania

Library of Congress Cataloging-in-Publication Data

Names: Allen, Amy, editor. | Mendieta, Eduardo, editor. | Jaeggi, Rahel.
Title: From alienation to forms of life : the critical theory of Rahel Jaeggi / edited by Amy Allen and Eduardo Mendieta.
Description: University Park, Pennsylvania : The Pennsylvania State University Press, [2018] | Includes bibliographical references and index.
Summary: "An introduction to the work of critical theorist Rahel Jaeggi for English-speaking audiences. Essays by scholars in Continental and analytic philosophy assess and critique her efforts to revitalize critical theory"—Provided by publisher.
Identifiers: LCCN 2018010006 | ISBN 9780271078458 (pbk. : alk. paper)
Subjects: LCSH: Jaeggi, Rahel. | Critical theory.
Classification: LCC HM479.J34 F76 2018 | DDC 300.1—dc23
LC record available at https://lccn.loc.gov/2018010006

Copyright © 2018 The Pennsylvania State University
All rights reserved
Printed in the United States of America
Published by The Pennsylvania State University Press, University Park, PA 16802-1003

The Pennsylvania State University Press is a member of the Association of University Presses.

It is the policy of The Pennsylvania State University Press to use acid-free paper. Publications on uncoated stock satisfy the minimum requirements of American National Standard for Information Sciences—Permanence of Paper for Printed Library Material, ANSI Z39.48-1992.

CONTENTS

ACKNOWLEDGMENTS

First and foremost, we want to express our gratitude to Rahel Jaeggi for agreeing to have her work meet the scholarly scrutiny of some exacting and original thinkers. Next, we want to thank all our symposium participants for their superior contributions. The symposium that gave birth to this volume was generously supported by the Department of Philosophy, the Rock Ethics Institute, and the Max Kade Foundation at Penn State University—we are extremely thankful for their support. We are especially thankful to Daniel Loick, who delivered a very thoughtful commentary and who agreed to contribute a chapter at the last minute. Joel Feinberg also stepped in during a busy time to translate Daniel's text quickly and beautifully. We also thank Alexis Dianda, editor of the *Graduate Faculty Philosophy Journal*, for permission to reprint the dialogue among Amy Allen, Rahel Jaeggi, and Eva von Redecker, which appeared in volume 37, number 2, 2016. We want to thank our Penn State University graduate students who served as chairs and timekeepers at the symposium and who introduced all the speakers: Tiffany Tsantoulas, Emma Velez, and Nicole Yokum. This volume made it to print due to the diligent and efficient eyes and fingers of Kris McClain, who helped with the editing of the entire manuscript. We also had amazing logistical support from Jason Traverse, who coordinated travel, hotel, and meal arrangements. Finally, we want to thank our editor, Kendra Boileau, for her enthusiasm, support, and patience. We hope this is the beginning of a long and productive partnership.

Amy Allen and Eduardo Mendieta

STATE COLLEGE, PA

CHAPTER 1

Introduction

Amy Allen and Eduardo Mendieta

1. A LEADING VOICE IN NEW CRITICAL THEORY

Rahel Jaeggi is a leading voice of the new generation of critical theorists working in the rich and storied tradition of the Frankfurt School. Her major publications include *Entfremdung* (2005), published in English as *Alienation* (Columbia University Press, 2014), and *Kritik von Lebensformen* (2013), of which the English translation, *Critique of Forms of Life*, is soon to be published by Harvard University Press. In addition, Prof. Jaeggi has edited and coedited several volumes, including, most recently, *Nach Marx: Philosophie, Kritik, Praxis* and *Karl Marx: Perspectiven der Gesellschaftskritik* (both coedited with Daniel Loick and published in 2013), and she has published numerous essays and book chapters. Throughout this substantial and wide-ranging body of work, Prof. Jaeggi has inventively reappropriated key concepts of Hegelian-Marxist social philosophy, reading those concepts through the lens of such thinkers as Adorno, Heidegger, and Dewey while simultaneously putting them into dialogue with contemporary analytic philosophy. Her work offers a forceful and compelling articulation of the left-Hegelian tradition of critical theory, one that demonstrates how the core concepts and methodological approaches of that tradition can be updated, stripped of their dubious metaphysical baggage, and made fruitful for critical theory in the twenty-first century.

2. ON THE METONYMY OF THE FRANKFURT SCHOOL

Rahel Jaeggi's work can only be properly understood against the background of the "critical theory" of the "Frankfurt School." The "Frankfurt School" is in fact a metonymy for "critical theory," a rich and generative interdisciplinary research agenda and theoretical paradigm that was launched nearly a century ago in 1923, when the Institute for Social Research was endowed and established in Frankfurt am Main. Since its birth, the Frankfurt School's philosophical agenda and orientation have been neither unified nor homogenous, and its interdisciplinary agenda has continually evolved as it has taken on the challenges of its times. Few movements, schools, or philosophical movements exemplify the Hegelian insight—that "philosophy is its time comprehended in thought"—as has the Frankfurt School.

Thus it would be instructive to briefly disentangle both the conceptual and material history of this "school." As Rolf Wiggershaus notes in his massive, comprehensive, and indispensable history of the Frankfurt School,[1] it is a "school" in virtue of the conceptual and material, intellectual and institutional, matrices that have held together its philosophical attitude, method, and paradigm. Following Wiggershaus, we identify the core features of the Frankfurt School as the following: First, a shared institutional framework to bring together research agendas and intellectual works. There would be no "Frankfurt School" without the *Institut für Sozialforschung*, the Institute for Social Research. Over nearly the last century, both the institute and Goethe University in Frankfurt with which it is institutionally linked have remained geographical points of reference. Second, there were and there are "charismatic," "inspirational," and "coalescing" figures who lend a name and personality to the project: Horkheimer, Adorno, Marcuse, Habermas, Honneth, and arguably now a new generation of scholars, which includes Jaeggi. Third, there were and there are "manifestos" that (re)articulate the agenda of the school in the light of contemporary challenges. Fourth, the school, however, is not a mere conglomeration of thinkers and researchers under a shared institutional roof; they are also thinkers who share a "conceptual paradigm," a way of asking questions and aiming to answer them that share some "family" resemblances. The name for that paradigm is "critical theory," which already in its name announces its basic orientation: a philosophical refusal of conceptual conciliations or accommodations with the status quo and the subordination of theory to any affirmation of extant reality. Still, what "critical theory" is and how it should be conducted are the objects of sustained and intensive reflection by members of the school. The Frankfurt School remains from its birth hyperreflexive of its own relationship to theory, to what counts as critical and traditional theory, and to how the latest developments in the natural and social-historical sciences can be marshaled to enhance the critical attitude toward both social reality and theoretical reflection on it. Fifth, a school is also held together by a venue or venues for its projects and results. The Institute for Social Research has had its publication venues in the form of the *Zeitschrift für Sozialforschung*, and later through its affiliation with Suhrkamp Verlag, which became the main venue for the publications of many of the affiliates of the Frankfurt School, members of the school disseminated their research and studies. Building on Wiggershaus, we could add two additional elements that give further warrant for the designator of "school" to the Frankfurt School: Sixth, and perhaps just as important as any of the factors already mentioned, the members of this school all engage in immanent, critical, generative, and transformative appropriations of the philosophical, sociological, and political canon in Western thought. Each figure and generation of the Frankfurt School has offered elucidating and provocative readings of key figures, beginning with Homer and Plato, Kant and Hegel, Marx and Freud, and culminating more recently with the works of Niklas Luhmann, John Rawls, Michael Tomasello, Hannah Arendt, and Michel Foucault, to mention only a few recent figures. To paraphrase Whitehead's words, philosophy is always a critical footnote to those who came before us but at the same time is one that not only allows us to understand better what the original thinker aimed to think but also challenges us to think our own thoughts. At the very least, the Frankfurt School is also a school of some of the most illuminating critical readings of the Western intellectual canon. And finally, seventh, a school is a school if it is so recognized abroad. The closeness of home only breeds neglect and misrecognition. Because of the exile of its founding members and the cosmopolitanism of its later generations, the Frankfurt School has developed an international reception that is unparalleled by any single individual, tradition, or movement. In fact, in its latest iterations and developments, the Frankfurt School has been advanced by individuals who are from neither Frankfurt nor even Germany. The school has become truly international, turning Frankfurt into not a geographical reference point but a state of mind, an intellectual and philosophical commitment. Without question, however, the Frankfurt School and its theoretical paradigm, critical theory, has retained a modicum of continuity over what some refer to as four generations of critical theorists.[2]

While the "Frankfurt School" may have been born on February 3, 1923, when the Institute for Social Research was established, it is often claimed that "critical theory" was born in 1931, when Horkheimer delivered his 1931 inaugural lecture as the new director of the Institute for Social Research, "Traditional and Critical Theory."[3] Interestingly, in this lecture, Horkheimer did not use the term "critical" in an affirmative sense, although he did make reference to "uncritical" and "critical" elements within Hegelian philosophy. Nonetheless, Horkheimer's "The Present Situation of Social Philosophy and the Tasks of an Institute for Social Research"[4] did articulate clearly the interdisciplinary and radical character of its research agenda, even if in rather Aesopian and conciliatory terms. In this lecture, Horkheimer is at pains to argue that what the institute should be doing is precisely taking up both the oldest and yet most pressing issues. He argued that the institute should be guided by "the question of the connection between the economic life of society, the psychical development of individuals, and the changes in the realm of culture in the narrower sense (to which belong not only the so-called intellectual elements, such as science, art, and religion, but also law, customs, fashion, public opinion, sports, leisure activities, lifestyle, etc.)," and yet, taking up this three-pronged research agenda, he exposed investigators to "nothing [else] but a reformulation—on the basis of the new problem constellation, consistent with the methods at our disposal and with the level of our knowledge—of the old question concerning the connection of particular existence and universal Reason, of reality and Idea, of life and Spirit."[5] Here "critical" appears in the guise of "reformulation on the basis of a new problem constellation," which is summarized in terms of the old antinomies of individual existence and universal reason, reality and the concept, object and subject, or to use the language of Jaeggi, unalienated agency and nonpathological lifeworld.

From Martin Jay, who offered the earliest intellectual history of the Frankfurt School;[6] Raymond Geuss, a British philosopher who provided one of the most acute and succinct overviews of the very idea of a critical theory;[7] and Stephen Eric Bronner, a political philosopher who has written on critical theory and its theorists,[8] we can gather a set of key terms, ideas, and approaches that give coherence to the paradigm called "critical theory." This paradigm has the following characteristics: an aversion to closed philosophical systems (and Habermas is not an exception, as his *Theory of Communicative Action* is not a system but a research project that is underwritten by a "fallibilistic" and "reconstructive" methodology); a critical but forward-looking appropriation of thinkers and social science research agendas; a philosophical focus on the subjectivity, interiority, and agency of social and moral agents; a materialist orientation that is attentive to the economic, political, legal, gendered, ethnic, and of course social conditions of agency and subjectivity; a positive but critical appropriation of enlightenment and bourgeois rationalism, which has either turned into ideology or has turned against itself in forms of irrationalisms and aestheticism; a resolute commitment to think through the "dialectical mediations" among the material conditions of the reproduction of social existence, the way in which these modes of existence are reflected in subjective and agential attitudes, and the ways in which they are captured both in "culture" and "social theory"; a complex and ambivalent articulation of modernity that critically appropriates the crucial insights of the great "masters of suspicion"—namely, Marx, Freud, and Nietzsche; and perhaps most importantly, a steadfast refusal to identify or assimilate any form of freedom with the extant institutional arrangements that claim to deliver any modicum of freedom or nonalienation. All these themes or research agendas could be gathered under two basic headings: moral autonomy and the becoming, or history, of freedom, both of which are united in the self-consciousness of a society that is able to direct its own moral development. At the core of critical theory is the rejection of all positivisms, empiricisms, pseudopragmatisms, and naturalisms and the affirmation of self-reflexive critical theory at the service of social emancipation, which has a commitment to the morally autonomous, though not autarkic, subject, who is part of a social project that aims at both individual and collective dignity.

The unruly expansiveness of the category of critical theory is both exhilarating and bewildering. We twenty-first-century critical theorists are alike inspired and challenged children trying to decipher who were our intellectual mothers and fathers but also how, whether, and to what extent we want to claim their bequest. The "school," "paradigm," "tradition," "method," or "movement," sheltered under "critical theory," however, claims us, because it is guided by a set of imperatives. We are standing at the foot of the scaffolding of a great edifice still under construction, attempting to articulate the common meaning that we invoke in that name: critical theory. *From Alienation to Forms of Life: The Critical Theory of Rahel Jaeggi* is a contribution not only to the appropriation of that history but also to the articulation of its future(s).

3. FROM EXTERNALIZATION TO REIFICATION TO ALIENATION

Alienation and reification are pillar concepts of critical theory, and they have been at the heart of the Frankfurt School's theoretical innovations. Yet the terms have a vexed and confusing history, as they are part of a cluster of related concepts, each with subtly different connotations and valances. Thus we have *Entäusserung* (externalization), *Entfremdung* (alienation), *Verfremdung* (estrangement), *Verdinglichung* (reification), and *Verschalingung* (objectification). To this list, we would have to add *fetish* and *fetishization*. As Ernst Bloch noted in his two-volume *Verfremdungen*, the word *Entfremden* has an old etymology and history in German, having been applied in the context of commerce, which competed or was used in tandem with *veralieneren*, which combined elements of Latin's *alienare* and the German prefix *ver* to indicate the transformation of a noun into a verb, or transitive action.[9] If we follow Walter Kaufmann's genealogy of the concept, the locus classicus for the emergence of alienation and reification as philosophical concepts are Hegel's *Phenomenology of Spirit*, Karl Marx's *1844 Philosophical-Economic Manuscripts*, Georg Lukács's *History and Class Consciousness*, and Erich Fromm's *Marx's Concept of Man*.[10] Insofar as critical theory is an appropriation of left Hegelianism and elements of Western Marxism (Lukács, Korsch, Gramsci), it has also contended with the centrality of alienation as a concept that gives a critical edge to its analysis of society and processes of individuation and subjectification.

Jaeggi's *Alienation* is a superlative contribution to the elucidation and reactivation of this key concept. In the first section of this book, Jaeggi offers a conceptual analysis of alienation that aims at its reconstruction, which for her means articulating what is useful and illuminating in the concept and how it can be transformed and renewed in light of recent developments in social philosophy. Her argument proceeds through close readings of classic discussions of alienation from Rousseau and Marx through Heidegger to Theunissen, Tugendhat, MacIntyre, Taylor, Nagel, and Geuss. Here Jaeggi argues that we ought to understand alienation as a "relation of relationlessness."[11] Alienation, as a critical concept, aims to diagnose or illuminate precisely a failure, rupture, disruption, or thwarting of the constitutive relationality of social agents, who always already are in relation to their social world and themselves. If we attend to the connotations of alienation, being alienated, or alienating, then we can note how alienation means *loss of meaning*, which is entwined with *powerlessness* and impotence, and thus, it refers to *relations of domination* that have rendered agents impotent and subordinated and to ways of being and feeling as if one were an *alien* or in a state of *alienness*, in which we are able to establish relations with neither ourselves nor others. For Jaeggi, then, *alienation* is a diagnostic concept that discloses the ways in which *self-determination* and *self-realization* have been disrupted, impeded, blocked, or hindered. The insight, more specifically, is not that alienation is the blockage or rupture of relationality. Alienation is indeed a type of relation, but one that short-circuits the return of the subject to itself and to its "proper" relationality to its social milieu. It is for this reason that Jaeggi translates and reactivates the concept of alienation by articulating it as a relationality of "relationlessness"—a form of being sundered from that which in fact "belongs together."

In part 2 of the book, Jaeggi develops four cases, culled and profiled through close readings of classic texts, in order to exemplify the ways in which alienated subjects come to live their lives as "an alien life."[12] In these readings, Jaeggi demonstrates herself a perspicacious and sensitive phenomenologist, detailing the phenomenology of alienated existence. It is not until part 3, however, that we find Jaeggi's exposition of what she takes to be still important in the concept of alienation. Here she develops the idea of alienation as "disturbed appropriation" of oneself and one's world. Jaeggi is quick and careful to clarify that she is not working with an existentialist conception of the human being, in which there is something that preexists relationality and that then is distorted or misshapen by alienation, nor is her view that the agent is capable of establishing an authentic or undistorted relation to something that could or should be transparently and authentically one's own. Rather, Jaeggi argues that hers is a "performative-constructivist" conception of social agency. By this she means that we are our actions, of which we take charge or assume authorship, and in so doing, constitute our selves in loops of directed and intentional self-appropriation. Our selfhood is never given ahead of time, nor is it ever complete. To be alienated, then, is precisely to be unable to appropriate ourselves, to make ourselves available or accessible to ourselves. Using existentialist language, we could say that it is part of the human condition to be "thrown" into a world, into "existence," and to find oneself a stranger or alien but still being at one's command, to make that world into one's world and then claim a selfhood that then inhabits that world, which can be claimed to be one's creation.

For Jaeggi, alienation is a fundamental concept of ethical theory, as it directly articulates conditions that impede the actualization of freedom. But it is also a key concept in social philosophy, as it can be used to diagnose social pathologies, as well as a foundational concept in social theory, because it can operate not only as a diagnostic but also as a "descriptive and explanatory" category.[13] Nearly half a century ago, Walter Kaufmann wrote, "Henceforth, nobody should write about alienation without first reading [Richard] Schacht's book [*Alienation*]."[14] Today, anyone who wants to think about the radical potential of the Frankfurt School's critical theory has to contend with Rahel Jaeggi's masterful and generative text. As Neuhouser writes in his introduction to *Alienation*, the book "is an astonishingly good representative of the work of an impressive new generation of German philosophers who, with roots in both of its major traditions, seem well positioned to reanimate Western philosophy."[15] We agree that this is an exemplar of the best that members of the Frankfurt School can still offer.

4. THE CRITIQUE OF FORMS OF LIFE

In her forthcoming book *Critique of Forms of Life*, Jaeggi continues her groundbreaking work in ethical theory, social philosophy, and critical social theory. Drawing on the rich legacy of left-Hegelian social theory read in conjunction with the American pragmatism of John Dewey, Jaeggi's new book seeks not only to articulate what is distinctive about the critique of forms of life but also to defend the importance of this type of critique. By forms of life, Jaeggi refers to ensembles of practices and value orientations, together with their institutional and practical manifestations, that structure and shape human cultures and communities. The plural in the phrase "form*s* of life" is central to Jaeggi's analysis, which explores conflicts among the divergent cultural forms that human life in common can take and seeks to establish criteria for the rational justification of forms of life.

On Jaeggi's view, the critique of forms of life opens up a rich field of questions in practical philosophy that are not reducible to a narrow concern with justice or correct moral action. Forms of life are normative frames of reference or orientations within which we act (morally or otherwise), hence they cannot be evaluated or justified using the tools of moral philosophy alone. Rather, a form of life is akin to the Hegelian notion of ethical life (*Sittlichkeit*), and its critique draws on a correspondingly thick ethical conceptual vocabulary. In defending the distinctiveness and importance of the critique of forms of life, Jaeggi is also thereby mounting a serious challenge to the tendency within post-Habermasian critical theory to construe normative questions in neo-Kantian terms alone. Unlike those, such as Habermas and Rawls, who are committed to what she calls "ethical abstinence"—the refusal to judge or evaluate forms of life unless they contravene universal moral norms or requirements of justice—Jaeggi questions the neo-Kantian priority of the right over the good or the supposed knife-sharp distinction between morality and ethics.[16] On Jaeggi's view, the distinction between morality and ethics itself has an ethical character; it is the expression of a particular (modern) form of life. Thus the retreat to ethical abstinence is anything but neutral—on the contrary, it is at least potentially ideological. In light of this, critical theorists are better off developing criteria for critiquing and justifying forms of life than pretending that such a task is impossible or unnecessary.

The core of Jaeggi's positive proposal is to view forms of life as "complex bundles (or ensembles) of social practices geared to solving problems that are in turn shaped by historical contexts and are normatively constituted."[17] This way of defining forms of life already contains a clue to how they can, in Jaeggi's view, be rationally justified—namely, by assessing the validity of their developmental dynamics as an ongoing social or ethical learning process, one that leads to gains in the ability to solve problems.

In part 1 of the book, Jaeggi focuses on reconstructing the concept in such a way that distinguishes forms of life from closely related concepts such as ways of life, lifestyles, customs, traditions, and cultures. This reconstructive analysis reveals forms of life to be clusters or ensembles of social practices that are characterized by a certain degree of inertia—they are both enabling conditions for human actions and the results of human activity; they are, as Jaeggi puts it, "simultaneously given and made."[18] The fact that they have been made means that they are in principle open to change, though whether or not they *should* be changed turns on the question of the normativity of forms of life, which Jaeggi takes up in part 2. Here, she analyzes the specific type of validity claims and normativity that are embedded in forms of life such that they can be subject to rational, critical evaluation. The key to this analysis is the idea that forms of life are problem-solving strategies, which means that they can be rationally evaluated in terms of how well they succeed (or fail) in solving the problems that arise within them. In part 3 of the book, Jaeggi draws out the conception of critique that has up to this point been implicit in her talk of a *critique* of forms of life. In Jaeggi's view, critique is neither merely internal nor wholly external to the forms of life that are criticized. Rather, on the model of a left-Hegelian and Marxist notion of ideology critique, critique starts from an internal perspective but transcends this starting point in an emancipatory or transformative way. Thus Jaeggi defends a model of immanent critique that "takes its orientation from the crises to which social practices and ideas can succumb, hence from the critical ferment of the self-transformation of a form of life."[19] In part 4, Jaeggi explores the notion of ethical or social learning processes that is implicit in her conception of immanent critique, drawing on the pragmatist tradition to develop a reconstructed philosophy of history according to which the development of forms of life is an open-ended but directed learning process.

The Critique of Forms of Life ends with a discussion of ethical and social learning processes that would enable critical theorists to speak of some notion of historical progress—this is the sense in which Jaeggi offers a pragmatist reconstruction of certain core themes in the philosophy of history. The English-speaking academic world eagerly awaits the publication of the translation of this important book, an event that will undoubtedly spark a new round of debates between the neo-Kantian and neo-Hegelian camps within critical theory. Many of the chapters in this volume take up themes related to the critique of forms of life based either on readings of the German text or on a partial draft of the English translation that was made available to the contributors to this volume.

5. OVERVIEW OF THIS VOLUME

In her current work, including the piece that opens our volume, "'Resistance to the Perpetual Danger of Relapse': Moral Progress and Social Change," Jaeggi seeks to further develop her understanding of progress and defend it against certain common criticisms. Resituating the question of moral progress within a more comprehensive analysis of the dynamics of social change, Jaeggi offers a further refinement of the conception of progress that underpins her critique of forms of life. Progress, for Jaeggi, is the possible (but certainly not necessary) result of a dynamic and crisis-ridden process of social change, and such processes count as progress or changes for the better just insofar as they solve problems. As Jaeggi emphasizes, this amounts to a nonteleological, pragmatist-materialist, and pluralistic concept of progress.

The six chapters that follow Jaeggi's take up various themes in Jaeggi's work. John Christman's "Decentered Social Selves: Interrogating Alienation in Conversation with Rahel Jaeggi" discusses Jaeggi's analysis of alienation, arguing that this account is incomplete without a deeper discussion of agency and reason-giving, both of which are also central to deliberative democratic practices. Christman offers a notion of self-governing rational, autonomous agency as an important companion concept to alienation. The remainder of our authors focus their attention on Jaeggi's more recent work on the critique of forms of life. Frederick Neuhouser, in his "The Normativity of Forms of Life," explores the deeply Hegelian social-philosophical roots of Jaeggi's work. Although he is in fundamental sympathy with her approach, he does raise some friendly amendments to her account of the relationship between functional and ethical modes of justification for forms of life. Max Pensky's "In Search of the Negative in Rahel Jaeggi's *Kritik von Lebensformen*" develops a more critical perspective. Pensky focuses on Jaeggi's conception of immanent critique, arguing that by attempting to combine dialectical critique with a pragmatist, melioristic, progressive understanding of social learning processes, Jaeggi's account underplays the force of the negative. Like Pensky, Rocío Zambrana also focuses on immanent critique. Comparing Jaeggi's Hegelian-Marxist critique of capitalism as a form of life with the recent work of Nancy Fraser, Zambrana argues that Fraser's account is superior to Jaeggi's insofar as it also entails a critique of coloniality—thus putting the spotlight on Jaeggi's inattention to questions of colonialism and imperialism. In his contribution, Daniel Loick contends that Jaeggi's critique of forms of life neglects the confrontational and transgressive dimensions of conflicts over forms of life. Building on Jaeggi's work, he offers an analysis of what he calls the politics of forms of life. Robin Celikates continues this focus on political struggles while also bringing the conversation back to the topic of progress in his contribution, "Forms of Life, Progress, and Social Struggle: On Rahel Jaeggi's Critical Theory." Celikates asks whether the categories of problem solving and learning processes are really apt for capturing transformations of forms of life that often take place instead through violent social struggles.

Finally, our book closes with two pieces: a further discussion of the perils and promise of the concept of progress for critical theory in the form of a conversation between Jaeggi and Amy Allen, mediated by Eva von Redecker, and Jaeggi's reply to her critics in this volume.

NOTES

1. Rolf Wiggershaus, *The Frankfurt School: Its History, Theories, and Political Significance*, trans. Michael Robertson (Cambridge: MIT Press, 1995).
2. See Max Pensky, "Third Generation Critical Theory," in *A Companion to Continental Philosophy*, ed. Simon Critchley and William R. Schroeder (Malden, MA: Blackwell, 1998), 407–16.
3. Max Horkheimer, "Traditional and Critical Theory," in *Critical Theory: Selected Essays*, ed. Max Horkheimer (New York: Continuum, 1975).
4. Max Horkheimer, "The Present Situation of Social Philosophy and the Tasks of an Institute for Social Research," in *Between Philosophy and Social Science: Selected Early Writing*, trans. G. Frederick Hunter, Matthew S. Kramer, and John Torpey (Cambridge: MIT Press, 1993).
5. Horkheimer, 11–12.
6. Martin Jay, *The Dialectical Imagination: A History of the Frankfurt School and the Institute for Social Research, 1923–1950* (Boston: Little, Brown, 1973).
7. Raymond Geuss, *The Idea of Critical Theory: Habermas and the Frankfurt School* (Cambridge: Cambridge University Press, 1981).
8. Stephen Eric Bronner, *Of Critical Theory and Its Theorists*, 2nd ed. (New York: Routledge, 2002), as well as the very useful *Critical Theory: A Very Short Introduction* (New York: Oxford University Press, 2011).
9. Bloch's 1968 two-volume *Verfremdungen* was translated into English in one volume, along with another of his writings on literature. See Ernst Bloch, *Literary Essays*, trans. Andrew Joron et al. (Stanford: Stanford University Press, 1998); for the discussion of alienation and estrangement, see pages 239–46.
10. See Walter Kaufmann, "The Inevitability of Alienation," in *Alienation*, ed. Richard Schacht (Garden City, NY: Anchor Books, 1970), xv–lviii.

11. Rahel Jaeggi, *Alienation*, trans. Frederick Neuhouser and Alan E. Smith, ed. Frederick Neuhouser (New York: Columbia University Press, 2014), 25.
12. Jaeggi, 42–50.
13. Jaeggi, xviii.
14. Kaufmann, "The Inevitability of Alienation," xvi.
15. Jaeggi, *Alienation*, xv.
16. Rahel Jaeggi, *Critique of Forms of Life*, trans. Ciaran Cronin (Cambridge: Harvard University Press, forthcoming), introduction.
17. Jaeggi, 33.
18. Jaeggi, 80.
19. Jaeggi, 192.

CHAPTER 2

"Resistance to the Perpetual Danger of Relapse"

Moral Progress and Social Change

Rahel Jaeggi

My chapter deals with a question that has repeatedly preoccupied contemporary philosophical discussion and that seems to me to be indispensable for a critical theory of society in the tradition of left-Hegelian critique in particular—namely, the question of moral progress. The questions I would like to ask are the following: How should we conceive of social change and moral progress? How do they occur? How are the two phenomena, moral progress and social change, related to each other, and how can they be evaluated—as change for the better? In fact, my thesis is already implicit in the combination of the previously mentioned aspects: (1) Moral progress, I want to claim, can be understood, assuming it can be understood, only in the context of a more comprehensive dynamic of social change. (2) Social change is, in turn, a reaction to crises; that is, it is a reaction to the pressure of problems that necessitates change. (3) Whether such change is merely a matter of alteration of circumstances or in fact constitutes "progress" in the sense of a change for the better can be seen only from the form assumed by this dynamic of change itself—although perhaps only through a negative diagnosis of phenomena of regression. My aim in these remarks is to lay the groundwork for a nonteleological, pragmatist-materialistic, and in this sense plural or multidimensional (hence, no longer ethnocentric) concept of progress.

DISCLAIMER: WHAT I'M NOT DOING

Now since the topic of progress is both inescapable and *heavily disputed*, it might be important to let you know not only what I actually *am* going to talk about but also what I will *not* be talking about.

First and most importantly, I'm neither talking about progress as an *empirical fact* nor dealing with progress as an *imperative*—to use the helpful distinction Amy Allen has suggested in her book *The End of Progress*. That is to say that neither am I claiming (or even dealing with the claim) that history is actually moving toward progress nor is my interest in reconstructing a notion of progress motivated by the idea of progress as a *positive goal*—a point of reference that informs our utopian hopes and directs our emancipatory efforts.

Rather, the intuition that has led me to reassess or rethink the topic is the intuition that we can't even make sense of our social world and its wrongs and cruelties without the notion of *regression*—and its counterpart, progress.

Adorno and Horkheimer certainly have not thought of actual world history as an irresistible and irreversible process toward the better, and yet they still couldn't do otherwise than analyze fascism in terms of *regression*. But then, it obviously makes a difference whether we judge fascism as an instance of "moral evil" (which is indisputably also true) or *analyze* it in terms of regression. The notion of regression (as it is dependent then on the notion of progress) thus adds an important dimension to what we can do as social philosophers. It is not only a fruitful concept but a concept suited for the specific character and task of a social philosophy[1] and for a critical theory that refrains from working with freestanding normative standards and instead adopts the perspective of an immanent crisis critique.[2]

Thus if I am concerned neither with progress as an empirical fact nor with progress as an imperative, it turns out that I'm rather interested in reconstructing *progress* (or even progressiveness) *as a category* and *evaluative criterion* within social philosophy. Which is disputable enough but still different from a substantial claim about the course of history.

Second, in talking about the "course of history" and evoking some idea of world history, I should clarify that I'm not asking about *global progress* but (at least this is what I start with) about local or sectorial instances of progress. That is, I'm disentangling the "idea of progress" as it has evolved in the eighteenth century from its connection with a heavyweight concept of a unified world history as we find it, most prominently, in Hegel's vision of history as a unified process with a center and with margins that, in the worst case, are situated entirely "outside of history" (and some who stay in the "waiting area of history," as Chakrabarty puts it[3]). If progress can occur with respect to this or that local institution or practice, it doesn't have to add up to progress "as such" or "for mankind"; to the contrary, progress with respect to one sphere of life may even lead to *regress* in another. Also, progress, once achieved, might *not be stable*. (Still, in the end, it might be possible to spell out the interdependencies between the different instances of progress and regression from a point of view informed by "global history," a bottom-up view rather than the unifying picture that a Hegelian account of world history might give us, at least in a superficial reading.)

Third, I start my chapter with an inquiry into *moral progress*—that is, into the *changes in the generally accepted conceptions* in terms of which we understand and evaluate morally relevant questions of social life—not only because I react to an ongoing discussion within contemporary moral and political philosophy, led, for example, by Elizabeth Anderson, Anthony Appiah, Michele Moody-Adams, Joshua Cohen, and Philip Kitcher, but also because I react to the fact that the supposed *unity or harmony between technological, scientific, social, and moral progress*, presupposed in the classical idea of progress as it has been "invented" in the eighteenth century[4] and was responsible for much of its optimism, seems to be out of the question today. That social and moral progress comes as a necessary result of technological progress, that social domination would *decrease* with the *increase* of mankind's mastery over nature—Marx is only mouthing an enlightenment axiom in this respect—is not a thesis anyone is likely to adopt. (Rather, some of us are convinced that, as Adorno/Horkheimer say, "in the unjust state of society the powerlessness and pliability of the masses increase with the quantity of goods allocated to them."[5])

The reaction to this is most often to give up the connection at all and to investigate into "moral progress" as an isolated phenomenon. If this now is my starting point as well, my chapter will (tentatively and cautiously) *widen* the perspective again in order to conceive of social change (and progress) as a multifactorial process (and, as it is, in a somehow materialistic-pragmatist spirit).

My chapter starts by spelling out the question or the set of questions involved in the idea of progress as a change for the better, suggesting that we should investigate the *form of change* here rather than its content (section 1), then discusses various (and unsatisfying) answers to the character of moral changes (section 2); in the next section (section 3), I then suggest an understanding of moral change that is embedded in a wider range of social changes. After discussing how these changes occur as results of a certain kind of mismatch (section 4), I sketch out a dynamic and crisis-driven understanding of social change before coming back to the question of how to evaluate the changes (section 5).

1. THE QUESTION CONCERNING MORAL PROGRESS

What led to the demise of the institution of slavery? How is it that—notwithstanding all the problems of implementation and enforcement—marital rape is today regarded as a crime that is subject to legal prosecution, whereas for centuries it was considered to be the self-evident right of a husband to make his wife "compliant" even against her will and if necessary by force? And how can one explain that beating children, which until relatively recently was considered to be an obvious educational measure, is today frowned upon in our societies and is subject to legal sanctions, even though it has not disappeared entirely?

In recent years, these and similar changes have received increasing philosophical attention and have been studied under the heading of "moral progress."[6] Notwithstanding the reservations that are now common in philosophy and in "real life" about the notion of general (or *global*) social and moral progress, there seems to be a relatively broad consensus about such individual and restricted (*local* or sectorial) instances of change. Only very few authors do *not* regard the developments described as positive. And for all the skepticism, there is a pronounced tendency to evaluate developments that would annul the state of affairs achieved as a result of a kind of *relapse*. One is tempted to say with Adorno, "What at this time should be understood by the term 'progress' one knows *vaguely, but precisely*."[7]

But what are we actually asking about when we raise the question of moral progress?

In such discussions, *moral progress* refers to *changes in the generally accepted conceptions* in terms of which we understand and evaluate morally relevant questions of social life and to the corresponding changes in the shape of the social practices and institutions, where a positive evaluation is attached to the changes in question. Such a process is conceived as *progress* insofar as it is a matter not just of *change* or alteration but of *change for the better*.

The pitfalls are obvious: whether something counts as progress, as regression, or as neutral is a question of how the change is *evaluated*. A particular development may not represent progress for all concerned. The corresponding innovations are generally highly contentious, especially at the beginning of transformation processes. And some change is more than superficially ambivalent.

But then, even though it is correct to point out that the concept of progress has an *evaluative component*, it would be inappropriate to follow von Wright in separating talk of moral progress into two independent aspects: "the notion of change and the notion of goodness."[8] A detachment of the *descriptive* aspect (the norm-free *description* of change as change) from the *ethical-evaluative* aspect (namely, the *evaluation* of this change as change for the better) would miss the point: it robs the question of progress of its independence. But such a decomposition not only fails to capture the political-historical semantics of the concept of progress; it does not capture its systematic content either.

My point is that to call something progress is to identify a quality that does not coincide with the evaluation of its effect—that is, the *result*—but instead refers to the *form of change*, to the *process of transformation* toward the good or the better as such. To assert that the abolition of slavery represents progress is not the same thing as to say that it is right. And vice versa, to interpret fascism or different forms of fundamentalism as *regressive phenomena* means something more and different than to say that they are morally *wrong*.

Apparently, the development in question is progressive or regressive as a movement or in its dynamic. When we speak of progress or improvements, we take our orientation from the process of *becoming better* or of productive or even accumulative transformation—and, conversely, we assume that there can be regressions behind a state already achieved.

The question about progress then is transformed: it is about the *form of change* that, as I suggest, we should ask.

Even though I initially focus in what follows on how the *change* that we call moral progress *comes about* and subsequently return to the question of how this change should be *evaluated* as change for the better, I nevertheless specifically do not want to separate these two moments from each other. Instead, my thesis is that the dynamic of the change conceived as progress in particular has implications for how it can be evaluated. Or even stronger, it is only after we understand *how these changes come about* that we will be able to understand whether or not we are in a position to evaluate them as progress, as change for the better.[9]

2. CONTINUITY AND DISCONTINUITY, THE OLD AND THE NEW: HOW DOES MORAL CHANGE COME ABOUT?

How, then, do moral improvements *come about* (assuming that they do)? How is it that social practices like those described above, which were accepted as completely normal for centuries and were interpreted as morally unobjectionable, become an object of public opprobrium and (at least in regards to the self-understanding of a society) are abandoned? *What kinds of* changes are involved and what *triggers* them? Do they come about all of a sudden and unexpectedly or not so suddenly and as a result of long-term and awaited developments? Do they bring about something *new*? And *who* is the moving force with respect to these transformations—human agency or anonymous forces?

Many contemporary authors[10] point out that progressive moral developments are less a matter of changes in the moral principles *themselves* than a matter of changes in the "catchment area" of morality—that is, in the domain of the addressees and the potential domain of the application of moral considerations and deference. Where moral progress occurs, previously excluded groups such as strangers, slaves, children, and women are elevated step by step to the status of morally relevant citizenship with all that this entails. The "morally relevant we," the description of the circle of those whom we owe a certain kind of treatment, is extended; the circle has become *more inclusive* and hence *wider*. As Michael Walzer puts it, "Insofar as we can recognize moral progress, it has less to do with the discovery or invention of new principles than with the inclusion under the old principles of previously excluded men and women."[11] And in concrete terms, "before the ethical change, black men and women did not count as *full people*; after it they did, and old proscriptions now applied to them, too."[12]

Moral progress, if we follow such a conception, is a matter of *correcting epistemic errors*, even if we grant that such correction calls not only for cognitive "insight" but also for heightening moral awareness or extending the capacity for empathy. We already have the correct norms for how we should treat people, but until now we were mistaken about who "counts" as a person.

A second approach to moral progress describes it in terms of *improved institutional implementation* of moral principles. Moral progress in this understanding is a matter of doing ever better justice to what is *meant* by certain moral principles or what is implicit in them and of realizing them in "deeper" or more complex ways in our institutions.[13] Assuming that the institution of civil marriage is based on the idea of love, then—this seems to be the suggestion—the idea underlying marriage is realized only if marriage is lived as a relation between autonomous human beings and, for example, rape is also outlawed within marriage.

As we see, common to both versions of the understanding of moral progress is the notion that moral progress is *not* a matter of inventing and implementing *new* moral principles. Rather, it is a matter of reinterpreting, realizing, or rightfully attributing already existing principles.

There is certainly something to be said for this:

- It is not at all evident that such a thing as a total innovative transformation—that is, an invention of *radically new* practices and principles unconnected to the ones that are overcome—could even be conceivable at all.
- Also, to conceive of moral progress as a deepening of already existing principles has the indisputable advantage that the problem of the evaluative standards—"Why should these changes count as progress?"—doesn't even come up.

Despite these advantages, for my part, I consider it more than doubtful that all moral improvements really adhere to this pattern of moral progress. And more than that, I doubt that when it comes to the moral principles themselves, we somehow *already have what we need.*[14]

Even in those cases where interpreting progress as a widening and deepening of already existing principles seems to be especially reasonable, sometimes the plausibility is merely apparent. When slavery is abolished or women included, it is not just that "slaves or women are suddenly also people" in the full sense. Rather, our understanding of *what it means to be a human being* or a person has changed. As Timothy Jackson writes, "Moral principles and their human application cannot be so neatly separated. The very humanity of slaves was at issue in the civil war, and America's 'old principles' themselves had to be changed if black men and women were to be included in civil society."[15] But then it is not just that the "circle" has expanded; it (and hence our conception of morality) has *changed* its character. And even where it seems especially obvious that moral progress involves a kind of *deepening* of the understanding of our institutions, it is not easy to draw the boundary between the progressive *adaptation to the idea* and the genuine *renewal* of an institution. If today the social institution of marriage is no longer restricted to heterosexual relations and the idea of a "family" no longer solely associated with heterosexual reproduction, does this really mean that we only now have *realized* that the deeper meaning of these institutions is that of enabling and protecting intimate relationships, no matter the sexual and/or gender orientation of the involved? Isn't it at the same time a pervasive *renewal* of these institutions?

However, a more important point is the following: perhaps the present-day prohibition of sexual violence gets in fact closer to the normative understanding of marital relations because it developed in the context of the bourgeois nuclear family since the eighteenth century. But since this understanding of marriage is itself a historically *specific* phenomenon, *how does this transformation come about*? And if it is *additionally* a matter of moral progress, how can we understand this transformation itself—the transformation leading to the concept of the bourgeois nuclear family—as progress? How can it be understood as a change for the better if the *framework* for such an evaluation no longer exists here and if the framework itself has changed?

The dilemma here is, the benefit of "solving" the normative (evaluative) questions with an expanding-the-circle / deepening-our-understanding approach comes at the price of leaving the social innovations that transcend this framework in the dark of a no-longer-intelligible paradigm change of some sort.

But if I'm right here, this seems to be a good reason for adopting a different approach to the question of moral change.

The approach that I suggest aims at overcoming the alternatives of *either* (1) conceiving progress or progressive change as somehow *continuous*, as it is implied in the idea of expanding or deepening our understanding of existing institutions, *or* (2) conceiving of it as *discontinuous*, as a real innovation or paradigm change. My intuition is, most of the social transformations that interest us—the "moral revolutions" (Appiah) as well as the "real" ones, the radical and thoroughgoing transformations as well as the local ones—are *continuous* and *discontinuous* at the same time, discontinuous in their continuity and continuous in their discontinuity.

The orientation that I will adopt here consists of *not* treating moral change *in isolation* and of not regarding it *as a purely endogenous phenomenon.*

Locating the problem of "moral progress" within the broader realm of social changes and inquiring into those processes of transformation (as I suggest doing) will enable us to face the possibility of "rational paradigm changes." At the same time, this allows us to avoid assimilating the all-too-strong (or even deterministic) "logics of history" that the critiques of progress rightfully question.

The thesis that I will pursue here is thus: in order to understand moral progress, we must understand *that* and *how* it is embedded in overarching social changes and transformation processes, *and* we must understand that and how those, in turn, depend on erosions and crises in the existing moral and social order. I will start with a remark from Marx in order to introduce the first point.

3. SOCIAL CHANGE AS A CONDITION OF MORAL PROGRESS

In the third volume of Marx's *Capital*, we find the following, in many ways remarkable, statement: "From *the standpoint of a higher socio-economic formation*, the private property of particular individuals in the earth will appear *just as distasteful* [*abgeschmackt*] as the private property of one man in other men."[16]

What interests me about this quotation is less the character of the earth as property, as important as it is, than a small, at first sight inconspicuous but nevertheless quite astounding accentuation. Marx claims here that the notion that human beings could fall under the legal form of private property must seem "distasteful" to us today. This way of describing our attitude toward slavery is disconcerting. Most of us surely think (as Marx certainly also did) that private ownership of other human beings—enslavement or servitude—is not only somehow "distasteful" but profoundly abhorrent. Why does Marx use what is in effect an aesthetic category—"distasteful"—to refer to such a degradation of persons? It is as if he were talking about a mere lapse of taste, a somehow inappropriate, despicable, deflated, but also slightly ridiculous, ugly, vulgar social institution or even one lacking in style.

Normality and the Ethical Context of Moral Evil

I suspect that this expression was no mere slip of the pen of such a great polemicist and stylist as Marx. That ownership of human beings now strikes us as "distasteful" indicates that today the institution of slavery is in a certain sense completely *unthinkable* for us. As something "distasteful," this social institution is not only morally outrageous but also *no longer intelligible* in the (in Hegelian terms) "ethical context" of practices, beliefs, and institutions in which we live. To treat a human being as property—to treat *someone* as a *thing*, therefore—is not, for example, worse or less bad than deceiving him, stealing from him, or murdering him; insofar as slavery has been overcome, it is a *category mistake*.[17]

Therefore, when Marx asserts that "from *the standpoint of a higher socio-economic formation*, the private property of particular individuals in the earth will appear *just as distasteful* as the private property of one man in other men," he means that today private ownership of the earth seems to us to be completely unproblematic and without alternative. Unable to imagine a different relation to the world than that of property, it does not dawn on us that this could be a problem. But a different time and *a different social order are conceivable in which* precisely this basic understanding and agreement (i.e., our moral sense) will have changed, just as what has already occurred with regard to ownership of human beings. Understood in this way, the designation "distasteful" points to the *ethical background conditions*—the changes in the protovalues of the society and possibly also in its fundamental social ontology—that make the institutions and practices described possible or impossible, conceivable or inconceivable, at a basic level.

But then, how do we get from here to there?

It seems to be something about the phenomenology of our moral experience that, in particular when it comes to what are for us such salient moral wrongs, we are sometimes confronted with changes that seem at first sight to present us with something like a *gestalt switch*, akin to the famous duck-rabbit switch. At the same time, however, the Marxian interpretation suggests that we are *not* dealing with an unconnected paradigm shift but with a motivated and intelligible transition.

As is well known, the Marxian "solution" to the problem is to claim that "underlying" the seemingly abrupt change in our moral sensibility is a material transformation that follows an intelligible and necessary logic. The social dynamic involved then doesn't originate from a transformation of our moral sensitivity itself but stems from somewhere else, the development of the forces of production, whereas morality (conceived of as ideology) "does not have a history,"[18] hence a dynamic of its own. Now there are a number of reasons why I do not want to embrace (or even, because it is well known enough, further discuss) the whole orthodox-materialist narrative in its one-sided determinism.

Nevertheless, the insight that changes in our moral conceptual world are *not purely endogenous phenomena* but are interconnected with other social changes seems to me to merit serious consideration.

The "Embeddedness" of Moral Practices in the Other Social Practices

Thus we can derive an initial thesis about the dynamics of moral progress from this first approximation inspired by Marx. Moral progress, this thesis asserts, *does not stand on its own.* It is framed by *social context and background conditions* and is reliant on them, even if moral virtuosi exist whose judgments are ahead of their social context. Therefore, the change in the normative evaluation of institutions *and* in their practically effective form described as "moral progress" would not be the result of a freestanding moral insight or of a freestanding development of the faculty of moral empathy. It would instead be the effect of a change of whole social formations, of a change in the *surrounding or adjacent practices* and of the social horizon of interpretation within which the practices in question can be understood and stabilized.

Let us take the example of "marital rape" mentioned at the beginning. The de facto toleration of marital rape (in Germany until 1997, rape was defined by law as an "extramarital occurrence" with the effect that marital rape is ruled out for conceptual reasons) is situated in the context of other provisions of marriage law. Take, for example, the bizarre state of affairs (again, in Germany) that a husband could dissolve his wife's employment contract at will and also dispose his wife's property freely, provisions that remain in effect until 1953. The legal status of marital rape is furthermore situated in the context of a social arrangement in which women are typically economically dependent on their husbands. And it fits closely with the interpretation of marriage as an intimate community of fate and an "organic unity" that would be disrupted by the interference of law. From the general "duty of obedience" of the wife operative here, it seems to be but a small step to the duty of sexual obedience. A specific interpretation of male and female sexuality may also have contributed to the fact that the violent-dominant violation of the woman's sexual integrity could even be conceived as a variety of *sexual relations* and not instead under the aspect of *violence*—or as we nowadays say, "sexual violence" (with an emphasis on violence!).

Similar embedding relationships could be demonstrated for the institution of slavery and for the problem of violence in education. Thus slavery in its manifold forms is situated in a practical continuum both with other practices of social domination and of racist exclusion and with other forms of (unfree) labor and with social practices of exchange. Corporal punishment of children, as well, is connected with the guiding concepts of childhood in education in general, and it becomes intelligible if one assumed that the nature of the child is essentially wild and untamed and must be tamed by civilization. But it is also situated in the context of the different social ways of dealing corporal punishment and the respective changes they undergo.

Contexts, Ensembles, Constellations

Thus morally relevant practices and interpretations are connected with a whole variety of other practices and interpretations within an *ensemble of practices*, which bear on the domain of "morality" but also in part on more wide-ranging life problems. These ensembles of practices also include technical skills and the "material" with which we deal practically. It is when a whole constellation changes that a specific moral institution can become peculiar, weird, repugnant, or even outlandish and can be thematized, rejected, and denounced by social actors or social movements.

The "ensemble structure" that we encounter here is diverse: moral practices and interpretations exert influences on other practices and are influenced by the latter in turn; they *make* other practices possible and are *made possible* by them in turn. Some of these practices are functionally interconnected or interwoven, but there are also elements that just "fit together" somehow, that are interlinked, that stabilize each other or belong to the same context of interpretation in a broad sense. And because practices are never "raw facts" but are always interpreted *as something*, the possible interpretations change along with the constellation of practices involved. Thus if (moral) practices are framed in a context of other practices, then they are also interpreted from out of this context and are intelligible within it. If marital rape is (in the context I referenced) interpreted *as* a version of sexuality or the beating of children *as* education, then the fact that these practices have not been *morally condemned* for the longest period of time is related to this context and the respective interpretations.

We should expect then that *change* within our moral behavior occurs within this context as well.

The formation of our "moral sense" or our faculty of moral perception that we asked about earlier, then, is *not an unmediated gestalt switch* that leads from one moral evaluation of a situation to another. It is actually not merely a change in our "moral sense" or "moral awareness" after all. Instead, it can be attributed to the *change* in the background conditions—the subsequent practices and interpretations—that transforms the *surroundings of the morally relevant practice* in such a way that they appear in a different light.

However, now the question arises, of course, of how these *changes, the transformation of such ensembles*, can be conceived. Thus our initial question about the genesis of *moral* change has shifted to the *questions of social change, its interrelation with moral change*, and its dynamic in general.

4. RELATIONS OF FIT, MISMATCHES, AND THE CRISIS DYNAMIC OF SOCIAL CHANGE

As we will see, social change is a somewhat messy affair, with a variety of components and a variety of interdependent dynamics involved.

Still, the conception of social contexts of practice suggested here yields some initial clues for answering these questions. If different practices are interconnected in the ways described, then the changes that they undergo can be explained in terms of *shifts* in a nexus of practices—shifts that are caused by the dissolution of the relevant "*relations of fit*": tensions (or even contradictions) between coexisting practices and their interpretations.

As is well known, Marx (as a historical materialist) has *a very specific relation of fit* (as I would like to put tentatively) in mind, which he expresses pointedly—perhaps even somewhat overpointedly—as follows: "The hand-mill gives you society with the feudal lord; the steam-mill society with the industrial capitalist."[19] The dissolution of this relation of fit (which in this case is a relation of functional conditioning) now gives rise to the dynamic of change. Maintaining feudal relations under conditions of the steam mill would be a mismatch leading to social upheavals and (according to Marx) ultimately to a social revolution. Or to put it in terms of historical materialism, the development of the forces of production represents a dynamic within which the relations of production that no longer "correspond" to these forces become dysfunctional and a "fetter" on their further development.

Again, I do *not* want to defend these theses. They involve thoroughly problematic assumptions whose functionalism is too one-sided and too deterministic to be of help in a world of complex webs of practice.

Still, if we try to understand the "ensemble structure" in a "looser" and more open sense, a "weaker" version of the idea of "relations of fit"—and, conversely, of *mismatches* between different practices and ideas as the origin of social change—seems to me to be still instructive and worth defending.

Shifts

If one inquires into changes that actually happened in the practical field, one will often observe that in such situations, relations of fit have become eroded and correspondingly vulnerable. New practices (and new technologies) are added to an ensemble of practices and interpretations; the conditions under which the latter are exercised, as well as their interpretation, undergo change. Some practices *fit* into the ensemble, whereas others seem to break it apart—so that in some cases an entire context or nexus of social practices undergoes a complete or partial shift.

A well-documented example of this is the social shifts in gender relations that occurred during and after World War II as a consequence of women entering into work relations that had previously been closed to them and assuming sole responsibility for the upkeep of the family. But even aside from such dramatic impulses, social relations of work can change in such a way that the institution of the "head of household" (and the "housewife marriage") no longer fits—or fits only poorly—into social life. But at first sight, inconspicuous technical inventions can also "trigger" social and moral changes. What makes the television series *Downton Abbey* so ingenious is its depiction of how love, war, radio, the telephone, and the typewriter combined with the ineffectiveness of aristocratic agriculture generated an irresistible dynamic of transformation that undermined—and would ultimately destroy—the way of life of the English aristocracy.

Thus there are *shifts in structures of practice*—caused by developments, innovations, or different kinds of crises involving change or the detachment of individual moments from structures of practice—that lead to changes in a whole ensemble of practices and their interpretation. Spaces (or gaps) *open up* as a result.[20]

Nonintentional Concatenations

Social (and moral) change, then, is sometimes a result of a complex concatenation of intended and *unintended consequences of action*.[21] *Changes in one complex of practices*—the invention of the typewriter, the invention of the pill, or the invention of gunpowder—can give rise to *changes in another area* without anyone actively intending the changes in question. (Indeed, such changes may be essentially impossible to *foresee*, let alone actively *intend*, by anyone.)

In his book on moral revolutions,[22] Anthony Appiah defends the (in my view convincing) thesis that it was the new high social regard for and *dignity of work*, a recent development in the bourgeois world, that contributed to generating the solidarity of the newly self-confident working classes with the abolitionist movement—against the disparagement of work expressed in slavery. This is certainly only one aspect of the many stories to be told—including a whole set of narratives that include social struggles, acts of resistance, and the agency of those involved. But nevertheless, with respect to this thesis, we have to ask what in turn led to the estimation of work. If we inquire further back, we will find that this change in the social regard in which work is held was conditioned in turn by a whole complex of social and economic factors, ranging from the loss in social relevance of the nobility, through the change in the technical boundary conditions of work and the new requirements for organizing it based on the division of labor, to the formation of the collective consciousness of the proletariat and the decline of aristocratic values. Insofar as this is conditioned in turn by a multiplicity of causal factors and already began with the invention of gunpowder[23] that rendered the martial virtues of the aristocracy superfluous, one could develop an (admittedly rather simplistic) narrative according to which the invention of gunpowder led (however indirectly) to the abolition of slavery. Similarly, it could be claimed that the inventor of the typewriter or the pill contributed to the prohibition of marital rape without—over long stretches of the plot—any of those initially involved having intended, or even having been able to intend, this development.

The Dynamics of Moral and Social Change

From what has been, we can derive a couple of initial insights for the question of the *emergence and the dynamic of both moral progress and social change in general.*

First, assuming that *moral progress* (as described) *unfolds within the broader context of social change*—hence in situations in which, together with the established moral judgments and institutions, other ethical, technical, and cultural practices also undergo change or become "obsolete"—then it develops in a non*endogenous* way. On the other hand, if we proceed from a web of different practices—each with its own developmental logic, its own specific normative character—and the resulting dynamic, moral progress is not one-sidedly dependent on or determined by the other changes, thus not completely exogenous either.

Second, with this, the locus of (moral) change has shifted in another respect: it is not the ideas that *first* undergo change, followed by the practices, so that the new (or newly interpreted) moral principles are subsequently applied at the practical-institutional level. To the questions Who *influences* whom *here?* and *Do the moral convictions and practices influence the other social practices, or vice versa?* one can answer, in case of doubt, *They both influence each other*. They form different constellations with different logics whose dynamics can become interlinked.

The practical dynamic intimated here suggests that the decisive processes can be represented as a somewhat "messy" tangle of ideas, practical changes, and (their) interpretive "recuperation." Sometimes newly emerging interpretations lead to practical changes, while at other times practical changes lead to new interpretations. Sometimes (as Pascal famously had it) we "*kneel down*, move our lips in prayer, and start to believe,"[24] and sometimes it is the other way around—and in cases of doubt, dynamics are at work in which these two moments can no longer be easily separated or unraveled.

Third, by embedding moral attitudes and practices in a more comprehensive context of the practice, they are placed in a continuum with other dimensions of social practice, together with their respective forms of knowledge and reflective capacities. As a result, it becomes possible to regard them (in the pragmatist spirit) as something that plays a role in the practical life of society and contributes to coping with its "life problems." Morality as a reflective capacity merges with reflective capacities of other kinds. How we think about organizing our social lives—how we should treat each other—turns out to be informed and influenced by other kinds of knowledge about the social and the human world and the world as such. Coming back to the relation between technological, social, and moral progress mentioned in the beginning, one might say as plausible as it is not to take for granted that one would be the result of the other, and as important as it is to grant an independent dynamic to the manifold transformations in play, it might also be decisive to retrieve insights to their respective influences, interdependencies, and intersections.

A (Very) Short Theory of Social Change

A tentative theory of social change (roughly pragmatist in spirit) then evolves, which can be outlined in three theses.

First, social transformations *do not arise out of nothing*. They are motivated by problems and crises such that existing practices and institutions "no longer function" or confront a problem they cannot solve. Social (and moral) change becomes possible where there is a mismatch between different social practices and institutions, thus where the relation of fit between them is no longer exact. It becomes necessary when the erosion of social institutions and practices calls for the formation of new institutions. If social change is triggered by crises and upheavals, it is a response to the need to adapt to social situations that have become unclear, hence to "problems" (in the pragmatist sense) or even "contradictions" (in the Hegelian sense). The question of how social change occurs, then, does not take the form "Why is it changing at all?" Rather, social formations present themselves as intrinsically dynamic formations that are "driven beyond themselves" by problems of all kinds in a crisis-prone dynamic. Progress, then, is a dynamic within an already dynamic situation.

Second, as an effect of challenge and response, the "new" (the new social practice, institution, or formation and the new understanding of our practices) is a transformation within a constellation that springs from the manifestations of erosion, of the "old order." The question of how "innovative" moral progress or change can be (and whether it can be conceived only as a deepening or extension of existing ideas and positions) is thereby defused in a certain sense. Problem-solving transformations, as they can now be understood, are at once continuous and discontinuous with previous practice. The "solutions" neither "really" already belong to our moral household nor arise in an entirely innovative way "out of nothing."

Third, as for the role of social movements and human agents, a multilevel picture comes into view: If the possibility of *change*—the possibility of turning moral wrong into an *object of opprobrium* (as feminists did in the case of rape and revolting slaves and abolitionists did in the case of slavery)—is bound up with shifts and with disjointed relations of fit, as I have argued, it is both correct and a simplification to say that social change rests on "social struggles" or social movements.[25] Neither the existence nor the success of social movements rests exclusively on the will and resoluteness of the actors involved. These will depend rather on social and material *enabling conditions* that must be fulfilled if social actors are to be able to make practical interventions. Against a "voluntaristic" interpretation, (radical) social change (following Marx) calls as much for *a passive* as for an *active element*. Or put differently, social conflicts and struggles contribute to changing the "aggregate state" of possibly latent crises or phenomena of erosion.

5. HOW DO WE RECOGNIZE PROGRESS AS CHANGE FOR THE BETTER?

Thus far I have dealt with the *first* of the questions raised at the beginning—namely, how social change (as moral change) occurs in general and how its dynamic should be understood. In conclusion, I want to turn briefly to the problem of understanding progress as *change for the better*.

The Evaluative Framework

Such an evaluation of social change *as* progress is so difficult (and hence in many cases so controversial) because we clearly need a frame of reference in order to be able to judge that—and in what way—something has become not only *different* but *better*.

This is why it seems easy to define in reference to *technical* what *progress* is—and difficult, on the other hand, when it comes to social and moral progress.

The invention of the washing machine represents progress over the laborious practice of washing by hand; the invention of antibiotics and vaccines led to major progress in combating life-threatening diseases. The fact that we find it so easy to identify improvements in the case of these examples—notwithstanding all the ambivalences that are also possible here—is not because they concern such basic spheres of life but because here we can define the progress achieved within the framework of an existing *means-end relation*. Progress with regard to washing or healing means quite simply that we now have better *means* to realize our *purposes*.

Social and Moral "Ethical" Progress

But how do things stand with *social and moral progress*—improvements in how we conduct our lives and organize our social life? If a "purpose" could be specified—either of human conduct or of social life as a whole—then it would be fairly easy to identify social or moral progress.

Now we are confronted not only (as a matter of fact) with ongoing controversies (in philosophy and in real life) regarding the objectives that should direct social life. Beyond this, the very attempt to determine overarching purposes, or the aims of human or social life as such, seems to be somehow misguided—if only because the individual instances of social life would then be reduced to a means to a predetermined end.

The Solution Resides in the Dynamic Itself

And more than that: regardless of the opportunities and possibilities of reaching at least a philosophical agreement here, such an attempt would—with regard to social life—occasion a shift from the question concerning progress to the question concerning the good (or the right) and how it should be defined. As a result, the question of progress, as I mentioned at the beginning, would no longer be posed as a *genuine* question but would be replaced by a discussion about how to define the *telos*, the *content* of a good life or the just society. Let's therefore take up the issue of progress as a certain kind of (normatively charged) dynamics itself.

From the proposed (pragmatist) perspective I have sketched out so far, this dynamic is a result of social crises, conflicts, and contradictions and an ongoing attempt to *solve* these problems—to adjust to the "new" and reintegrate the situation but also (in a more Hegelian spirit) to accumulate experiences, to "learn" from whatever has come up as a crisis and, as a result, establish new demands.

Now this dynamic of problem solving doesn't run smoothly. It is permeated by relations of domination and prone to systematically and structurally induced learning blockages and upheavals.

This opens up the possibility of evaluation qua evaluation of change as change itself: a social change is a *change for the better because and insofar as* it is a problem-solving process[26] of a certain kind. With this, the question of the *criterion* for progress shifts to the question of whether *the dynamic of this movement* is progressive—or, alternately, *regressive*. The brief formula that suggests itself is the following: progress is part of an accumulative problem-solving process that is not hampered by blockages or moments of regression. Progress would then be an *experiential process that is becoming constantly richer*—thus one in which experiences are accumulated and conflicting experiences are not systematically blocked. A typology of such experiential blockages and moments of regression—extending from ideological distortions and hermeneutic "gaps" to experiential impoverishment, alienation, and blockages to collective action—must then provide the normative criteria that in my project take the place of a positive description of the *goal* of progressive development.

That things get *better* (if they do), then, is not because we are approaching an already fixed and normatively demonstrated goal; rather, it is a matter of the character of the "progressing" itself. It is this *process* and not (first) its *result* that provides philosophical orientation. Progress in this way is conceived, as it were, as *freestanding*—and hence as a *principle* of movement.

Conclusion: Nonteleological, Formal, Plural Negativistic

This is, to come back to the aims I sketched at the beginning, a nonteleological approach toward progress. Not only are problem-solving dynamics open-ended; within such a process, the problems themselves also undergo change—and with them the means-end framework as well. Then progress is not the ongoing mastering *of a basic problem or a set of basic problems*; instead, it is a matter of ongoing and progressive problem solving in the course of which its ends and means can undergo transformation—without a definite end.

An advantage of such a conception is that it can be conceived as *plural.*

We will then be confronted with a variety of versions of a change for the better (of a "progressive transition" movement) and a variety of changes for the worse. And these transformations can be evaluated relative to the respective contexts in which they evolved—relative to the diverging problem-solving narratives. There is, then, not the one and only path *to* (or rather *of*) progress. Nevertheless, we still have the capacity to judge the very quality of these processes. That is, their specific dynamic can be judged as more or less "progressive"—as adequate or inadequate with respect to the (second-order) problems as they historically emerged.

This is, to conclude, a somewhat "formal" account. It doesn't say anything substantial about the "content" of progress—"progressive" would then be an evaluative means to judge a certain social dynamic of change. In other words, we would use it as a critical (as well as analytical) concept. And it might very well be that progress then turns out to be a category that we can only use in retrospect.

It is also a deeply negativist approach that is informed by the *metacategory of nonregression*, which brings me to a supposition already expressed by Adorno in a short essay on progress—namely, what progress is can be understood, assuming we want to do justice to the "dialectic of progress," only in terms of the concept of *regress or regression*: "A situation is conceivable in which the category [of progress] would lose its meaning, and yet which is *not the situation of universal regression* that allies itself with progress today. In this case, progress would transform itself into the *resistance to the perpetual danger of relapse*. Progress is this resistance at all stages, not the surrender to their steady ascent."[27]

NOTES

1. Axel Honneth, *Pathologien des Sozialen: Die Aufgaben der Sozialphilosophie* (Frankfurt: Fischer Taschenbuch Verlag, 1994).
2. See for this Rahel Jaeggi and Robin Celikates, *Sozialphilosophie: Eine Einführung* (München: C. H. Beck Verlag, 2017), and my *Critique of Forms of Life*, chapters 5 and 6 (forthcoming).
3. See Dipesh Chakrabarty, *Provincializing Europe* (Princeton: Princeton University Press, 2000).
4. See Peter Wagner, *Progress: A Reconstruction* (Cambridge: Polity Press, 2015).
5. Max Horkheimer and Theodor W. Adorno, *Dialectic of Enlightenment: Philosophical Fragments*, ed. Gunzelin Schmid Noerr, trans. Edmund Jephcott (Stanford: Stanford University Press, 2002), xvii.
6. Cf., for example, Elizabeth Anderson, "The Social Epistemology of Morality: Learning from the Forgotten History of the Abolition of Slavery," in *The Epistemic Life of Groups: Essays in Collective Epistemology*, ed. Miranda Fricker and Michael Brady (Oxford: Oxford University Press, 2016), 75–94; Elizabeth Anderson, *Social Movements, Experiments in Living, and Moral Progress: Case Studies from Britain's Abolition of Slavery*, The Lindley Lecture (Lawrence: University of Kansas, 2014); Kwame Anthony Appiah, *The Honor Code: How Moral Revolutions Happen* (New York: W. W. Norton, 2010); Michele Moody-Adams, "The Idea of Moral Progress," *Metaphilosophy* 30, no. 3 (1999): 168–85; Philip Kitcher, *The Ethical Project* (Cambridge: Harvard University Press, 2011).
7. Theodor W. Adorno, "Progress," in *Critical Models: Interventions and Catchwords*, trans. Henry Pickford (New York: Columbia University Press, 2005), 143.
8. See Georg H. von Wright, "Progress: Fact and Fiction," in *The Idea of Progress*, ed. Arnold Burgen et al. (Berlin: Walter de Gruyter, 1997), 1–18: "Progress is change for the better; regress is change for the worse. The definition splits the concept in two components: the notion of change and the notion of goodness" (1); cf. also Gereon Wolters, "The Idea of Progress in Evolutionary Biology: Philosophical Considerations," in *The Idea of Progress*, ed. Arnold Burgen et al. (Berlin: Walter de Gruyter, 1997), 201–17: "Phenomena are never progressive as such, but only with respect to at least one feature that seems 'positive,' 'desirable,' or 'better' to somebody for some reason. 'Progress' means that this feature or these features, respectively, increase quantitatively or qualitatively" (201).
9. For those for whom the very notion of progress has become a nonword, you might give the conception of change that is involved a thought (and therewith my underlying claim that social philosophy has to engage with the problem of social transformation and understand its dynamic) even if you think of the evaluative undertaking as absurd.

10. Cf. Peter Singer, *The Expanding Circle: Ethics, Evolution, and Moral Progress* (Princeton: Princeton University Press, 1981).
11. Michael Walzer, *Interpretation and Social Criticism* (Cambridge: Harvard University Press, 1987), 27.
12. Kitcher, *The Ethical Project*, 214. Kitcher himself is critical of the "expanding circle" thesis.
13. For such a notion, see, for example, Axel Honneth, "Rejoinder," *Critical Horizons: A Journal of Philosophy and Social Theory* 16, no. 2 (2015): 204–26.
14. See "No circle is expanded; one circle is replaced by another" (Kitcher, *The Ethical Project*, 215). Philip Kitcher has argued convincingly in his book *The Ethical Project*, using several examples, that changes in legal conceptions—such as the abolition of the *lex talionis* (but the same argument could be made for blood revenge in general)—cannot be understood so easily as an *extension* of the domain of moral consideration. These changes cannot be easily conceived as a more appropriate realization of the "meaning" of *our* legal institutions either—that is, not unless we extend both the idea of law and the "we" (i.e., the community that has such intuitions or ideas) to such a degree that they drift into vagueness (726).
15. Timothy P. Jackson, *Political Agape* (Grand Rapids, MI: Eerdmans Publishing, 2015), 79.
16. Karl Marx, *Capital: A Critique of Political Economy, Vol. 3*, trans. David Fernbach (London: Penguin Classics, 1981), 911 (translation amended).
17. In order to avoid misunderstandings, I am not denying here that we are faced with various new forms of unfree labor as in human trafficking that might with good reasons be called "modern slavery." But even if social practices exist that resemble slavery in various ways and even if it might be useful to denounce them as slavery, it is important to note (and this is what I am referring to here) that these institutions do not openly claim a right to property in human beings, thus they do not openly legitimate slavery as an institution. As important as it might be to disclose the similarities, it is important to spell out the differences as well. This at least is what Marx did when he articulated the differences between exploitation under feudal regimes of direct domination and exploitation within the framework of (double) free labor and contracts.
18. See Karl Marx, *The German Ideology*, ed. C. J. Arthur (New York: International Publishers, 1970), 47.
19. Karl Marx, "The Poverty of Philosophy," in *Marx-Engels Collected Works: Volume 6: Marx and Engels, 1845–1848* (New York: International Publishers, 1976), 166.
20. For an account of social change that takes place in the interstices, see Eva von Redecker, "Metalepsis und Revolution" (PhD diss., Humboldt University of Berlin, 2015).
21. For the classic text on unintended consequences of social action, see Robert K. Merton, "The Unanticipated Consequences of Social Action," *American Sociological Review* 1, no. 6 (1936): 894–904.
22. Anthony Appiah, *The Honor Code*.
23. I would like to thank Terry Pinkard for a very helpful discussion of these matters.

24. This is attributed to Blaise Pascal and famously quoted by Louis Althusser, *Lenin and Philosophy and Other Essays*, trans. Ben Brewster (New York: Monthly Review Press, 1971).
25. See also Anderson, "*Social Movements*."
26. For this, see Rahel Jaeggi, *Kritik von Lebensformen* (Berlin: Suhrkamp, 2014).
27. Adorno, "Progress," 161.

CHAPTER 3

Decentered Social Selves

Interrogating Alienation in Conversation with Rahel Jaeggi

John Christman

It is rather difficult to embark on a critical engagement with work that one agrees with as deeply as I do with Rahel Jaeggi's views on alienation and the self. In fact, as I hope to bring out in what follows, we have been traveling parallel paths through these issues over the last two decades or so, though her journeys have been so much more wide ranging and profound. Specifically, Jaeggi's work on alienation developed in her book on the subject is a paradigm of sensitive, critical, and momentous social theorizing, and what I have to add to it should only be considered friendly extensions and amendments.[1]

That said, part of my motivation here is to push some of her ideas in directions that point toward her later work on forms of life, though I won't say much about that material directly. Jaeggi's powerful claim that alienation is an endemic pathology of modern social existence develops and makes more precise sociological claims from the early twentieth century woven into a broader critical fabric. Such alienation, she argues, runs counter to the ideals and aspirations of the ethical world of modern democracies, and as such the critique she develops is an immanent one.

But what is alienation exactly, and how is it a special deficiency of democratic societies? These are the central concerns of my chapter, as I will answer them first in Jaeggi's voice but then suggest that in order to capture the *special* deficiency that modern alienation manifests, more must be said in that voice (or at least as harmonious partners to it). I will suggest a certain incompleteness in Jaeggi's original account but argue that connecting alienation with deficiencies of agency captures the special status of that pathology. For as I will try to explain, agency and will formation connect directly to the normative requisites of democratic social practices and, as such, highlight the ways that failures of collective agency via alienation threaten democracy.

I'll proceed in three steps. I will first attempt to reconstruct Jaeggi's view of alienation (and the corresponding conception of the self that aligns with it) drawn from her seminal book on the subject. I will conclude, however, by noting certain aporias in the account but then suggest, in the second section, that we can further develop the account by tying alienation to agency and agency to reason-giving, something required for deliberative democratic practices. I will then conclude by trying to show that such connections are needed to provide critical force to the diagnosis of social alienation with which we began.

1. JAEGGI ON ALIENATION AND THE SELF

The central aim of a theory of alienation, in Jaeggi's view, is for the diagnosis of pathologies of modern capitalist societies, specifically the way that self-realization is undercut in such settings. It is an ethical critique, but one motivated by the inherent ideals and values operative in such settings. Being immanent in this way, the critique attempts to avoid two problematic positions that would threaten any view of self-realization, (positive) freedom, autonomy, and related notions. These are, first, the assumption of an overly reified conception of an essential self that is structured independently of social forces and the dynamics of power and, second, the use of an externally generated normative order—a perfectionist ethical framework—in grounding a critical appraisal of social conditions.

The first of these dangers can come in many forms. Traditional atomistic notions of the self as a rational agent with fundamental self-defining commitments once dominated the theoretical landscape of Western social theory.[2] But this has given way in current thinking to an understanding of persons as more porous and fluid and structured by social dynamics. Identity categories by which we understand ourselves are not fixed, nor are they immune from varying interpretations, both social and individual. Our self-concepts may contain social elements (about which more in a moment), but those elements are not given in advance of our own and others' reflective interpretations of them.

To underscore this last point, Jaeggi looks critically at Harry Frankfurt's approach to this issue, where he defines certain "volitional necessities" as definitive of the self. These are commitments in reference to which our second-order acceptance of first-order motives gains its agentic force. But as Jaeggi points out, defining the self in terms of these core commitments—faithfulness to which is essential to being true to oneself—fails to account for the many ways that people adapt and change, especially to losses of loved ones or forced separations (172–73). There are better and worse ways to adapt to such life alterations, but seeing commitments to them as simply ineluctably fixed is wrongheaded. As she writes, "The question whether someone is 'herself' is not about whether she remains true to certain projects and commitments but whether in passing through various fundamental commitments she is able to tell a coherent 'appropriative story' of herself that can integrate the ruptures and ambivalences in her life history (including radical revaluations of her own values). I remain true to myself not when I remain loyal to projects I once entered into but when I can integrate both my holding onto projects and my giving them up into a meaningful narrative about myself" (170).

The crucial notion in Jaeggi's account of the nonalienated self is "appropriation"—the capacity for and ongoing process of constituting ourselves in our actions and productions. When we move and act, we take in elements of our social world through the effects of those actions and the residue of our interactions with others. In a way reminiscent of Christine Korsgaard's "self-constitution" view of agency,[3] Jaeggi argues that appropriation involves a genuine relation to oneself, others, and one's social world in ways that one can identify with and pursue aims for her own sake. This does not assume or require an eradication of all conflicts, of course, in that, for Jaeggi, "identity is what perseveres in the balancing out of inner ambivalences or of (externally caused) conflicts and in securing continuity in the face of changing commitments" (175).

Nonalienated appropriation requires the extension of the self into the world in ways that make the ongoing process of self-formation intelligible to the person, establishing a hermeneutic unity wherein the person can see herself as an ongoing subject of a life narrative. Additionally, this is by no means a solitary endeavor, in that appropriation takes place within self-defining social roles. But such roles are not merely masks to be put on and removed (implying a self that exists independent of them); they are a function of involvement by the person wherein she identifies noninstrumentally with the goals inherent in them.

Alienation, then, is the systematic disruption of this process of appropriation—that is, "alienation [is] an inadequate power and a lack of presence in what one does, a failure to identify with one's own actions and desires and to take part in one's own life . . . One is not alienated when one is present in one's actions, steers one's life instead of being driven by it, independently appropriates social roles and is able to identify with one's desires, and is involved in the world" (155). This can emerge in any number of forms, including rigidification of one's life trajectory in a way that prevents experimentation and adjustment; anomie or indifference relative to the momentum of a life course wherein one feels not only that the directionality of that momentum is not of your own choosing (as this is often the case) but that one's actions and experiences become "unrecognizable" as one's own (54). Similarly, one can be self-alienated in failing to see one's own impulses and desires as part of an autobiographical narrative that is personally and socially intelligible. (This last condition is necessary to avoid the pitfalls of views such as Frankfurt's that see self-identification as merely another subjective response to one's own motivations.)

This picture of the self and of alienation is powerful and robust, and I have much sympathy with virtually all of it, although I have developed similar views under the rubric of "autonomy," and Jaeggi insists that the nonalienated self is not identical to the autonomous self and alienation is not the same as heteronomy. I will return to this issue, but for now let me merely note that the way I and others have conceived of alienation as part of our view of autonomy echoes this view in many of its details and sensitivities.

However, I want to raise two points about this view of alienation, points that are meant not as criticisms but only as requests for further elaboration so that the phenomenon of alienation can play the critical role that theorists like Jaeggi and others (including myself) want it to play. And while it would be felicitous to simply ask Jaeggi to provide this elaboration, I will here provide my own version of it.

The two aporias I want to underscore here are these: First, can the notion of narrative intelligibility that is so central to the notion of appropriation at work here bear the weight it is asked to carry in defining the nonalienated self? Second, how can this account of alienation ground the critical stance we want to maintain regarding that condition in the contemporary world? That is to say, what is *especially* problematic about alienation? Let me explain each of these questions in turn, albeit only briefly.

Although she does not emphasize the point, the idea of agency Jaeggi develops here relies crucially on the narrative conception of the self, in that proper, genuine, and authentic appropriation is defined as that which results in an ongoing self-understanding that meets narrative or hermeneutic standards of intelligibility. I myself have developed a narrative component to a conception of practical agency, although I have also expressed some ambivalence about narrative accounts of the self generally.[4] This ambivalence stems from the open-endedness of the narrative standard: it is not exactly clear what it requires, for virtually any sequence of experiences and actions can be woven into a story if only in the minimal diegetic sense of a sequence of related elements. Dream events can be told as a story no matter how surreal they seem. And events that entirely disrupt a life—catastrophic accidents, illnesses, violence, and destruction—can be recounted as a survival narrative or a victim narrative.[5]

So some orienting framework must be in place and operating to determine when an appropriation sequence (in Jaeggi's sense) is intelligible as the person's own and not artificially constructed or externally imposed.

The second question to be raised in some ways suggests a connection between Jaeggi's work on alienation and her recent research on lifeworld critique—namely, what exactly is the *harm* or *loss* that alienation represents, and what does our critique of the lifeworld that produces it amount to? How is the pathology of alienation to be distinguished, say, from general lack of flourishing, or experience of anomie or malaise, or simply pain and suffering? There is nothing fatal in blurring these distinctions; however, the critique of social forms and political systems based on their tendency to produce alienation may want to avoid bundling this together with other social ills so that balancing and rectification are envisioned all of a piece. Alienation cuts deeper, as it were.

As I said, Jaeggi can certainly provide answers to these questions, but for my part, I will attempt to suggest an answer by providing an analysis of alienation that links it to autonomy and, as such, to the basic conditions of agency presupposed in democratic ways of life. Alienation in this sense, then, threatens the normative core of contemporary aspirations for democratic practices and institutions. In this way, I will try to both clarify its conditions (hence answering the first worry) and show its fundamental value (answering the second) in a way that I hope is congenial to Jaeggi's overall normative outlook.

2. ALIENATION AND AUTONOMOUS AGENCY

In what follows, I want to sketch an account of nonalienated agency that echoes many of the positions Jaeggi takes but couches this view in the idea of self-government or autonomy.[6] (I acknowledge Jaeggi's claim that alienation should not be equated with heteronomy or nonalienation with autonomy, and later I will comment on that view, but I put it aside for now.) Central to the account will be a view of the moral orientation of the person, her practical identity, a model I take from Christine Korsgaard but adapt in several ways. Practical identities, in Korsgaard's sense, are those self-descriptions under which one sees one's life as worth pursuing. Such an identity, akin to what some psychologists refer to as a self-schema, can be characterized by a set of identity categories that carry with them core normative commitments. To be this or that type of person—a professor, a parent, a loyal friend—is to be committed to a set of values that provide reasons to act in particular ways. I would insist, further, that such identities be understood diachronically in that they can only be conceived over a span of time that makes sense of memories but also organizes future plans.

In addition, the practical identities that guide our reflective evaluations in this way do more than provide a propositional basis for arguments in support of our lower-order judgments, such as our decisions to treat particular desires as action-guiding. Practical identities perform this function in fact—when they are articulated in this form, they often are part of practical syllogisms comprising our reasons for actions. But more than this, basic commitments of this sort perform what we can call an *orienting* function: they order the moral world in a way that sets the stage for our evaluations themselves.

This is akin to what Barbara Herman called "rules of moral salience,"[7] though I think they function more broadly as evaluative structures and not simply moral ones. Also, I am not sure they are best understood as "rules." Still, Herman describes these normative factors as aspects of the self that "structure an agent's perception of his situation so that what he perceives is a world with moral features. They enable him to pick out those elements of his circumstance or of his proposed actions which require moral attention."[8]

A committed Catholic looks at (and swallows) a consecrated host as the body of Christ. Such a person does not merely believe that "this object is the body of Christ"; she *experiences* that wafer as a holy object. Were it to fall to the ground or be stomped on by an unconcerned passerby, she would be shocked and offended, in a reaction that shows the function of a practical identity as ordering her mode of understanding the world, not merely a set of beliefs that she can consider as propositions.

This functional feature of practical identities is important in understanding how they can speak for the agent. Other features of practical identities ground this point further: First, practical identity structures and guides reflection so that when we consider our motives and decisions, we do so in a way that manifests our basic commitments. Such identities explain our motives over a variety of conditions and over time more consistently than other characteristics of our bodily or psychic selves. Practical identities also organize memory, in that having a working self-concept structured by value commitments of this sort is necessary to engage in active construction of narrative first-person memories.[9] Narrative remembering is more than a passive replaying of an already-structured event sequence; it is always an active reconstruction of events in ways that make sense from our current perspective. This intelligibility reveals both how our basic commitments organize what we recall and how those commitments define who we think we are. Without such an organizing device, remembering our actual past would be more like recalling a dream—things would happen with no identifiable structure or meaning. Actual memories are veridical (in part) because they are organized by our self-understanding, which is shaped by our basic values.[10]

In this way, I contend that this account of alienation avoids the first of the worries I raised earlier—namely, that simple narrative unity was not demanding enough to uniquely pick out genuine agentic selves. In the view developed here, narrative intelligibility is anchored in one's practical identity, the evaluative orientation that shapes one's world and guides one's judgments (and without which such activities could not function). So not *any* story of ourselves will meet this condition, only those that echo our functional self-concepts.

Following Jaeggi's "process" view of the self, we could call this an *adverbial* conception of the agent. It refers to the unique manner in which a person experiences the world from her own embodied (and socially structured) point of view. Practical identities in this sense organize reflection and experience, explain reactions (both automatic and considered), and justify judgments.

The model of intentional action I sketch here also mirrors Jaeggi's view of appropriation in that action extends the self into the world, constituting itself as it acts. Moreover, when one acts intentionally, one is guided by a standard of success or failure, a standard that is given both by the teleological structure of action (in a local sense, one chooses an action with a purpose in mind) and by the evaluative organization of the practical identity that grounds the choice. In this picture, acting is always value-conferring in two directions. When our actions are guided by our practical identities, we both project value onto those actions and reflexively inherit their value in being their source. In this way, we constitute ourselves in action and we reflexively affirm the value of the identities that underwrite those actions when we choose them. As we will see, this is crucial to understanding alienation.

Also, it should be emphasized that there are important interpersonal and social elements to the normal operation of these self-schemas. The nomenclature of practical identities, the terms in which value orientation expresses itself, involves a rich language of roles, social categories, and standards of behavior. We see ourselves and act *as* a certain kind of person, such as being a mother or a teacher or a Muslim or a brother, and those self-descriptors carry with them socially structured expectations and motivations. These terms do not merely refer to a set of values or propositionally structured commitments that one can say one *believes in* (though those surely figure in our identities). Rather, these categories orient our way of seeing the world and prioritize values and options.[11] The core of the postulate of self-worth, I suggest, is that those descriptors can be understood as naming a life worthy of pursuit from one's own perspective. They are self-validating in practical reflection because they stand in for a host of interconnected values, which, in turn, justify action.[12]

The crucial functional aspect of practical identities is that they are able to provide reasons for acts and continuation of action plans. Only if the feedback mechanism of reflexive self-affirmation I have described is functioning can such identities play this reason-giving role. When one acts from reasons grounded in one's practical identity and succeeds in achieving a desired end, a sense of satisfaction results as well as a judgment that such a sequence was worth doing. If one is frustrated in one's attempt, regret ensues. If one's actions have a moral character, one feels moral satisfaction from their success and guilt or shame from their failure. In all four cases, the valence of the affect tracks the relation between the action and the structure of the self-schema grounding the reasons to perform it. This reaction involves affect—satisfaction or regret to varying degrees (ranging from beaming pride to repugnance and deep shame)—but also involves judgment, the determination that the success was worthwhile or the failure was regrettable.

Of course, many other mechanisms operate in the generation of motives, judgments, and actions, be they internal, subconscious, or social. And many of these mechanisms work pervasively to structure the behavior and actions of any subject. But laying out such mechanisms performs a *diagnostic* function, explaining and dissecting actions rather than justifying them. From a practical perspective, however—one that emerges from the space of reasons accessible to the agent herself—the reflexive self-affirmation (or criticism) that results from acting out of the frame of one's practical identity will be the dominant operative mechanism in human action.

Only if this recursive mechanism functions in something like this manner will one have a *continued* reason and motive to act from the practical identity that frames deliberation and choice. If no such response is ever elicited, one would have no continued reason to trust the perception and judgment that one's practical identity provides one with when one next engages in deliberation and choice.[13] As we will see, this is a crucial implication of the view as it connects with communicative reason-giving in our interactions and deliberations with others.

However, in order to further clarify alienation against the backdrop of this model of the self, it is necessary to discuss self-*reflection*, for the relationship between reflection and alienation is a complex and subtle one. Despite what I just said about the merely diagnostic role of subconscious explanations of action, it is clear that even the most straightforwardly intentional, voluntary, and "rational" actions emanate in part from habit, automatic and unreflective processes, and uncontrollable impulses. Further, it is clear that postulating a completely detached, disembodied, and unembedded consciousness as the seat of self-governing agency is a fiction that is misleading at best and dangerous at worst.

So I must say a word to clarify the role of self-reflection in this model of agency in ways that avoid this pitfall. Keeping in mind the functional role of practical identities in orienting deliberation, perception, and choice, we should distinguish at least three "levels" of reflection, though again these are not levels in the simple sense of higher and lower orders. Level 1 is simply the consideration of action; it is a reflection on what is best to do given one's situation. Level 2 reflection involves the interpretation and application of the normative commitments of one's self-conception so that one asks, "Given the kind of person I am and the commitments I have, what do I have reason to do in this situation?" This is different from level 1 in that it is not merely the application of a hypothetical imperative or the use of instrumental rationality (as might be the case at that level). It is a broader consideration of what one has reason to do in light of one's normative orientation.

Level 2 reflection involves deliberation about whether a person like me should do the act in question. As a result, it recursively reflects on what it means to be a person "like me"—to have the practical identity I have. It need not involve a focused consideration of what it means to have such an identity, for it may well be simply the *use* of the orienting function of that self-conception. One might reason, "As a mother, should I allow my young son to sleep over at his friend's house tonight?" It utilizes the orienting frame of "being a mother" and recursively involves consideration of what that identity means in such contexts. But the thought process may be relatively automatic and untroubled.[14]

Next, there are moments when one does turn one's introspective attention to one's identity itself, asking more directly about what the value of being such a person *is*. This is level 3 reflection. But again, such deliberation need not require a complete separation from one's identity as a whole. Rather, it involves questions of the *meaning*, *value*, and *social impact* of having the identity one has. It need not be phrased as the question "Should I be an X?" but rather "Being an X, what is the meaning, value, and social impact of this way of being?"

This can be distinguished from the fully separated reflection that we could label level 4—namely, the depersonalized viewpoint from which one asks about whether *anybody* should occupy the identity in question. This is the unencumbered self reflecting on her life and commitments in toto that I mentioned earlier that various critics of Kantian liberalism and other modernist accounts have rejected.[15]

But we need not involve ourselves in such debates, for the relevant kinds of reflection for autonomous action need include only levels 1–3.

What is involved in deliberate action in this picture is consideration of what it is (instrumentally) rational to do, reflection on what a person with my identity has reason to do, and reflection on the meaning and importance of being that kind of person. Level 3 need not be involved in everyday habitual actions or those exercises of plans and projects that one is fully committed to and hence never has reason to question one's commitments or identity.

To sum up, I have developed a picture of normal human agency as it emanates from a person's practical identity functioning over time (her diachronic self-schema). I have tried to explain how this identity not only grounds the justification for an action but orients the person in her perception of her options and the relevant evaluative aspects of the world she faces. Deliberate action involves reflections at least up to level 2—namely, deliberation about actions as well as the interpretive application of one's self-concept as a generator of reasons to perform that act. Further reflection—level 3—functions at least implicitly in that the interpretive application of one's practical identity carries with it a recursive endorsement of the having of that identity so as to generate reasons now and in the future. Finally, normal agency also involves an affective/judgmental feedback process that confers value on the identity that frames and supports one's decisions. This reflexive self-affirmation is an aspect of self-trust that operates to endorse the reason-giving function of the normative commitments that structure that identity.

This is agency. But what is *self-governing* agency? And more to the point, what is alienation and how does it disrupt autonomy in this sense? Let us now turn to that issue so as to circle back to Jaeggi's views.

The view of autonomy I have tried to develop over the years has relied heavily on the notion of alienation in that I attempted to avoid the (to my mind) overly demanding requirement that we *identify* with our desires and deepest cares in the sense of wholeheartedly embracing them. In this way I follow Jaeggi in resisting Harry Frankfurt's view of action as emanating from volitional necessities, but I also eschew talk of identification with roles and relations altogether. In earlier versions of this view, I characterized autonomous agency in terms of hypothetical reflection, such that one is autonomous if (among other things), *were* one to engage in sustained critical reflection on a central aspect of oneself over a variety of conditions in light of the historical processes that brought them about, one would not be alienated from that factor.[16]

However, using this hypothetical test as a defining element of autonomy presented difficulties and ambiguities. What I now see is that this hypothetical test is a *mark* of heteronomy, in the sense that it can be used as a test for it, but it should not be expressed as the definition of that state. The problem with defining autonomy in terms of a hypothetical is that it leaves open the possibility that one is autonomous even if one *never in fact reflects* on one's actions. But this has struck some as implausible.[17]

The refinement I would now add to this picture is that one is *disposed* to reflectively accept one's values and desires in a way that is enacted in deliberative action. As I have described everyday agency, one reflectively orients one's reasons by way of a practical identity and recursively affirms its value (as an orienting mechanism) when one acts. In this way, one enacts the general disposition to reflectively accept that identity, in the sense in which level 3 reflection is engaged when one acts for reasons, as explained earlier.[18]

Let us consider this last point with an illustration from literature (and film). In the novel *The Remains of the Day*, Kazuo Ishiguro describes the character of Stevens, a (head) butler in a British manor house who has served in this fashion for much of his adult life, as his father did before him. He never asks whether being so, in this house, is worthwhile overall, as this is thought obvious to him because it is a position of *honor*. Being honorable means being self-affirming in the social terrain in which he defines himself. At one point, in fact, a character asks him to reflect on serving his employer, Lord Darlington, who in the 1930s engaged in a misconceived attempt to appease the Nazi regime, and Stevens replies that he never thought about it, that doing so would have distracted him from his work. It is true that at some moments during the time he served with such single-mindedness, certain experiences jarred him into feeling conflict about that broader social structure and his part in it, pangs of guilt, stirrings of romantic love, and so on. But during the earlier (main) period in the plot, these do not succeed in short-circuiting his motivational/reflective feedback loop. His sense of himself as leading an honorable life of obedience continues to affirm itself in functionally effective ways. During such time, I submit, he remains autonomous.

Later, however, he is induced to reflect on that life and feels the tragedy of it, how his devotion prevented him from gaining true happiness, seeing his chance at finding love, and grasping the evil folly of his employer. At that point, there *is* a crisis, and his reflections on himself and his life do cause him great misery. At this point his autonomy is shaken. But it is not counterintuitive, I think, to say that during his time in service, he was autonomous as an obedient servant who does not reflect in any way more deeply than level 2. And only later, when subsequent encounters and reflections shake his commitment to this identity and cause a crisis of faith, is his autonomy compromised.[19]

So the view is that autonomy requires a disposition to reflectively accept one's practical identity in being able to experience the recursively self-affirming affective and judgmental feedback that occurs when one acts as oneself. One is in effect saying, "This is how I am, and it is good to be this way." "Good" here means simply that it is acceptable as a governing perspective that generates further reasons and motives for one to continue acting in this way, as this sort of person.

One is alienated, then, when one feels deep cognitive and affective dissonance in acting on a desire (in a socially structured setting). More specifically, one's reactions to acting (or desiring to act) do not line up with the normal satisfaction-regret matrix I outlined earlier. Moreover, one has a desire that one cannot shed or resist being moved by in the current context (without great psychic or social cost).

Reflection plays a role in this model, but not as a *means* by which alienation is produced. Rather, reflection at the levels I earlier described engages the feedback mechanisms I refer to here so that one reflectively chooses an action for instrumental reasons (level 1), one reflectively applies an interpretation of one's values to justify one's choice (level 2), and perhaps in cases when challenged, one reflects on the meaning and importance of being the kind of person one is (level 3). In the normal case, such deliberations deliver a recursive sense of self-acceptance as a result of acting over time for the reasons in question. However, if such reflections consistently produce feelings of self-abnegation, guilt, frustration, or worse, then one is alienated in the sense that one cannot include the reasons in question within an ongoing autobiographical narrative shaped by one's working self-conception.

3. THE SOCIAL PATHOLOGY OF ALIENATION

In closing, let me return to the social level at which alienation in the broader sense has been pitched and in this way return to my dialogue with Jaeggi's views. This will help us connect the conception of alienation I have been attempting to clarify here to the critique of forms of life—say, of living conditions in capitalist societies or in overly rationalized and bureaucratized social settings. Insofar as some social forms or modes of social organization systematically cause breakdowns of the sort described, they can be called alienating even in my (narrow) sense. That is, as modes of production and/or social organization prevent members of those societies to feel that their identities and evaluative perspectives are being recognized as the "sources of normative authority" typically afforded to agents as worthy of respect, then such modes undercut the self-affirming reflexivity I described and are thus alienating in my sense.[20]

More specifically, the conditions of autonomy I set out here, specifically lack of alienation relative to one's practical identity, manifest the requirements of authentic reason-giving that deliberative democratic practices require and presuppose. That is, collective will formation requires that participants interact in reciprocal exchanges whereby they convey the reflective importance of their value orientations in cooperative discourse with fellow citizens. Only if people can feel at home in these orientations can the self-expression involved in this deliberation have the normative authority it has. Moreover, the *outcomes* of such deliberative will formation will have normative authority over their participants only if (among other things) they are the genuine expressions of the reflective value orientations of participants. Alienation, in my view (as perhaps in Jaeggi's), marks a systematic disruption of this process of authentic reflection and recursive reason-giving, and in this way, alienation strikes at the heart of the normative aspirations of democracy.

Although stated all too briefly, this last point helps answer the second worry I raised about Jaeggi's earlier work on alienation. Or if *worry* is the wrong word, it helps continue that valuable work by describing and emphasizing the central normative importance of alienation and the companion idea of self-governing agency I think is linked to it. In my view, alienating practices and institutions undercut the capacity of persons to give self-supporting reasons for the value orientations that define and motivate them. This inability undermines the normative presupposition behind collective self-government characterized by sincere deliberation, communication, and exchange. The "special harm" of alienation I alluded to earlier, then, amounts to this threat to egalitarian democratic practices and the forms of social life that they require.

As I said, this picture is meant as a companion view to the conception of alienation developed in Jaeggi's work. So my further reflections are merely meant as a choral harmony in the background of the melodious patterns of her original reflections, reflections that should always remain at center stage in our considerations of the pathologies and promises of our current condition.[21]

NOTES

1. See Rahel Jaeggi, *Alienation*, trans. Frederick Neuhouser and Alan E. Smith, ed. Frederick Neuhouser (New York: Columbia University Press, 2014). Unmarked page numbers in the text refer to this volume. See also Rahel Jaeggi, *Kritik von Lebensformen* (Berlin: Suhrkamp, 2014).
2. See, for example, Charles Taylor, "Atomism," in *Philosophical Papers, Volume II* (Cambridge: Cambridge University Press, 1985), 187–210.
3. Christine M. Korsgaard, *Self-Constitution: Agency, Identity, and Integrity* (Oxford: Oxford University Press, 2009).
4. See John Christman, "The Narrative Self," in *The Politics of Persons: Individual Autonomy and Socio-historical Selves* (Cambridge: Cambridge University Press, 2009), 66–85.
5. For a sensitive treatment of this dynamic, see Susan Brison, *Aftermath: Violence and the Remaking of a Self* (Princeton: Princeton University Press, 2002).
6. This material draws from the view I work out in *The Politics of Persons*.
7. Barbara Herman, "The Practice of Moral Judgment," *Journal of Philosophy* 82, no. 8 (1985): 414–36.
8. Herman, 418.

9. For discussion of memory and its relation to self-concept and autonomy, see my "Why Search for Lost Time: Memory, Autonomy, and Practical Reason," in *Practical Identity and Narrative Agency*, ed. Catriona Mackenzie and Kim Atkins (New York: Routledge, 2008), 146–66.
10. This claim has been made explicitly in the psychological literature on memory: "Another way to put this is that normal autobiographical memory and reflective, temporally extended agency, is mutually constitutive," according to Stanley B. Klein, Tim B. German, Leda Cosmides, and Rami Gabriel, "A Theory of Autobiographical Memory: Necessary Components and Disorders Resulting from Their Loss," *Social Cognition* 22, no. 5 (2004): 460–90.
11. Cf. David Velleman, "Identification and Identity" and "The Centered Self," in *Self to Self* (Cambridge: Cambridge University Press, 2006), 253–83.
12. This is akin to what Stephen Darwall labels "recognition self-respect" in his "Two Kinds of Respect," *Ethics* 88, no. 1 (1977): 246–61. Also, I do not take up the details of these similarities or the complexities of self-respect itself. For discussion, see Robin Dillon, "Self-Respect: Moral, Emotional, Political," *Ethics* 107, no. 2 (1997): 226–49.
13. The literature on self-trust attempts to characterize this very phenomenon. See, for example, Keith Lehrer, *Self-Trust: A Study of Reason, Knowledge, and Autonomy* (Cambridge: MIT Press, 2002), and Trudy Grovier, "Self-Trust, Autonomy, and Self-Esteem," *Hypatia* 8, no. 1 (1993): 99–120.
14. Cf. Bernard Williams, "Internal and External Reasons," in *Moral Luck* (Cambridge: Cambridge University Press, 1981), 101–13.
15. See, for example, Michael Sandel, *Liberalism and the Limits of Justice* (Cambridge: Cambridge University Press, 1998).
16. John Christman, "The Historical Conception of Autonomy," in *The Politics of Persons*, 133–63.
17. See, for example, Marilyn Friedman, review of *The Politics of Persons*, *Ethics* 121, no. 2 (2011): 424–29.
18. This also represents an attempt to resolve an ambiguity in the earlier account described insightfully by Michael Quante—namely, the ambiguity between saying that the heteronomous person is alienated *because* she reflects and saying that she is alienated, full stop, but her (hypothetical) reflection would *reveal* this to her. If the latter is the view, we need a separate account of alienation to explain what it is that reflection reveals (and this also shows that reflection is not part of what constitutes heteronomy; alienation is); reflection merely exposes it to the person. See Michael Quante, "Autonomy by Default" (unpublished manuscript).
19. Kazuo Ishiguro, *The Remains of the Day* (New York: Vintage International, 1988); see also the film version, *The Remains of the Day*, directed by James Ivory (Columbia Pictures, 1993). K. Anthony Appiah also discusses this case in relation to the question of autonomy. See K. Anthony Appiah, "The Ethics of Individuality," in *The Ethics of Identity* (Princeton: Princeton University Press, 2005), 1–35.
20. The phrase "source of normative authority" comes from Catriona Mackenzie's account of (relational) autonomy. See Catriona Mackenzie, "Relational Autonomy, Normative Authority and Perfectionism," *Journal of Social Philosophy* 39, no. 4 (2008): 512–33. For an account of oppression in the modes mentioned here,

see Iris M. Young, *Justice and the Politics of Difference* (Princeton: Princeton University Press, 1990).

21. An earlier version of this chapter was part of a workshop on the work of Jaeggi at Penn State University on April 22, 2016. I am grateful for the participants in that workshop and to Professor Jaeggi for comments on that presentation.

CHAPTER 4

The Normativity of Forms of Life

Frederick Neuhouser

Rahel Jaeggi's *Critique of Forms of Life* is an ambitious attempt to construct a comprehensive critical social philosophy around the idea of a form of life—an idea that, as articulated by her, springs from a marriage between Hegel's conception of ethical life (*Sittlichkeit*) and Dewey's thoughts on experimentation and problem solving. In my view, this is not precisely a marriage between equals: Jaeggi's concept of a form of life appears to have inherited considerably more from Hegel than from Dewey. While this claim should in no way be construed as a criticism of Jaeggi's book, it does explain why my response to it here is formulated primarily from the perspective of Hegel's social philosophy.

My focus in this chapter is on one central Hegelian element of Jaeggi's position—namely, her claim that forms of life are "normatively constituted entities" (*normativ verfasste Gebilde*).[1] This is first and foremost an ontological claim that echoes Hegel's distinction between nature and objective spirit, an idea that he in turn inherits from Rousseau's contrast between the natural and the artificial: it is central to the kind of thing human societies are that they are normatively governed in a specific, "spiritual" way. What distinguishes human sociality from merely natural forms of life is not that one is norm-governed while the other is not (since, as Kant pointed out, living beings too are normatively organized). The difference, rather, is that natural life is governed by norms or rules in a way that does not require consciousness on its part of its governing norms—life is not self-conscious—whereas the norms governing human societies (forms of objective spirit) are operative only insofar as conscious beings follow those norms, as opposed to merely behaving in accordance with them "externally," as ants and bees do when they engage in their naturally determined "social" activities. In other words, forms of life are essentially self-conscious phenomena, although this claim must be qualified in two ways: first, they possess no collective consciousness independent of that of their individual members, and second, the self-consciousness that characterizes forms of life can be both implicit and distorted. Rule *following*—not mere conformity to rules—is essential to forms of life, and it is what makes them "normatively constituted" in a spiritual way.

Jaeggi's view goes beyond the metaphysical claim that normativity in this sense is essential to something's being a form of life. She also makes the causal claim that normativity is what "holds forms of life together";[2] normativity is the "social glue" that makes what can look like merely a multiplicity of interactions among individuals into a single, identifiable entity—a human society—and this is crucial to the capacity of forms of life to maintain (or reproduce) themselves over time as the unified entities they are rather than disintegrating and ceasing to exist. This talk of "social glue"—it is my phrase, not Jaeggi's—is potentially misleading, however, since glue (or cement, to use Jon Elster's metaphor[3]) is a "sticky" substance that holds together independent building blocks that preexist the glue that joins them. In contrast, Jaeggi's conception of a form of life—although this remains largely implicit in the book—rests on a different, and *holistic*, conception of the relation between normativity and the interactions among individuals that make up the material substrate, as it were, of a form of life.[4] The actions of and among individuals that constitute social reality are existentially and conceptually dependent on the rules or norms of a form of life; viewed as isolated motions, apart from the normativity that informs them, they are incoherent and could not take place qua actions. Forms of life, then, are normatively constituted in the strong sense that social norms explain and make possible the very parts—the individual actions—of which forms of life are made up. This thought is relevant to another way in which Jaeggi formulates her central thesis—namely, that forms of life are "structured by norms":[5] the latter make up the framework within which the characteristic actions of the former become possible.

Even if it is correct to regard these as ontological claims, social ontology is not Jaeggi's main project, and this distinguishes her from John Searle and Vincent Descombes, whose positions, though they overlap significantly with hers, are more narrowly focused on articulating the kind of entity societies (or social institutions) are. What makes *Critique of Forms of Life* a work in critical theory is that its interest in social ontology is inseparable from the task of understanding what type of social critique it is fruitful and appropriate for us to engage in, given the kind of thing human societies are and the kind of norms they are governed by. This means that it is not enough merely to establish that forms of life are normatively structured; Jaeggi also wants to investigate, more than Searle or Descombes, the kind of normativity they possess, including what the sources of that normativity are. Here too it is instructive to compare Jaeggi's project with Searle's. There is a sense in which Searle also asks about the source of the normativity characteristic of social institutions. His answer is that it derives from the collective "acceptance" of norms by the subjects who participate in institutions, norms that assign "deontic status functions" to objects, and persons who do not have those functions intrinsically—that is, independently of the "collective agreement or acceptance" (or "recognition") of the norms on the part of the subjects who follow them.[6] Searle's version of the Hegelian view that social reality is spiritual might be expressed as the claim that collective intentionality is essential to its being what it is or that, as he puts it, in the case of social institutions, "the attitude . . . we take toward the phenomenon is partly constitutive of the phenomenon."[7] (This, it will easily be recognized, is roughly consonant with Fichte's and Hegel's conceptions of the fundamental nature of subjectivity and spirit, respectively.)

I take it that Jaeggi is in broad agreement with these social-ontological claims in the very general form in which I have expressed them here. She goes beyond Searle, however, in wanting to know more about the kinds of normative considerations we appeal to in order to justify, or legitimize, our acceptance of the status function-assigning rules that are constitutive of social life. Moreover, Jaeggi is interested in legitimation in a sense that goes beyond that of the sociologist or social ontologist: she wants to know not merely what kinds of collective acceptance the existence of social life in general depends on but also what kinds of norms (and acceptance) genuinely legitimize a form of life—or, put another way, what considerations in fact justify the collective acceptance of norms without which forms of life could not exist. When Searle, in contrast, says that collective acceptance "authorizes"[8] the social actions it makes possible, he is not claiming that this acceptance genuinely justifies the practices in question but only that social participants' de facto acceptance of them is what makes social action possible, regardless of whether those participants have good reasons for accepting the norms they do. When Searle broaches the question of what grounds for accepting institutions social participants might have that would render their acceptance rational, he rests content with the vague and unsatisfying suggestion that such institutions make us "better off" than we would be without them.[9] (What is unsatisfying here is that "we" and "better off" are completely undefined: Who precisely is made better off? Everyone? And in what sense better off?)

One of the most interesting parts of Jaeggi's book is its consideration of three ways of justifying norms that are relevant to understanding what forms of life are and what kinds of critique of them are appropriate. She labels these forms of justification *conventionalist*, *functional*, and *ethical* and characterizes them as follows: conventionalist justification points to some de facto agreement among social members that establishes a certain norm, or practice, as legitimate; functional justification grounds the legitimacy of a norm by reference to "its role in maintaining or establishing a specific practice"; and an ethical justification of norms appeals to the goodness (in some ethical sense) of the practices they make possible.[10]

When initially presenting her position on what justifies forms of life, Jaeggi declares her intention to reject the conventionalist mode of justification and to endorse some combination of the other two.

Much of what she goes on to say about functional and ethical justification is enlightening, and I am in agreement with the main thrust of her arguments there. Moreover, the position she articulates is deeply Hegelian; it is very close, for example, to what Hegel means when he names "the living good" as the normative principle of *Sittlichkeit*, where "living" points to the functional and "good" to the ethical modes of justification.[11] I believe, however, that it is a mistake to reject conventionalist justification altogether and that Jaeggi herself is dimly aware of this, since the position she goes on to develop allows some space for conventionalist justification, understood in a specific way. Essentially her rejection of conventionalist justification goes wrong by confusing two very different senses of "convention": one in which the conventional is equivalent to the merely arbitrary and another in which the conventional is that which has been determined by actual human agreement—as in Rousseau's claim that *convention*, the coming together of human wills, is the source of right within society.[12] Rejecting conventionalist justification *tout court* is a mistake because norms that are conventional in the second sense I have distinguished can acquire a limited degree of legitimacy simply by having been agreed upon by those subjects affected by them.[13] Indeed, some of Jaeggi's statements appear to support precisely this view.[14]

The most interesting justificatory questions raised by Jaeggi, however, arise in the context of her account of the functional mode of justification. In the remainder of this chapter, I will explore whether that account is convincing as it stands. I will argue that it is not, and in doing so, I will outline the account of functional justification that I think Jaeggi ought to have embraced. Much of my critical reconstruction involves making use of points that can be found somewhere in Jaeggi's text but that do not make it into her "official" statement of what functional justification is. So here too I hope that my critical remarks will be understood as friendly amendments to the position she explicitly endorses.

I begin with the parts of Jaeggi's position that I find most persuasive: her distinction between functional and ethical modes of justification and her understanding of their relation. First, it is important to be clear (since it is possible to be misled by the text on this point) that

Jaeggi does not claim that there are two distinct types of arguments that purport to justify forms of life, as if it were sometimes fitting to offer a purely functional justification and at other times a wholly ethical justification. Her claim, rather, is that the most important justifications of human (or with Hegel, "spiritual") forms of life are always *at once* functional and ethical; these two modes of justification are typically, as she puts it, "intertwined."[15] Notice, however, that in characterizing the justifications in this way, Jaeggi commits herself to distinguishing *conceptually* between the functional and ethical moments of such justifications, even if, in any specific argument evaluating a form of life, the two are always intertwined. I do not believe Jaeggi is wrong to take on this commitment, but it is not easy to say what a functional justification—or the functional moment of justification of forms of life—consists in, and it is worth spending some time trying to figure out how she means to do so.

I will begin by outlining one possible way of distinguishing functional and ethical modes of justification that, I believe, can be found in Hegel. Recall my earlier suggestion that Jaeggi's view regarding the intertwining of functional and ethical justification is similar in spirit to Hegel's making "the living good" into the grounding principle of *Sittlichkeit*, since "good" points to the ethical character of forms of life and "living" suggests a functional justification of a certain type familiar from the study of living organisms (or species). This kind of functional argument is exemplified in a biologist's response to the question of why, for example, higher animals have hearts—namely, because the heart functions to pump blood throughout the animal's body, supplying it with oxygen and nutrients without which the animal would die. If we want to call this a biological "justification" of the animal heart—an account of how it functions so as to satisfy a vital need of the organism—then the benefit that explains why certain animals "ought" to have hearts is the purely natural good of remaining alive, as opposed to, as in the case of justifying human forms of life, a good that, though perhaps partly biological, is at the same time always ethically tinged. In Jaeggi's words, the norms that justify human forms of life are oriented toward "*das gute Funktionieren einer Praxis*,"[16] where that phrase must be translated not as "the well functioning of a practice" but as "the (*ethically*) good functioning of a practice."

I have introduced the idea of proper functioning in the purely biological sense both because Jaeggi's explanation of functional justification sometimes refers to this idea and because it is central to Hegel's understanding of life, which in turn is central to his understanding of spiritual phenomena, including those that count for Jaeggi as "forms of life." This might lead one initially to think that what she means by functional justification is closely tied to the biological values, as it were, of material self-maintenance and reproduction. This interpretation is made more tempting by the fact that Hegel, along with many of the social philosophers who follow in his footsteps, lean heavily on the biological analogy when thinking about the proper functioning of societies and take social reproduction (or social self-maintenance, in the guise of "stability") as central to the defining ends of a rational social organism. I am thinking here of the priority Hegel assigns to the family, civil society, and (to a lesser extent) the state, precisely because of the central role they play in the material reproduction of society. Applied to the family, one Hegelian version of how functional and ethical justifications are intertwined in social philosophy would run as follows: in the case of spiritual beings (like us), there is always more at stake in raising children than merely reproducing life—although this is part of what a rational society must be able to do and part of what makes the family a rational institution. As a spiritual activity, child-rearing at the same time promotes, and in some manner is taken by parents themselves to promote, an ethical end—namely, freedom broadly conceived. Clearly, child-rearing plays a vital biological function—in reproducing the species—although in a spiritual form of life, the family does not merely produce the bodies of the next generation; it also develops and nourishes the subjective resources children will need as adults in order to realize themselves as free, and it does so in such a way that participation in the family can itself be conceived of as a form of free activity. In this view, ethical and functional moments (where the latter is interpreted purely biologically) are always intertwined, even though it is possible to distinguish in thought two types of ends rational family life serves: the ends of life and the ends of freedom. To repeat, on this way of understanding what Jaeggi means by the functional mode of justification, it contributes to a justification of forms of life by pointing out how they serve the material (biological) reproduction of society.

For better or worse, Jaeggi means to give a different account of the functional element that she takes to be a necessary part of justifications of forms of life. (I say "for better or worse" because I believe that there is some merit to Hegel's "materialism" in this context—his keeping the needs of life firmly in focus when doing social philosophy—and I think this topic is in danger of falling out of sight, or being marginalized, in Jaeggi's version of social philosophy.) The problem is that once "functional" is decoupled from the ends of life, it becomes very difficult to say precisely what the term means, and Jaeggi's discussion does not completely overcome this difficulty.

Let us look carefully now at how Jaeggi characterizes the functional moment in the mode of justification on which critical social philosophy is supposed to depend. In elaborating on what functional justification in social philosophy is, she begins by pointing to an example of biological function: the function of the giraffe's long neck is to facilitate its nourishment, a requirement of life.[17] (Notice, by the way, that what is being functionally "justified" here is neither a norm nor a practice but a part of the giraffe's body. I will return to the question of the appropriate object of functional justification in social philosophy in a moment.) This is nothing more than the biological conception of functional justification we encountered in discussing the importance Hegel attributes to the ends of life in his account of *Sittlichkeit*. When explaining function in the social domain, however, Jaeggi appeals first to something quite different—namely, the idea of a professional ethos, which implicitly ascribes a certain point or aim, not necessarily a biological aim, to the practice it governs and therefore contains within itself standards that can be used to evaluate how well individual participants carry out that practice in terms of whether what they do conforms to the point of the practice or achieves its aim. (I will return later to Jaeggi's discussion of professional ethoses and argue that it implies an account of functional justification different from, and superior to, her "official," explicit account. It is interesting, by the way, that the example of a professional ethos she appeals to in order to elaborate her notion of function is the ethos governing the practice of doctoring. I am inclined to think that the aptness of this example derives in part from the fact that doctoring serves a life need of human beings—even if the doctoring of humans also involves much more than ministering to our purely biological needs.)

Immediately after discussing this example, Jaeggi formulates her "official view" on functional justification. This mode of justification, she says, justifies norms by pointing to the role they play in "maintaining or establishing a certain practice,"[18] and in the same vein, she characterizes functional justification as claiming that a certain norm is necessary for the existence[19] of a given practice. This talk of maintenance (*Erhaltung*) and of a norm being necessary for a practice to exist, or to continue to exist, retains some of the language used in biological conceptions of function, but as I have noted, Jaeggi means to distance herself from this sense of "functional" more than her language here might suggest. One notable difference is that her understanding of functional justification focuses not on the existence, maintenance, and reproduction of "the social organism" but on the existence and maintenance of social practices in general, which themselves might have nothing, or only very little, to do with social reproduction in the sense in which, for Hegel, both families and civil society function to maintain and reproduce life. For Jaeggi, "functional" is to be understood more broadly than this, such that something (in her case, a norm) can be said to serve a function and to be a candidate for functional justification, when it "contributes to the achievement or maintenance of a certain condition [or state of affairs] within a nexus" of social practices.[20]

These passages point out a peculiar aspect of how Jaeggi conceives of the object of functional justification: she speaks consistently of justifying *norms* and of doing so by showing how they enable certain *practices* to exist. This way of formulating her position runs into two problems, both of which come into view if we apply Jaeggi's account of functional justification to the case of doctoring. (Or perhaps these "two problems" are simply two ways of characterizing a single problem.) On this account, the normative rule "perform thorough physical exams even if doing so reduces profits" would be justified by showing how it maintains or establishes the practice of doctoring. If we are to understand this norm as necessary for maintaining or establishing the practice of doctoring—necessary for the practice's existence—then the only possibility for doing so is to see the rule in question as a constitutive norm of doctoring. Although Jaeggi wants to make room in her account of functional justification for this way of a norm being necessary for a practice (namely, its being constitutive of that practice), this does not, in the case of doctoring, seem like a functional justification to me. This is because when we consider a thing's function, we are asking what that thing "is good for," and in a sense that does not allow for a purely internal answer, such as a certain norm governing the practice of medicine is good, or justified, because following it is just part of what it is to practice medicine. To take a different example of constitutive norms, it seems perfectly fine to say that the rules of chess are "justified" because without them the game of chess would not exist, but it is less plausible that this would constitute a functional justification of them.

The second problem concerns not what a genuinely functional justification must be but the kind of relation between norms and practices that Jaeggi's official account seems to presuppose. This problem lies in the thought that we can functionally justify *norms* by appealing to the *practices* whose existence those norms make possible, as if the two things were distinct enough that the former could be justified by placing them in some (functional) relation to the latter. Does not this strategy require us to separate norms from practices in a way that neither Hegel nor Dewey nor Jaeggi endorses? Because in the case of doctoring, where the norm in question is in some sense internal to the practice, it seems artificial to claim that the norm is justified by pointing to the practice it makes possible, as if the rationality of the norm could be established by referring to something else—to the practice it is associated with. But in this case, our conception of the practice whose existence is supposed to justify the norm in question already contains that norm within it: we are trying to justify a part of a whole (a specific norm internal to the larger practice) by appealing to a whole that is already constituted by that norm. My suggestion is that we try to find some way of characterizing the specifically functional moment of justification in social philosophy in a way that avoids justifying a norm by establishing some relation between it and the "existence" of the practice it governs. Do not both Dewey and Hegel, for example, agree that norms are too internally related to practices for us to think of justifying one in terms of the other? The suggestion I will make is that norms and the practices they govern can be justified only together, as a unity. And since a practice is the more comprehensive of the two—a practice includes the norms that govern but is also more than just those norms—I suggest that we take the primary object of functional justifications to be practices. The question then is, What would it be to give a functional justification of social practices when, as Jaeggi persuasively establishes, their intimate connection with the good (in an ethical sense) places them outside the group of things we normally have in mind when evaluating how well something "functions"?

Fortunately, Jaeggi's book provides us with some of the resources we need to reformulate the idea of functional justification in social philosophy, and following up on these aspects of her discussion will lead us back to some of what she herself says about the functional character of practices when discussing the ethos of doctoring. Let us return to her definition of "function" most generally. As we have seen, Jaeggi claims that for something to have a function is for it to "contribute to the achievement or maintenance of a certain condition within a nexus of relations in which it stands," and in elaborating on this, she notes that a function is always defined in relation to "an aim or an end."[21] What I want to emphasize is that functioning involves achieving a certain state of affairs in accordance with a certain aim or end. Jaeggi's emphasis on the aims or ends of what is to be evaluated functionally helps us formulate a different account of functional justification from the one I have just considered (where a norm is justified by showing it to be necessary for the existence of a practice): Why not think of the basic criterion of functional justification simply in terms of how well something that has a function in this sense succeeds at achieving its own aims—of how well, in other words, it brings about some condition that realizes its ends? Since it makes sense to ascribe aims to social practices, they can be evaluated functionally by assessing how successful, or effective, they are in achieving their own ends, regardless of whether those ends are biological or ethical, or some combination of the two.

With this suggestion in mind, we can now return to the example of doctoring, where, as I have hinted, what Jaeggi implies about the nature of functional justification fits the model I am proposing here better than the one she officially espouses. In this case the functional justification we should be looking for does not justify a norm by showing how it enables the practice of doctoring to exist; instead, it evaluates the specific practice of doctoring sketched out by Jaeggi in terms of its effectiveness—which is to say, according to whether it produces results that realize its own ends (which she names as "correct diagnosis and appropriate therapy").[22] If we want to follow Jaeggi and functionally evaluate a specific norm within that practice, we should say that the rule "perform thorough physical exams even if doing so reduces profits" is justified not because it somehow makes the existence of doctoring possible but because it is a good rule to follow if we want to achieve the ends of doctoring.

If the functional justification of social practices involves assessing them in relation to how well they achieve their own aims or ends, then there are at least two kinds of considerations it might take note of: not only whether a practice in fact succeeds in achieving the aims that define it but also whether it achieves those aims with reasonable efficiency. I will not say anything here about what efficient functioning consists in, but with respect to the first consideration—whether a practice achieves its aims—I will merely point out that this criterion of functional evaluation has its place in the uncovering of contradictions that the critical method of the *Phenomenology of Spirit* depends on. In that text, configurations of consciousness—we might think of them as *practices* of knowing—fail, and fail functionally, when what they end up producing is at odds with what they took themselves to be aiming at when following the norms of their practices.

It is no objection to this view that it enables us to give functional justifications of even pernicious institutions such as the secret police. It is important to keep in mind that our concern here is to understand what the functional *moment* of justifications of forms of life might consist in, where, as Jaeggi emphasizes, this moment is always *supplemented* by ethical considerations when the objects of our evaluation are forms of life. In fact, different ways of organizing the secret police *can* be evaluated from the purely functional perspective: some do a better job than others of achieving their defining aims, but since this type of functional justification is only a part of the evaluative criteria at play in the critique of life-forms, the social critic can acknowledge these limited functional virtues of a social institution without concluding that it is, all things considered, good.

Finally, I want to note two additional considerations that are relevant to functional justification in social philosophy. Both play a role, I believe, in Jaeggi's text even though they are not explicitly incorporated into her definition of functional justification. Moreover, both considerations push us in the direction of *life* as Hegel conceives of it, not because they ascribe biological ends to social practices but because one of them ascribes a certain *structure* to societies (or forms of life) that mirrors the structure of biological organisms and because the other ascribes an *end* to social orders that mirror an end of biological species.

Let me begin with the second of these points: for both biological and social life, a central criterion of success resides in life's ability to reproduce itself and to do so as the kind of thing it is in its nature to be. In reintroducing the criterion of reproducibility into functional justification in the domain of social philosophy, I am not thinking of reproduction exclusively, or even primarily, in the biological sense. I am thinking, rather, that part of what constitutes the success of both forms of life and biological species is their ability to reproduce themselves over time rather than dying out after a generation or two. Moreover, both forms of life aspire to be *self*-reproducing, not in the sense that they can reproduce themselves wholly self-sufficiently—without interacting with their environment—but in the sense that they are "set up" such that the principal mechanisms for their reproduction are internal—inscribed into how their various parts, with specialized functions, are constituted and in what relations they stand to one another. In human forms of life, a large part of this self-reproduction consists in processes of *Bildung*, or socialization, in which the subjectivities of their members are formed so as to make them capable of *freely* reproducing the practices and institutions they are born into. In any case, mere reproduction (survival in any form whatsoever) is never the aim of either biological or social beings. In both domains, the thing's well functioning requires that it reproduce itself as the kind of thing it is in its nature to be, and in the case of social reproduction, this includes reproducing itself so as to realize the ethical goods it takes as its constitutive aims.

This thought is bound up with the second element I want to add to Jaeggi's account of functional justification. We can arrive at this point by paying close attention to one specific aspect of her definition of a function: something has a function when "it contributes to the achievement . . . of a certain state of affairs within a nexus of relations in which it stands."[23] What we should take from this definition is that functional justification in both biology and social philosophy presupposes that the thing being evaluated (a biological organ or a social practice) operates only within a *nexus* of organs or practices and that its successful functioning depends in part on how it relates to the other organs and practices (to the related subsystems, we might say) that make up the form of life to which it belongs. A social practice, for example, might be very good at achieving its own aims and at the same time inhibit other practices from realizing theirs. Or a practice might achieve its aims in such a way that it produces results that impede the functioning of other "vital" practices. If this is correct, then taking account of the nexus of practices that makes up a form of life means that, in functionally evaluating a practice, social philosophy must also take into account its implications for surrounding practices and, ultimately, how it affects the functioning of the larger "body" it is a part of. If this point is correct, then some (hopefully weak) notion of organic structure—invoking the interrelatedness and mutual dependence of specialized parts and functions—must be appealed to in understanding forms of life and assessing how well they function.

Consider, for example, certain practices within the institution of the family: hiring a cook to feed one's children might be an efficient way of accomplishing one of the ends of family life (nourishing the bodies of children), but it may stand in tension with another end of family life—caring for the good of children through acts of love—if neither parent actually labors on the food their children eat. Alternatively, a regime of stern punishment for misbehavior may be effective at instilling the capacity for self-discipline in children that family life aims at, but it may be inconsistent with another principal end of child-rearing: allowing children to have a free, noncondemnatory relation to their spontaneous impulses. It is equally easy to imagine how different institutional spheres might conflict: there may be good reasons from the perspective of (capitalist) civil society for laborers to work night shifts or to be highly flexible in their work schedules, as demanded by the rhythms of industrial production. But this can be criticized, even from the functional perspective, if irregular work schedules inhibit laborers in their roles as parents and hence fail to accord with the aims of family life.

In other words, a large part of the functional moment of the justification of forms of life will be concerned with how well social practices succeed in harmonizing the various ends, including various kinds of ends, that those practices aim at. The well functioning of a social practice, then, cannot be determined solely by regarding it in isolation from the other practices that constitute a form of life; a very large part of a practice's well functioning depends on how well *integrated* it is with the social organism's other vital functions. This point makes clear why the society-as-organism analogy is still (in this limited sense) valid, even though many of the ends of the social body extend far beyond those of biological organisms to include considerations of what is ethically good. As Jaeggi recognizes, a form of life is "a comprehensive system of mutually related practices."[24] Her point, I take it, is that forms of life must be regarded holistically, as a nexus of interdependent practices, none of which can be adequately evaluated in isolation from the other practices that make up a given form of life.

Let me try now to summarize what I think I have learned from engaging with Jaeggi's ideas on criticizing forms of life about the functional mode of justification that such critique depends on: In the first place, I have rejected the idea that functional justification in social philosophy is well captured by the claim that a functional justification of the validity of a norm points to its role in enabling a certain practice to exist. Rather than justifying norms by reference to the practices they make possible, I suggest that we take practices, including the norms internal to them, as the primary object of justification. Moreover,

I have argued that one reason it is so difficult to characterize functional justification in this context is that it brings together a variety of considerations, not merely one. The three components of functional justification I have suggested we pay attention to can be expressed in the following claims: First, whether a practice succeeds in achieving its defining aims, and with reasonable efficiency, is the basic criterion of functional justification. Second, since reproduction (as the kind of thing it by its nature is) is an aim of both biological and social forms of life, we can assess the latter functionally by looking at whether they are well equipped to reproduce themselves, finding many of the resources they need to do so internal to their own workings. Third, since social practices exist within a nexus of social practices, a practice can be evaluated functionally by examining how well it "fits together" with the other practices that larger nexus includes.

NOTES

1. Rahel Jaeggi, *Kritik von Lebensformen* (Berlin: Suhrkamp, 2014), 5.
2. Jaeggi, 142.
3. Jon Elster, *The Cement of Society* (Cambridge: Cambridge University Press, 1989).
4. A similar conception has been powerfully articulated by Vincent Descombes in *The Institutions of Meaning* (Cambridge: Harvard University Press, 2014).
5. *Strukturier[t] durch Normen*; Jaeggi, *Kritik*, 144.
6. John Searle, *The Construction of Social Reality* (New York: Free Press, 1995), 39.
7. Searle, 33.
8. Searle, 41.
9. Searle, 88. Again, answering this question is not Searle's main project here.
10. Jaeggi, *Kritik*, 165.
11. G. W. F. Hegel, *Elements of the Philosophy of Right*, ed. Allen W. Wood, trans. H. B. Nisbet (Cambridge: Cambridge University Press, 1991), §142.
12. Jean-Jacques Rousseau, *The "Social Contract" and Other Later Political Writings*, trans. Victor Gourevitch (Cambridge: Cambridge University Press, 1997), I.4.1.
13. For an account of the version of this view subscribed to by Rousseau, see Frederick Neuhouser, *Rousseau's Theodicy of Self-Love: Evil, Rationality, and the Drive for Recognition* (Oxford: Oxford University Press, 2008), 209–12.
14. See her admission later in the text that "conventional norms are only weakly normative" (Jaeggi, *Kritik*, 169). In making room for conventionalist justification, I take myself to be offering a friendly amendment to Jaeggi's view from a perspective that I find in both Rousseau and Hegel, and most likely in Dewey as well.
15. Jaeggi, 165.

16. Jaeggi, 165.
17. Jaeggi, 171.
18. Jaeggi, 165.
19. Jaeggi, 171.
20. Jaeggi, 171.
21. Jaeggi, 171.
22. Jaeggi, 169.
23. Jaeggi, 171.
24. Jaeggi, 171.

CHAPTER 5

In Search of the Negative in Rahel Jaeggi's *Kritik von Lebensformen*

Max Pensky

1. PROGRESS OR NEGATION?

I begin with a reconstruction of a debate over the nature and future of Marxist theory and practice between Eduard Bernstein and Rosa Luxemburg at the turn of the twentieth century. The debate may be little remembered now, but it is of far more than antiquarian interest. In fact, the respective positions that Bernstein and Luxemburg defended were, and were to remain, central for the branches of socialist and social-democratic theory and politics, critical theory included. It also remains highly explanatory for Rahel Jaeggi's project in *Kritik von Lebensformen*: developing an immanent social criticism of forms of life with a transformative dimension.

I'll suggest that Bernstein's progressive, functionalist orientation toward social theory and the nature of social democracy, on the one hand, and Luxemburg's dialectical logic, inferring the inevitable collapse of capitalism under the weight of its internal contradictions, on the other, are irreconcilable positions. They rest on incommensurable, and not merely opposed, theoretical assumptions. The temptation to embrace both—that is, to argue both sides of this divide in socialist theory and practice and to suggest a middle position encompassing both sets of such assumptions—arises from an appropriation of Hegel that badly underestimates and misconstrues the concept of negation. While Jaeggi's work does not address the Bernstein-Luxemburg debate directly, I want to reconstruct an aspect of her work that seems to yield to this temptation: a version of dialectics that replaces the work of negation with the (to me false) alternative of meeting halfway. Reading Jaeggi's work in this way sheds light on some of the more puzzling features of *Kritik von Lebensformen*. Or so I will argue.

Bernstein and Luxemburg were both confronted with the undeniable resilience of industrial capitalism in most of Western Europe and the Americas in the decades following the deaths of Marx and Engels. For Bernstein, the parliamentary success of the German Social Democratic Party and the increasing vitality and capacity of the German and European economies both suggested that Marx's prediction of the inevitability of capitalism's collapse at the hands of an impoverished postnational proletariat had to be revised significantly, if not rejected outright. If Marxism was to survive as a respectable social science, Bernstein argued, it would have to prove itself to be fallible in the face of refuting empirical evidence, capable of adapting its methodological commitments and even its axiomatic views about the dialectical nature of economic relationships, in order to respond intelligently to the obvious fact that the prediction of the inevitability of revolution had proven false.[1]

Bernstein recognized that capitalism was structured by recurrent crises, with severe and measurable human costs. But such cyclical events of creative destruction in themselves were insufficient to establish the economic system's overall dysfunction. On the contrary, Bernstein insisted, evidence pointed to capitalism's capacity to respond in an intelligent and adaptive manner to systemic disequilibria, whether internal or external to the economic system itself. For Bernstein, this realization had both theoretical and powerful practical implications. Theoretically, much of Marx's justification for predicting the inevitability of the collapse of capitalism had been empirically falsified, including dialectical materialism's fixation with Hegelian logic—the movement of sociocultural forms from actuality to negation to transcendence—as the privileged method for diagnosing social and economic crises.

This revision of Marxist theory went hand in hand with a dramatic shift in the political practice of social democracy. For Bernstein, social democracy without revolution entailed the commitment to achieving steady improvements in the welfare and prospects of the working class, via the "long march through institutions." By securing parliamentary majorities for European social democratic parties through the political process, the German Social Democrats could use those majorities to exert steady legislative pressure on the German government and other European states for progressive reforms: civil and political rights for workers, better governmental regulation of working conditions, rising wages, and a comprehensive social welfare system. That progressive movement would necessarily be open-ended, culminating in no revolutionary *Aufhebung*. If it resulted in something other or less than a classless society, then the preservation of a class system was, Bernstein reasoned, a fair compromise given the preponderance of evidence suggesting that capitalism would not be going anywhere anytime soon.

In defending orthodox Marxism against what she branded as Bernstein's "revisionism," Rosa Luxemburg insisted that Bernstein and other social democrats had blinded themselves to the nature and severity of capitalism's systemic crises, in large part by endorsing interpretations of the value and effect of democracy and law that were themselves ideological products of the system itself.[2] In other words, removing the clarifying lens of dialectical theory had blurred the contours of systemic economic crises, making increasingly feeble and ineffective compensations via noneconomic, symbolic mechanisms appear far more significant than they were.[3] Where the social democrats saw periodic cycles of boom and bust, requiring intelligent adaptive responses, a dialectician saw the playing out of internal contradictions that could only be "resolved" by the collapse of the system in its entirety in a transnational revolution that completed, rather than ameliorated, the internal contradictions of capitalism.

Where Bernstein saw *dysfunction*, Luxemburg saw *contradiction*. Where Bernstein saw adaptation and learning as autopoetic responses to dysfunctions, Luxemburg saw mere ideological defensive reactions to conceal the systemic nature of immanent contradictions. Bernstein saw open-ended progress—provided that the working classes endorsed a social democracy that worked within the capitalist economic system to reform it from within. Luxemburg saw impending global revolution and the advent of the first genuinely humane and decent form of socio-economic life—provided that the working class remained true to the doctrine of dialectical materialism.

Both of them did agree on one thing, however: the differences between their theoretical stances, and the political commitments they implied, were intractable. Bernstein observed with growing irritation that the stubborn insistence to see the economic and political world only through the categories of dialectical logic prevented socialism from emerging as a properly objective branch of applied social science. Worse, it came increasingly to resemble a mode of religious faith, impervious to empirical refutation, hostile to facts, and friendly to fanaticism. It was the classic case of the Marxist with a hammer, who looks at the world only seeing nails and spends her life hitting them.

Critical theorists need little reminder of the way this theoretical and political split widened in the subsequent years and decades into a chasm. The history of Luxemburg's and Bernstein's incompatible positions is a sorrowful one and can be told in ways that show each to have right, at least in part, on her or his side. Bernstein's version of Marxist revisionism was a crucial factor in the German Social Democratic party's rapid emergence as the largest parliamentary party in Imperial Germany. The concessions that the party was willing to make with the ruling power structure increased along with the party's size and influence, culminating in the near-unanimous vote in the Reichstag to support war credits in August 1914. The German Social Democratic Party in effect found itself compelled by political expediency to voice approval of what Luxemburg had insisted was the last and most complete form of bourgeois ideology: national war.[4] In doing so, the party placed Germany's military ambitions above international working-class solidarity—a decision that itself should be a strong candidate for an empirical refutation of the revisionist version of Marxist theory and practice.

The resulting fragmentation of the party led in short order to the formation of the Spartacist League and the Communist Party of Germany (the KPD). It was in effect the end of a united front between communism and social democracy in Germany and a split in the prospects for a socialist political organization that remains intact to the present day.

2. IMMANENT CRITIQUE AND DIALECTICAL CONTRADICTION

I've offered this potted history of the debate between the revisionists and orthodox Marxists around the turn of the twentieth century as a way of giving some structure and context to my response to Rahel Jaeggi's project of an immanent critique of modern forms of life. Let me put the response in a nutshell: Jaeggi is attempting to argue both sides of the debate at the same time. In the rest of my remarks, I will try to fill out this sense and offer some thoughts on why, if my sense is accurate, this goal may be neither possible nor desirable.

At the core of Jaeggi's project lies a distinctive version of *immanent critique* in which life-forms, *grosso modo*, can be seen as learning or nonlearning, rational or irrational, stagnant or vibrant, progressive or regressive. The rationality or vibrancy of life-forms is measured by their capacity to respond to crises in an intelligent and adaptive fashion. Crises, in turn, emerge from within the contexts of life-forms. Such forms undergo structural pressures as they cope with contradictory elements immanent to norms and corresponding practices that constitute the life-form's "concept."[5] Immanent critique identifies the relevant boundaries and formal enabling and constraining conditions of a given form of life. It discloses which norms its members must endorse in order to count as members; what practices, performed in what way, members mutually expect of one another as instances of satisfactory conformity to those norms; and how the spectrum of normative and pragmatic commitments in question do or do not successfully replicate the life-form across time and space.

Immanent critique refrains from evaluating either the higher-ranking normative commitments of respective forms of life or the suite of practices that conform to them by appeal to any normative standard external to the form of life itself. In this sense, immanent critique is meant as a conscious response to the standard objection that social critique is "merely" a hermeneutics of suspicion, in which the critic's own normativity finds that of the members of a form of life wanting, without offering a reason to think that the critic's internal standards are themselves any less open to normative critique than anyone else's.[6]

Immanent critique is also not merely *internal* insofar as the immanent critic is concerned with more than merely patrolling for inconsistencies between norms or among norms and their respective practices. Immanent critique also seeks to identify and make explicit those moments in which the formal structure of a form of life—a spectrum of coordinated norms and practices—*must* enter into contradiction. It is alert to moments where the "concept" of the form of life itself generates contradictory relationships in its norm-practice spectrum by the playing out of contradictory elements immanent in the structural core of the "concept" of the life-form itself.[7] Immanent critique identifies moments within a form of life where contradictions *must* occur, where they *cannot help but* occur.

The actualization of internal contradictions within a form of life registers as a crisis. The form of life must make use of its own internal resources to register this crisis *as* a crisis and find ways of responding to this crisis in an intelligent, effective manner.[8] Success in the intelligent mobilization of internal resources to internally generated crisis is how Jaeggi defines *learning*[9] and the capacity of forms of life to learn in this manner is for Jaeggi the equivalent of the form of life's *rationality*. Forms of life capable of responding rationally to crises are, insofar as they do so, also capable of *progress*, which for Jaeggi is indeterminate between a normative and a more normatively neutral, functionalist sense.

This conception of immanent critique has a strongly Hegelian pedigree. The idea of immanence and the methodology of immanent critique rest on the claim that forms of life embody internal contradictions. In the absence of this assertion, there is no reason to prefer immanent critique to any other critical approach, whether genealogical, reconstructive, hermeneutic, or for that matter an internal or transcendent approach of the kind Jaeggi analyses and rejects. Formal, immanent contradictions are *the* definitive trait of forms of life, marking them as appropriate objects of social critique. And contradictions taken in these terms are *irreducibly* tied to a Hegelian logic, in which contradiction—the relation of negation between internal, equally essential moments of a form of life's concept—is the phenomenal dimension of a dialectical logic in which such moments can be identified as bearing a specific set of relations with one another.

There are many ways to read Hegelian logic and many ways that any given reading can be illuminating for an existing social institution or practice. What I will argue here is that an indispensable moment—indeed for me, in my own Adornian reading of Hegel's logic, the most significant moment—is that of negation.

Immanent contradiction asserts the primacy of negation in the way the concept of a form of life dissolves analytically into its discrete moments. The norms constitutive of a form of life cannot be conformed to without the undermining and negation of those norms themselves as a foreseeable, unavoidable consequence. The form of life itself becomes unlivable: one cannot fully inhabit the form of life without being both obliged and forbidden to take one and the same course of norm-directed action, since the norm itself is in a relation of negation to itself, in distinction to external, contingent conditions that make practices demanded by the norm difficult or circumstantially impossible to perform.

Analytically dissolving the self-contradictory norm into its constituent moments discloses that what appears as a unitary object (the concept of the relevant norm) is in fact anything but: the obligatory character of the norm simultaneously issues a positive command but at the same time implicitly directs the conforming practices in ways that generate the opposite of the foreseen consequences of norm-conforming practice. Contradiction in this sense is the actualization of the moment of negation that is always already immanent to the normative order under which the form of life even emerged as a form of life, and the playing out of negation is diachronic and indeed narratively structured insofar as we can in principle always identify a real course of life in which norm conformity on the part of life-form members can be described phenomenologically as the playing out of a series of determinate negations that were identifiable analytically from the "mere" description of the logical moments of the norms themselves.[10]

Negation is not capable of sustaining itself as a logical moment in isolation. To negate is also to posit or assert: negation has effects. A form of life's internal process of self-negation possesses a logical structure that may or may not determine in actuality how that form of life will fare as its members attempt to inhabit it.[11] On this Jaeggi and I agree. Where we differ is my sense that Jaeggi's conception of immanent critique errs in effacing the work of negation implied in the claim of the contradictory character of forms of life. This loss (not negation) of the negative seems to me to lie behind and to make possible Jaeggi's distinctive combination of dialectical criticism with the pragmatic belief in the meliorist, progressive capacity of forms of life to learn from, rather than collapse under, their own self-negations. It's therefore the basis on which Jaeggi attempts to reconcile (rather than sublate) conceptions of the dynamic transformation of forms of life, as though attempting to split the difference between Luxemburg and Bernstein. In the next section, I'll try to make this claim more substantive.

3. NEGATION AND FORMS OF LIFE

Immanent critique is dialectical critique. Jaeggi gives three specific instances where such critique has been performed. The first is Hegel's critique of the immanently contradictory character of bourgeois civil society as a moment of *Sittlichkeit* in the *Philosophy of Right*. The second is Marx's critique of the self-contradictory bourgeois ideology of formal freedom and equality in its relation to a capitalist wage-based economy in *The German Ideology* and other early works. The third is Freud's writings on the psychoanalytic relation and the work of the analyst in disclosing the origins and nature of individual neuroses.

I confess to some degree of confusion regarding the last of these three paradigm cases of immanent critique, since I simply do not see it as critical in the relevant dialectical sense, nor do I perceive how to equate the category of immanence in Hegel's and Marx's sense with what such a term could plausibly mean in the context of the Freudian topography. (Nor does Jaeggi ever follow up on the assertion that psychoanalysis is immanent critique.) In the former two Hegelian instances, the clear difference is between Hegel's larger claim that the contradictory elements of a moment of ethical life are *compatible, even necessary*, given the conceptual core of that form, and Marx's view of ideology as legible only from the perspective of its impending real collapse.

In the former case, a form of life is immanently contradictory in the sense that inhabiting it—living the life that the form normatively promotes or requires—foreseeably generates forms of consciousness and directives for action that are incompatible with the norm the form of life imposes. The form, by being lived in, generates its own negation.

Hegel's description of the bourgeois family, for instance, shows how the immediacy of love (the norm in question, which Hegel defines in *The Philosophy of Right* as "ethical life in its natural form"[12]) constitutes a relation of the parent and the child that undergoes a series of mediations (determinations-negations), producing a child whose capacity to remain in the role of a hierarchically inferior being in relation to the authority of the parent is progressively undermined and destroyed by the very conformity of all concerned to that very same norm. The family rests on an immanent contradiction: its immediacy requires the absence of that reflective, mediated dimension in which the child's own consciousness asserts itself as a legitimate source of claims, preferences, and interests of its own. It is constituted as a being that must negate its own subordinate role as the (mere) object of love. Loving parents—loving their child with the immediacy that parents ought to do, if they are "really" parents—will by their conformity to the norm raise children in what Hegel calls "a circle of love and trust." This will, all things going well, produce children for whom that immediacy itself will, as a consequence of repeated mediations, transform into its other: an opposition to be cast off, a life no longer livable.

Raised in this enabling-confining circle, the child will acquire just the resources of self-confidence and independence she will need in order to recognize the need to break free from it. The child's childness, as the site of iterated negations, must itself be negated, and this can only be done by negating the form of life itself, which the *successfully raised* child does by asserting her own independence, moving from the loving immediacy of the family world into the distinctly nonloving mediation of the "system of needs" in bourgeois civil society, in which a lack of warmth and care is compensated by a gain in autonomy and equality and the achievement of a higher, more substantial form of her self-determinacy. The point, therefore, of any given family is its own dissolution as children leave and parents die. Hegel is clear that the "ethical dissolution of the family" consists precisely in "the fact that the children are brought up to become free personalities" (§177)—free, that is, to leave and enter a form of life characterized by its own specific forms of initial indeterminacy.

Hence logical analysis of the concept of "child" discloses a thoroughly dialectical term. "Child" is itself immanently contradictory, which is why even in everyday parlance, it makes sense for older parents to say, for example, that their "child" is in her forties and—provided she doesn't still live in her childhood bedroom—therefore both a child and not a child at one and the same time. But for Hegel, "child" could only be a dialectical concept insofar as the very concept of relations of love, on which the emotional reality of family must rest, is itself "the most immense contradiction."[13]

Moreover, this disclosure of the immanent contradiction of the form of bourgeois family life entails moments both of crisis and of transformation. Of course, those crises and transformations properly concern the individual members occupying and operating the form of life and not the form of life itself. Ontogenetically, the experiences of repeated negation as the child makes her way through the familiar forms of life are indeed crisis structured and transformative (as any parent of a teenager can attest); indeed, it's the *absence* of such transformative crises that should have parents worried about their kid's failure to launch. Families therefore dissolve through the actualization of contradictions indwelling in the "concept" of the family as an institution of bourgeois ethical life. And yet the dissolution in question of course is not a "problem" in Jaeggi's sense but the very opposite of a problem.

For Hegel, the crisis-and-transformation phenomenology of negation that is imposed on the *subjects* of life-forms only makes sense on the further assumption that there is *another life-form*, to which the life-form is itself dialectically related, in which the negated or mediated form of subjectivity generated by the self-contradictory life-form can find "satisfaction" or a form of subjective life appropriate to its new form. Ethical life for Hegel does not consist of a simple pluralism of various forms of life that offer themselves to the modern subject as menu options for the construction of a meaningful life. On the contrary, bourgeois civil society bears a specific negative relation to the life of the family that could not be replaced or modified by any other institution.

It's *because* family and civil society are constructed in a specific kind of relationship to one another that the internal contradictions specific to each—together with the crises and transformation that each predictably generates for its members—are not only compatible with the ongoing functional life of the respective forms of life but in fact equivalent to that very functionality. Insofar as this is true, for Hegel such forms of life *have nothing to learn because they are rational.* Their vitality and functional endurance presuppose no new thing, apart from the continued supply of new subjects to inhabit them. This same set of claims applies *mutatis mutandis* to the relation between bourgeois civil society and the state, where the "extremes" of the former—the otherwise unsustainable separation of individuals equally situated in a system of needs—are once again negated (and hence compensated) by a form of solidarity where individual freedom can acquire the ethical substance that is a condition for its actual value and meaning.

Hegel thinks that the disclosure of immanent contradictions, far from a source of problems that a form of life must solve to survive, is a form of insight into the form of life's normative rightness. In other words, self-contradiction is a documentation of the form of life's embodied rationality, not its irrationality. That rationality consists in this: what may *appear* as a problem from the limited, one-sided perspective of a given form of life is disclosed as *not really a problem* from the perspective of that form of life's successive, superior form.

This entails the claim—about which Hegel is famously specific in the preface to the *Philosophy of Right*—that philosophy's critical reconstruction of the rationality of institutions is not part of a larger intention to revise or reform those institutions according to some normativity external to them. The internal rationality of forms of life is only accessible as an object of philosophical analysis once the philosopher can *behold* how those contradictory elements, actualized, are taken up and resolved in a form of life superior to it.

In the case of Marx's critique of bourgeois ideology, this set of claims is itself negated in the critical project of disclosing how the formal freedom and equality of the isolated bourgeois individual cannot actually be lived—cannot be a practice-guiding norm in actuality—insofar as abstract freedom and equality are valid norms only in the context of a wage-based economy. That economy demands that the majority of subjects occupy social roles in which freedom and equality are incompatible with those roles. The relation of negation between equal formal freedoms normatively demanded by bourgeois civil society on the one side and the subjection to domination and immiseration actually required to operate that society on the other is no longer understood (merely) as a foreseeable crisis for the subjects attempting to occupy the form of life but as the functional capacity of the form of life itself to continue to replicate.

Those crises are material and immaterial at one and the same time. Marx wants to show that immanent contradiction extends to materiality's self-directed outcomes as well as the interplay between material and symbolic modes of domination. Even in the absence of an ideology of freedom and equality, the internal logic of capital accumulation is unsustainable for purely material reasons. Market expansion, technological innovation, and downward pressure on wages in concert generate the conditions of their own exhaustion. Add to this the inevitability of ideological factors to generate proletarian consciousness of the cui bono of this accumulation and the Marxist analysis completes its treatment of *crisis* with a distinct conception of the term's medical origin, the decisive moment in the etiology of a disease in which the course toward either death or recovery is announced. But for Marx, "crisis" acquires the distinctive sense of objective economic indicia for a process of dysfunctional collapse long since predecided by the incompatible dynamics embedded in its concept. The tendency of economic booms and busts to grow more severe and the human costs these conjunctures inflict are thus not crisis-structured systemic behaviors in the strict sense, insofar as each cycle provides further confirmation of a dysfunctional dynamic whose outcome was never in doubt.

To regard this dysfunctional dynamic as a *dialectic* is for Marx (and Luxemburg) to see it as unfolding according to the logic of negation. As a logic of negation, the playing out of capitalism's contradictions will also inevitably generate system-wide responses that will *take on the appearance* of intelligent coping from the perspective of those ideologically disposed to do so. But those appearances reverse under immanent critique, disclosing not just the lack of efficacy of those systemic responses but indeed their status as cosymptomatic of the exacerbating material conditions themselves.

What from an internal perspective still appears as a "learning process"—for instance, the kind of accommodations or adjustments, both material and ideological, that Bernstein welcomes as signs of progress—from an immanent-critical perspective reappears as the *opposite* of learning. It is certainly composed in part of the conscious efforts of social actors, mobilizing what resources they can to respond effectively to the perceptible drift of a form of life into dysfunction. But such reactive responses, whether in the meliorist guise of reform and inclusion or the resort to brute political force, cannot ultimately qualify as learning for this dialectical mode of critique. The initial commitment to the mode of contradiction determines instead that these efforts come into focus only as episodes of self-negation, with outcomes that must be assessed independently of the intentions of their initiating social agents.

4. THE MISSING MOMENT OF CONTRADICTION IN THE CRITIQUE OF FORMS OF LIFE

Hegel and Marx, in differing ways, understand negation as the driver of organic developments of forms of life and hence as an indispensable concept for dialectical analysis and criticism. Even where they differ in the implications of negation for the interpretation of the functional viability of respective forms, they agree that *negation is the primary object of attention* in such an interpretation. They are both, in that sense, dialectical thinkers.

For Jaeggi, who explicitly takes on this legacy of dialectical criticism, the role of negation in the actual performance of immanent critique is more difficult to discern. While the presence of immanent contradictions in life-forms remains for her the basic object of immanent critique, it is not easy to reconstruct the process of reasoning that leads from the identification of such contradictions to the assertion that "responding" to them creatively and intelligently is the criterion by which the institutional rationality of a given form of life is to be measured and its progressive or regressive potential is to be assigned.

In brief, it's not evident why *contradictions* in each case are to be interpreted as generative of potential *problems*, unless an additional, nondialectical premise is introduced. This premise (derived largely from the reading of John Dewey) is the claim that *contradictions are equivalent to dysfunctions*. But are they? Hegel, at least, the originator of immanent critique as a dialectical exercise, certainly doesn't think so.

Equating the unfolding of contradictions as dysfunctional requires that Jaeggi's form of Hegelianism conflates two dimensions in the analysis of forms of life that are in fact distinct: The first is the presence of contradictory elements or moments within a given form of life, the actualization and realization of which will take the form of a series of determinate negations. The second is the presence of factors that will lead to the (eventual) dissolution or fading away of a given form of life as it undergoes dysfunctional processes—typically experienced phenomenologically as anomie, in Robert Merton's sense—the loss of capacity of the form of life to reproduce itself in historical time and social space by replacing outgoing (dying) members with new ones via processes of socialization and normative integration. For Jaeggi, it appears that these two dimensions—contradiction and dysfunction—are equivalent, a claim that draws on Hegelian dialectics for support.

As we've seen, however, Hegel asserts the contradictory position in the *Philosophy of Right*, though he reserves this argument for a small subset of privileged forms of life corresponding to the moments of *Sittlichkeit* as such. It's the very immanent contradictions of a form of life that propel subjects through and out of them—that is, that characterize their *function*. Marx's view is that the self-contradictions inherent in bourgeois civil society have empirical, material entailments generating nonsurvivable outcomes for the metaform of life (capitalism) as a whole.

For Jaeggi, by contrast, individual life-forms in the context of a multiplicity of available life-forms can be analyzed separately, according to how robustly they respond to crisis-generating contradictions emerging as dysfunctions (problems) in the ongoing replication of the respective forms. However, what counts as a dysfunction will clearly depend on whether we take the point of view of the dialectical critic or the (distinct) viewpoint of the external observer merely measuring function in terms of the capacity of a life-form to replicate itself by generating new members. If Hegel is at all correct, then the microsociological phenomena of negation, as in young people feeling "expelled" from their family as a result of repeated, crisis-structured experiences, can be taken as functional, not dysfunctional, from the point of view of theory.

Further, to the extent that we accept Marx's reformulation of immanent critique as ideology critique, then the final confirmation of a theory describing the *macro*dysfunction of a form of social existence (i.e., its demise) resting on a contradictory relation between formal and actual freedom and equality depends on the plausibility of the claim of the *inevitable*—the conceptually and really necessary—collapse of the form of existence itself. No creative or rational response to alleviate the mere epiphenomenal emergences of minidysfunctions (miserable workers, exacerbated and quickened economic boom and bust cycles) matters one way or another, in the sense that *capitalism cannot learn*.

Jaeggi's response to these positions, in the ninth chapter of *Kritik von Lebensformen*, is to assert the equivalence of problems and contradictions. The pragmatist (Deweyan) understanding of problem solving as an open-ended, progressive, self-transformative, creative adaptation to blockages in the subject's behavior repertoire is transferred from the micro- to the macrolevel. Systemic crises are described as analogous to those interruptions of the individual subject's habitual suite of practices, and since those crises are understood to arise from within that suite of normed-but-habitual practices themselves, problem solving on the macrolevel involves both drawing on and transforming the reservoir of meanings and interpretations, norms and habits, constitutive of a form of life, so that the form both continues but changes—just as an individual subject, in Dewey's terms, grows and changes through a process of self-transformative developmental learning.

Pictured in these terms, it's clear enough why Jaeggi sees deep affinities between a Hegelian account of the unfolding or actualization of the subject through a series of determinate negations and Dewey's conception of growth and development as a learning process. Understood as dialectical contradictions, crises appear most dramatically as the "contradictoriness, fragmentation, and unlivability"[14] of a form of life that propels its members toward creative coping.

Of course it takes another logical inference to assert that members of life-forms themselves are capable of reflexively interpreting such crises *as* problems to be solved, and it is the special duty of immanent critique to assist them in doing so. As dialectic, contradiction problems present social members with a range of cognitive and affective disorders that Axel Honneth, less dialectically minded than Jaeggi, prefers to see as social pathologies.

To put my point no doubt too crudely: in her appeal to a powerfully Hegelian-dialectical vocabulary (unlivability, contradictoriness, fragmentation) to depict the crises that confront members of a life-form as second order, Jaeggi asserts—but does not argue for—the capacity of those members to interpret these crises as practical problems to solve. I don't regard this argument as very promising. It seems to me more intuitively plausible that actual social members would respond to such second-order crises—registering as the unlivability of a form of life—by leaving (if they can), not learning. In both Hegel's and Marx's conceptions of immanent critique, this is in fact the predominant route of explanation. Individual members of an unlivable form of life experience that unlivability as an impetus toward self-transformation via institutions, as in Hegel's moments of ethical life. Proletarians experience both the material and the psychic unlivability of bourgeois civil society as an impetus to act in ways calculated to bring that form of life to its natural end in Marx's revolutionary dialectical materialism. But the prospect of social members (or a form of life as a macrosubject) to translate *unlivability* into an occasion for *problem solving* seems to me at least to retain its plausibility only by downplaying, or indeed omitting entirely, the dimension of the unlivability of crisis-ridden forms of life as the *experience of negation*. Unlivability is the *loss* of meaning, of the validity of existentially significant norms. What must we impute to these subjects, macro or micro, such that these experiences of repeated negation would also generate the set of competencies and orientations characterized as a capacity to learn?

This would be an empirical question, provided we had some reasonable confidence in determining (in advance) that what registered as problems for social members were also what the critic determines as self-contradictions. But we can't solve this problem by fiat by merely asserting that the two are equivalent. Problems, Jaeggi reminds us, have an irreducible reflexive element (374). They are in a sense second-order responses to second-order crises. But insofar as those second-order crises are also negations of (and not just challenges to) a form of life in its concept, it's not clear why the form of life should be expected to respond to *negations* as just as many *problems*—as though Bernstein's idea of a patient working through the dysfunctions that capitalism generates can be reconciled with nothing further to Luxemburg's idea of a form of life incompatible with itself. This logic of both/and, so powerfully on display here, is the logic of nondialectical reconciliation, of meeting in the middle, of contradictions solved by averaging, rather than negating, the opposing poles.

5. CONCLUSION: ON HOW (NOT) TO HAVE IT BOTH WAYS

Contemporary readers of Hegel are faced with a dilemma. Either they approach Hegel's dialectic as historians of modern philosophy, in which case they have a more or less free hand to explore Hegel's project and its predecessors and influence at the risk of reducing the distinctive features of Hegelian philosophy to a limited antiquarian interest. Or they appropriate Hegel as a badly needed resource for political philosophy and social criticism with normative ambitions and set out to dissect and remove those resources from their setting in Hegel's larger philosophy.

There is nothing unique or even extraordinary about this second kind of (cherry-picking) reading, and certainly Hegel is not the only philosopher whose appropriation requires more or less ruthless pruning. But features specific to Hegelian thought do impose special challenges not found, say, in Kant or Hume. Hegel's logic is of a piece with both his commitment to the philosophy of spirit as well as the organicism that is definitive for Hegel's treatment of each and every philosophical topic. In terms of normative political philosophy, it's not clear which is more worth avoiding: Hegel's spirit monism and its entailment of the rational affirmation of the existent or the way in which that affirmation generates a celebration of the German state that many of Hegel's own reform-minded contemporaries found just as repugnant as we do.

What is distinctive, as far as I can see, in Jaeggi's place in this wider practice of Hegel appropriation is that her version of immanent critique, as well as her overall orientation toward the ends and procedure of a normatively ambitious political theory, asserts a dependence on a dialectical mode of argumentation in ways that her peers' appropriative projects do not. Immanent critique, as I described it in the previous section, simply *is* dialectics; in any event, it would be incoherent as a core methodological commitment without an explicit dependence on Hegel's original conception and application of the idea of the contradictory structure of social formations. The Marxist theory of ideology critique may break from Hegelian logic in important senses but remains internal to the family of dialectical approaches to social criticism, and Jaeggi's dependence on it is explicit and well defended. In this sense, Jaeggi is a Hegelian interpreter of Hegel, to a degree greater than most other contemporary critical theorists.

My disagreement with Jaeggi's project is simply that dialectical logic is not compatible, in my judgment, with the functionalist account (of the capacity of forms of life to respond intelligently to dysfunctional problems) that she sees as its supplement. Jaeggi's position, in anticipation of the concerns I voice here, is that of a *dialectical learning process*, diachronically perceptible now as "history," or at least as the concrete history of a given life-form.[15] And yet I remain unclear on how the direct and substantive appeal to Hegel and to a Hegelian conception of reason in history, which Jaeggi provides, amounts to a response to the worry that "learning processes" are precisely what Hegel does *not* find characteristic of the preeminent institutionalized forms of life characteristic of a developed, modern *Sittlichkeit*.

Jaeggi's defense of the unity of *dialectics* and the dynamics of *learning processes*, in other words, seems undermotivated. The former corresponds to a conception of historically articulated, contextually embedded reason, of Hegelian reason, which notwithstanding all postmetaphysical efforts at translation remains in some significant sense linked to Hegel's spirit monism: it is *Spirit*, in this conception, that is doing the learning, and universal history *is* that learning process.[16]

Transformative effects of that process on the level of particular forms of life would then have to be assessed as progressive or regressive by reference to a larger frame—the expansion of reason's freedom in the world *through the medium of* individual life-forms. But in this context, the latter conception of reason—the instrumental capacity to respond effectively to internal disequilibria, to counter tendencies toward dysfunction, and to increase the prospects of the self-replication of a life-form over historical time and in social space—has only a derivative and secondary significance for the normative evaluation of forms of life. Progress as a norm cannot reduce to mere survival. To count as progress in Hegelian terms, a form of life must be shown to have played its part in a larger historical narrative; otherwise, its passing has no special importance.

This I think is the true measure of Hegel's coldness. Where there is no negation, there is no life; there, Spirit is not at work. Such times of stagnation may be very fortunate for individual persons (or maybe even individual life-forms) lucky enough to pass an agreeable span of years in uneventful times. As Hegel succinctly puts it in the *Lectures on the Philosophy of History*, the periods of happiness in human history are "blank pages," the periods of "missing contradiction." One way of figuring the implications of this form of Hegelianism is that, in the absence of an expanded conception of reason beyond the internal instrumentality of forms of life, we lack a way of arguing why the "progress" of any given form of life, in the instrumental sense, matters.

This implies that the equation of a historically embedded dialectical process, on the one hand, and the internal learning processes of individual life-forms, on the other, is at best unconvincing and at worst tendentious.

The retrospective judgment concerning historical winners and losers is always, as Benjamin reminds us, an assertion of power as much as an objective evaluation of warranted outcomes. In the confrontation between Bernstein and Luxemburg at the beginning of the twentieth century, it may be best to refrain from making any such judgment at all. Bernstein's progressivism and meliorism, like Luxemburg's radicalism, proved both a success and a failure, on multiple registers. Bourgeois civil society did indeed progressively adapt itself to accommodate a range of workers' political and legal demands that would have been scarcely imaginable a generation earlier. Capitalism's capacity to generate wealth—and to obliterate forms of life standing in its way—would have astonished even the Marx of the *Manifesto*.

And yet the state of global economic and political inequality, unfreedom, and injustice remains stunning, and in many important respects has grown, not ameliorated, in the century following Bernstein's vision of a progressivist social democratic agenda. That very agenda may well have played itself out in the near total victory of a neoliberalism that has become synonymous with globalization. Luxemburg's insistence that radical transformation is not compatible with gradual progress remains as relevant now as it did during the brief window in which socialism showed prospects to be an international political movement. And yet Luxemburg's revolutionary program too has never been able to mount a satisfactory defense against the core of the social-democratic accusation: that the nonfalsifiable claim of the historical inevitability of capitalism's systemic collapse falls into dogmatism or worse.

But even if we resist the temptation for retrospective scorekeeping, I'd insist on one thing we can say about the respective positions of Bernstein and Luxemburg: they are different. They rest on distinct and (to me) irreconcilable methodological and social-ontological principles. Jaeggi's project nevertheless aspires to reconcile them. In my view, the plausibility of this attempt depends on a conception of dialectics that seriously undervalues the centrality of negation as the foundation of dialectical criticism.

In the absence of the negative moment, dialectics can often take on the appearance of mere addition: the logic of both/and. But mediation entails loss; one cannot reconcile everything. If, to take only the most pressing example, bourgeois civil society justifies its hegemony with a commitment to the norms of freedom and equality, norms whose realization capitalism renders impossible, then *either* that contradiction expresses a structural self-contradiction, a negation profound and systemic enough to indict the institution of bourgeois civil society as a whole, *or* it invites civil society institutions and practices to rationally adapt, to accommodate dysfunctional problems as they arise, as equality and freedom encounter internal obstacles to their progressive realization. But one cannot assert both—at least, so it seems to me.[17]

NOTES

1. See Eduard Bernstein, *Evolutionary Socialism: A Criticism and Affirmation*, trans. Edith C. Harvey (New York: B. W. Huebsch, 1911).
2. See Rosa Luxemburg, *Reform or Revolution?* (1899; repr., London: Militant Publications, 1986).
3. "When [Bernstein] directs his keenest arrows against our dialectical system he is really attacking the specific mode of thought employed by the conscious proletariat in its struggle for liberation. It is an attempt to break the sword that has helped the proletariat to pierce the darkness of its future. It is an attempt to shatter the intellectual arm with the aid of which the proletariat, though materially under the yoke of the bourgeoisie, is yet enabled to triumph over the bourgeoisie. For it is our dialectical system that shows to the working class the transitory nature of this yoke, providing to workers the inevitability of their victory, and is already realizing a revolution in the domain of thought" (Luxemburg, 66).
4. On hearing the news of the vote, Luxemburg promptly announced, "If they think we are going to lift the weapons of murder against our French and other brethren, then we shall shout: 'We will not do it!' "—a public proclamation that earned her the first of her two prison terms during the war years.
5. Typical is the following passage, where Jaeggi defines contradiction (in the context of Hegel's theory of bourgeois civil society) as "keine schlichte Inkonsistenz, er bezeichnet aber auch nicht eine logische Unvereinbarkeit, sondern ein *Spannungsverhältnis innerhalb einer Formation, das diese über sich selbst hinaustreiben wird*"; Rahel Jaeggi, *Kritik von Lebensformen* (Frankfurt: Suhrkamp, 2014), 287.
6. See Rahel Jaeggi, "Was ist Ideologiekritik?," in *Was ist Kritik?*, ed. Rahel Jaeggi and Tilo Wesche (Frankfurt: Suhrkamp, 2009), 266–95, 283. For an interesting commentary, see Oliver Krüger, "Die Normativität der immanenten Kritik," *Zeitschrift*

für philosophische Literatur 2, no. 3 (2014): 12ff. See also Robin Celikates, "Politique des formes de vie," *Raisons Politiques* 57 (February 2015).
7. See Jaeggi, "Was ist Ideologiekritik?"
8. "Immanente Kritik schließt dann insofern an das in einer Konstellation Vorhandene an, als die Mittel zur Lösung des Problems oder der Krise *in* dieser Situation selbst verortet werden" (Jaeggi, *Kritik*, 302).
9. Jaeggi, 315–17.
10. See the account in Titus Stahl, "What Is Immanent Critique?" (working papers, SSRN, 2013), http://ssrn.com/abstract=2357957.
11. On this, see G. W. F. Hegel, "Doctrine of Being," in *Science of Logic* (Cambridge: Cambridge University Press, 2015), §21.94, 88–91.
12. G. W. F. Hegel, *Elements of the Philosophy of Right* (Cambridge: Cambridge University Press, 1991), §158, 199.
13. "The first moment of love is that I do not wish to be an independent person for myself, and that, if I were, I would feel deficient and incomplete. The second moment is that I find myself in another person, that I matter in her, who, in turn, matters in me. Love is therefore the most immense contradiction; the understanding cannot resolve it, because there is nothing more intractable than this punctuation of self-consciousness, which is negated, and which I ought nevertheless to possess as affirmative. Love is both the production and the resolution of this contradiction. As its resolution, it is ethical unity" (§158). Translation amended. I know of few more touching definitions of love than Hegel's eccentric notion of a self-consciousness permitting its own "punctuation" by another person, and even though I suspect Hegel is referring to romantic love between a man and a woman here, the view strikes me as more relevant still for the decision of adults to become parents and the transformations they thereby will into being of their own selves by virtue of the voluntary creation of a third, a process that for Hegel allows romantic love between two people to "possess objectivity" (§173).
14. Jaeggi, *Kritik*, 368.
15. Jaeggi, 351.
16. Jaeggi, 352.
17. See Jaeggi's argument that critically fomented self-transformation of bourgeois civil society would lead to norms of freedom and equality "transformed to a fuller and more encompassing understanding of freedom as 'positive freedom' or to a 'material conception of equality' " (Jaeggi, 288).

CHAPTER 6

What's Critical about Critical Theory?—Redux

Rocío Zambrana

The work of our time [is] to clarify to itself (critical philosophy) the meaning of its own struggle and its own desires. This is work for the world and for us. It can only be the work of joint forces.

—MARX[1]

In her 1985 essay "What's Critical about Critical Theory? The Case of Habermas and Gender," Nancy Fraser offered a decisive critique of Jürgen Habermas's theory of communicative action.[2] Habermas's distinction between system and lifeworld—itself based on a distinction between the material and symbolic reproduction of society—ignores the gendered character of social reproduction. One could only consider the lifeworld as a site of communicative interaction, for instance, if one ignores the fact that women's exploitation in great part takes place within "socially-integrated action contexts" or if one ignores the feminization of work within "system-integrated action contexts."[3] Habermas's critical theory lacks critical power, Fraser argues, because it fails to "clarify the struggles and desires of the age." It does not offer an account of the gendered character of social reproduction because it fails to take seriously the insights of the feminist movement—insights that are not peripheral to an account of society, that ought to shape our understanding of social reproduction, and that ought to inform how we understand critique.

Fraser opens her essay with the suggestion that Marx's 1843 definition of critical theory as the clarification of the struggles and desires of the age is unmatched given its distinctively political character.[4] Critical theory remains critical if it is oriented by the potential for social transformation embedded in the concrete struggles of the present. This political commitment, however, sets a theoretical agenda for critical theory. Critical theory remains critical when it reflects on its own assumptions in light of the struggles of the age, when it is willing to revise its own assumptions in light of the strictures of those struggles. The theoretical task, then, is to work out a conception of critique that inscribes within itself the idea that critique takes its bearings from social reality while at the same time aiming to transform that very reality for the better. The theoretical task is thus working out what has come to be known as the dialectic of immanence and transcendence at a methodological level. Rather than a retreat to the abstractions of philosophical reflection, the theoretical task prepares the ground for research programs that heed to the struggles and desires of the age.

Marx himself understood that, with all its shortcomings, Hegel's dialectics were best suited for tackling this theoretical task. He famously sought to turn Hegel's idealism on its head in order to recover dialectics for a materialist account of capitalist modernity. He rejected Hegel's speculative philosophy while understanding the power of Hegelian negativity. He understood that Hegel's insistence on characterizing contradictions as objective rather than logical helps us grasp the dynamic character of reality. He sought to develop the Hegelian thought that objective contradictions disclose the truth of the matter at hand, suggesting concretely their own overcoming. Rahel Jaeggi has taken up the theoretical task of critical theory along these lines, developing a thoroughgoing Hegelian conception of critique as immanent critique. Following Hegel's critique of Kant and Marx's critique of liberal political economy, she has characterized liberalism's insistence on "neutrality" as a form of "ideology."[5] She has transformed Hegel's concepts of contradiction and determinate negation, offering a critical theory of "forms of life" (*Lebensformen*). She has thereby prepared new ground for clarifying the struggles and desires of the present.

In what follows, I assess Jaeggi's conception of immanent critique by examining her proposal for a critical theory of forms of life. Focusing on her transformation of Hegel's key concepts of contradiction and determinate negation and her brief articulation of the concept of emancipation, I evaluate the claim that critique is based on an assessment of a form of life's capacity to enable collective self-determination through learning processes. In order to assess Jaeggi's proposal concretely, I turn to her account of a critique of capitalism as a form of life and contrast this account with Fraser's recent essays on capitalism. I argue that Fraser's recent work displays a latent Hegelianism that is radically different from Jaeggi's. Rather than progressive learning processes, Fraser emphasizes the mediating force of capitalist accumulation and the normative ambivalence that such mediation yields. I argue that the differences between Jaeggi and Fraser's deployment of core Hegelian motifs matter a great deal, given the aims of critical theory as defined by the Hegelian-Marxist commitments sketched earlier. In closing, I suggest that Fraser's emphasis on mediation and normative ambivalence ought to be taken in a different direction, one that reframes a critique of capitalism by arguing that it entails a critique of coloniality.

1. CONTRADICTION, DETERMINATE NEGATION

Kritik von Lebensformen takes on the remarkable task of revitalizing Hegel's dialectics for a critical theory of society. Rather than focusing exclusively on Hegel's social or political theory, Jaeggi breathes new life into the core Hegelian concepts contradiction and determinate negation. This is a bold task, given the ambivalent relation that, throughout the twentieth century, critical theory has had to these concepts.[6] On the one hand, they are central to the very idea of immanent critique, to the idea that critique takes its bearings from social reality while aiming to transform reality for the better. On the other hand, they are central to conceptions of historical necessity and progress that, with good reason, have been called into question within and beyond critical theory.[7] Notwithstanding these significant objections, Jaeggi's undertaking is important and welcome. Although I will argue for a different understanding of Hegel and of the role that Hegel's master concepts should play in critical theory today, I share with Jaeggi the view that what is most productive in Hegel is not the content of his dialectics but rather the form.[8]

In the fourth part of *Kritik von Lebensformen*, Jaeggi pursues an ambitious rewriting of Hegel, thereby developing her proposal for a critical theory of forms of life. In order to mitigate some of the problematic features of Hegelian contradiction and determinate negation, Jaeggi draws from John Dewey and Alasdair MacIntyre's work. She rewrites Hegelian contradiction and determinate negation in light of Dewey's pragmatic understanding of learning processes and MacIntyre's conception of the retrospective integration of traditions.[9] Dewey and MacIntyre are helpful since they allow Jaeggi to articulate a Hegelian conception of historical development that walks a fine line between contingency and necessity. Indeed, Jaeggi aims to articulate the contingency of social practices *and* the necessity of both the tensions that the problems they confront express and the solutions to these problems. She also aims to think through the discontinuity of forms of life in light of the continuity of a form of life's historical development, understood as a learning process. Ultimately, she aims to develop a conception of historical development as experimental and open yet one that can be assessed as progressive or regressive in view of its capacity for enrichment. This Hegelian-pragmatic account of the dynamic of learning processes pays heed to social reality yet yields a metacriterion for critique and transformation.

It is instructive to begin by recalling the social ontology grounding Jaeggi's conception of history. Forms of life are "inert bundles of practices." Practices are a set of actions that are repetitive and habitual yet are nonetheless interpreted and understood. They are norm governed and have a *telos*, a goal or aim. They are "inert" because they contain "sedimentary elements," features that are not transparent or explicit but that can be made explicit. Forms of life are therefore "something that human beings do and therefore could do otherwise."[10] Moments of crisis are crucial since they "force reflection and/or adjustment."

So understood, forms of life are "instances of problem solving." They are the "best solution" to problems they "face and pose." They address problems understood by commitments structuring any given practice.

Hence problems are "normatively predefined." But they respond to functional deficits, to crises that refer to the aim of the practice at hand. A problem is understood and addressed then in light of functional *and* normative commitments. Now to speak of forms of life as instances of problem solving is to speak of a social formation in terms of its history rather than an anthropological ground or "need."[11] Forms of life are "historical processes of problem solving."[12]

This social ontology guides Jaeggi's conception of immanent critique and her rejection of external critique (guided by a norm or perspective that purports neutrality with respect to the practice at hand) and internal critique (guided by a norm structuring that practice but measured by the practice's inconsistency with its own norm). Immanent critique is the appropriate critical method for forms of life since it conceives of the form of life as normatively articulated, understands the functional-constitutive character of norms, considers crises as inversions within the very effectiveness of the norm, is oriented to crises immanent to the practice, articulates the parallel tension between reality and norm, and is transformative rather than reconstructive.[13] Immanent critique, then, takes its bearings from social reality by paying heed to the contradictions immanent to the practice at hand. But it understands these contradictions not as inconsistencies between norm and reality but rather dialectically—as the inversions of *both* norm and reality *within the very effectiveness of the norm*. This entwinement of the functional and normative structure of a practice is the key feature of Jaeggi's conception. Immanent critique thematizes and seeks to revise *both* social arrangements and their normative commitments. For this reason, it is not reconstructive. It does not attempt to reestablish continuity between norm and reality. It is transformative. It attempts to revise norm *and* reality in light of the contradiction at hand.

Contradiction and determinate negation, reread in light of Dewey's and MacIntyre's works, are central to Jaeggi's social ontology and conception of immanent critique. Dewey conceives of social change as experimental problem solving. On his pragmatic conception, experience is a shared learning process. We only undertake an experiment when practical problems arise, and we only come to understand hypotheses in light of their practical consequences.[14] Solutions are thus contingent, fallible, and open-ended. They are necessarily subject to revision. Learning and hence social change can be critically assessed in light of the extent to which they "block" or "enable" experience. This negative criterion is crucial for Jaeggi. Problem solving is assessed in light of its capacity to identify and address "blockages of experience." Learning processes can thereby be understood as enriching or not a form of life. MacIntyre in turn understands the inner rationality of a tradition in light of standards developed and employed in addressing limitations or deficiencies.[15] Processes of justification must thus be understood retrospectively. It is only after the fact, in light of the fact, that an interpretation of the limits encountered as well as the continuity between such limits and forms of address can be established.[16]

Accounting for the *systemic* character of blockages of experience, Jaeggi argues, requires understanding problems in a stronger sense than Dewey did.[17] Hegel's notion of contradiction here is insightful. For Hegel, contradictions are objective rather than logical.[18] They take different forms given the tensions within a specific institutional arrangement, forms of self-understanding or conceptual structure. In Hegel's work, normative expectations revert to their opposite, the unfolding of an action undermines its very actualization, and incompatible expectations generate a clash between subjects, institutions, and concepts. Contradictions refer to the work or "function" of a given institution, self-understanding, and concept and its normative structure. Hegelian contradiction, then, captures the entwinement of the functional and normative aspects of a form of life. Social crises, Jaeggi thus argues, express a deficiency *within that entwinement*. Problems should be understood as contradictions then when a practice cannot *function* within its *normative* self-conception.[19] Contradictions express a tension within the realization of the norm in reality *and* the functioning of reality in relation to its normative self-conception.[20]

Because contradictions are systemic, they are not merely obstacles to action. They are "conditions of possible action."[21] This means that the mode of address is tailored to the contradiction at hand. Also, because contradictions lie within the very effectiveness of the norm and hence call for a revision of function and norm, justification for social change relies on criteria developed immanently. Hegel's notion of determinate negation is fruitful here. It describes a process of enrichment that specifies address and justification immanently and retrospectively.[22] In *Phenomenology of Spirit*, determinate negation refers to a process whereby a new object arises from the negation of a specific contradiction. Negation improves on the object since a contradiction is addressed in light of the tension at hand. Criteria are therefore developed within the unfolding of the contradiction; justification must refer to the way in which the contradiction was addressed.[23] The necessity at hand, however, is not causal.[24] It is the "practical-rational necessity" of the very logic of the contradiction and its mode of address, of the problem and its solution.

A form of life, Jaeggi maintains, can thus be criticized in light of its "history of problem-solving attempts." The "rationality"—indeed, the "success"—of a form of life can be measured in light of its capacity to address its problems and to learn from its history of problem solving. Learning processes can therefore be "regressive" or "nonregressive." Problem solving represents progress if "blockages of experience"—"hindrances that prevent a form of life from opening up to further experiences"—are "observed." This delivers a metacriterion for a critique of forms of life. A learning process makes transformations for the better if it provides emancipatory possibilities. Emancipatory possibilities are grounded in "the degree of insight" into the "configurability" (*Gestaltbarkeit*) of one's own form of life and into the ability to give shape to one's form of life. As such, emancipation is tied to the possibilities for learning that a form of life offers.[25] A form of life can be said to be rational—transformations can be said to be for the better—when it affords opportunities for collective self-determination through learning processes. A critical theory of forms of life is thereby grounded in an "experimental pluralism" since openness to other forms of life makes learning possible.

Jaeggi's articulation of the entwinement of the functional and the normative is extremely insightful, yet her understanding of Hegelian contradiction and determinate negation neutralizes the critical purchase of her account. She remains squarely within classical readings of Hegel based on a conception of history as progressive and contradiction as the motor of progress. To be sure, Jaeggi works hard to rewrite the modality of Hegelian dialectics (necessity is not ontological but rather practical) and to dispel the specter of dialectical closure (learning processes are fallible, provisional, and pluralistic). However, her rewriting of contradiction and determinate negation does not allow her to fully develop the implications of her own account of the entwinement of the functional and the normative. The inversions of both norm and reality imply a *thwarting* of the goal at work within the entwinement of the normative and the functional that complicates any conception of historical learning. Forms of addressing blockages of experience are not free or safe from such thwarting. This is not a future possibility and hence a feature of the fallibility of solutions. Rather, it is a feature of any solution in its very work—a feature that Fraser's work captures quite well, as we will see.

In addition to the linearity that they reintroduce to Jaeggi's view of historical learning, contradiction and determinate negation so understood complicate her conception of immanent critique. It remains squarely within a revisionist rather than transformative paradigm. The thwarting of the goal at work in any practice at both normative and functional levels calls for the transformation of norm *and* reality. However, it is hard to see how the metacriterion she offers would be able to guide the work of transformation at both registers. As a form of life's insight into its configurability and hence openness to other forms of life (pluralism), the notion of emancipation is too thin. It suggests that emancipatory possibilities only lie in a form of life's self-reflexivity but without reflecting on the inversions that any concrete solution might suffer. This is especially pressing when attempting to articulate what a critique of capitalism entails and wherein its transformative possibilities lie.

In an a recent essay, "What (If Anything) Is Wrong with Capitalism?," Jaeggi sketches a critique of capitalism as a form of life. She is concerned not with a sociological account of capitalism but rather with considering forms of criticizing capitalism.[26] She examines three forms of critique: a functional critique, which traces its deficiencies as a social and economic system; a moral critique, which traces the dehumanizing effects of exploitation; and an ethical critique, which traces the alienated character of life under capitalism. All three critiques express the entwinement of the functional and the normative, but they fail to articulate such entanglement. The functional critique points to the ways in which capitalism's economic efficacy undermines itself, whether under the guise of the pauperization theory or the Marxist theory of the fall of the rate of profit, yet ends up appealing to value judgments about economic distribution. The moral critique seeks to assess the dehumanizing character of exploitation yet ends up appealing to functional features of exploitation, whether by providing analyses of surplus value or accounts of labor conditions. The ethical critique points to the impoverishment of "life relations" as articulated by a critique of objectification, marketization, and commodification but appeals to accounts of the unfolding of capitalism and to values tied to such unfolding.

The entwinement of the functional and the normative establishes the need for a multidimensional perspective. A critique of capitalism as a form of life entails understanding these perspectives as "dimensions" of capitalism and grasping each in relation to the other two. Precisely by "coming together," the three critical perspectives can "generate criteria" for assessing capitalism's deficits. But all three dimensions become *critical* perspectives when guided by the "metacriterion" developed in the closing pages of *Kritik von Lebensformen*. As she puts it in the essay, "A successful form of life would then be one that has the feature of not hindering but facilitating successful collective learning processes—learning processes that may be triggered in part by crises of a functional sort."[27] As a form of life, capitalism should be assessed in light of its capacity to address, for example, the inversions of the norms of equality and freedom within the very work of exploitation. Addressing such contradictions requires revising its arrangements (exploitation) and its normative commitments (equality and liberty). Yet such revisions are transformations—they are progressive—if they enable learning and openness to other forms of life.

To be sure, Jaeggi states that whether capitalism enables learning "is more questionable." I would put the point more strongly, however.

As Marx taught us, capitalism learns very well to expand in light of its inversions, indeed in light of the entwinement of its functional *telos* and its main normative commitment: profit and freedom respectively. And it learns very well to do so by being open to other forms of life, not only changing in light of alternative forms of life, but changing those forms of life that it has deemed "other" according to its own functional-normative aims. I would thus argue that precisely the entanglement of the functional and the normative within capitalist modernity makes processes of learning as Jaeggi conceives of them quite unlikely. Furthermore, I would also argue that the thwarting of concrete solutions to the normative-functional crises of capitalism could not be curbed by a commitment to pluralism. From the perspective of capitalist societies then, Jaeggi's notion of historical learning loses its critical force.

I have argued that Jaeggi's notion of historical learning is compromised by the conception of contradiction and determinate negation involved. This is not to suggest that we ought to abandon Hegel's master concepts for rethinking critique. On the contrary, it is to argue that we ought to recover resources within these very concepts that remain untapped in Jaeggi's account. Precisely because they are "large-scale" categories, contradiction and determinate negation help us think through the ambivalent mediation at work in the multiple logics and sites of domination that arguably compose capitalist modernity. Rather than progress, they help us conceptualize the normative ambivalence at the heart of solutions to the functional-normative crises of capitalism. Instead of turning to Hegel or Marx, I want to turn to Fraser. Her recent work on capitalism displays a latent Hegelianism in line with my own intuitions about the power of Hegelian categories for critique.

2. MEDIATION, NORMATIVE AMBIVALENCE

There are two straightforward points of convergence between Jaeggi's and Fraser's critiques of capitalism, and they point to a Hegelian understanding of social reality. They both conceive of social reality as a functional-normative order, or, as Fraser calls it, an "institutionalized social order."[28] Furthermore, they both conceive of critique as a matter of assessing and addressing inversions within the functional-normative workings of social reality. Fraser's explicit Hegelianism, however, ends here. She does not understand history as a learning process nor believe that contradiction is the motor of progress. Nevertheless, we find distinctively Hegelian motifs in Fraser's work that are promising. Fraser's Hegelianism is perhaps best understood as a Hegelianism post-Marx, whereby contradiction is understood as inversion and determinate negation as ambivalent mediation. These Hegelian motifs become important for "reviv[ing] the project of large-scale social theorizing,"[29] which she argues is necessary in light of the current crisis of neoliberal capitalism, one that can only be understood as multidimensional.

Fraser's starting point is crucial. Rather than grounding her account of critique in a social ontology, she seeks to assess the current crisis of neoliberal capitalism. The crisis must be understood in at least three dimensions: ecology, political economy, and politics. These dimensions, however, should be understood as "structuring principles and axes of inequality in capitalist societies."[30] Ecology, political economy, and politics are not ontological regions but rather differentiated sites of capitalist accumulation expressing differentiated logics of oppression. This understanding is grounded in the "stakes and premises of social struggle," as developed by feminism, ecosocialism, and other social movements. In order to further conceptualize this multidimensionality, in her essay "Marx's Hidden Abode," Fraser turns to Marx's *Capital*. There, Marx provides a two-tiered account of capitalism. His analysis is based on an account of private property, free labor market, self-expanding value, and the distinctive role of markets. But he also provides an account of "background conditions" necessary for capitalist accumulation, specifically under the banner of primitive accumulation. Fraser seeks to deepen the latter by thinking through the "functional imbrication" of marketized and nonmarketized aspects of society within neoliberal capitalism. For both Marx and Fraser, then, an account of the logic of capitalist accumulation requires an account of its background conditions. It requires moving from the "foreground of exploitation" to the "background of expropriation."

Fraser examines three examples of the functional imbrication of foreground and background conditions within neoliberal capitalism. First, following the contributions of feminism, she examines social reproduction. Highlighting the contributions of critical accounts of "care," "affective labor," and "subjectivation," Fraser conceptualizes the "proletarianization" of activities geared toward sustenance and socialization as background conditions of neoliberal capitalism. Second, following the contributions of ecosocialism, she highlights the simultaneous presupposition and disavowal of nature as a background condition for capitalist accumulation. A new round of enclosures and the fact of ecological disaster are nodal points for thinking about nature as the material condition for accumulation. Finally, following the contribution of critiques of the nation-state as well as critiques of "imperialism," Fraser points to geopolitical power as a background condition for neoliberal expansion. The shifting boundaries of the Westphalian division between domestic and international *and* the imperialist division between core and periphery are background conditions. Accordingly, Fraser argues, Marx's notion of the contradictions of capitalism should be understood as the tensions between the economic system and background conditions. Contradiction here refers to the destabilization of necessary background conditions, which jeopardizes social reproduction, ecology, and political power.[31]

The entanglement between foreground and background conditions is not only a functional imbrication, however. It also expresses the entanglement between functional and normative aspects of neoliberalism. Fraser argues that this entwinement should be conceptualized by thinking through "boundary struggles," whereby agents "challenge or defend the established boundaries separating economy from polity, production from reproduction, human from non-human nature."[32] Boundary struggles draw on normative perspectives associated with the "zones" that compose foreground logics and background conditions. Crucially, Fraser argues that agents contest the functional entanglement of foreground logics and background conditions by appealing to norms embedded in the noneconomic orders that enable capitalist accumulation in the first place. For Fraser, "far from being exhausted by or completely subservient to the dynamics of accumulation," these background zones harbor "distinctive ontologies of social practice and normative ideals." Background conditions, then, are at once sources for and against accumulation.[33] Boundary struggles, then, draw sources for critique and transformation from the complex normativity that results from functional-normative imbrication.

In "Marx's Hidden Abode," Fraser argues that a critique of capitalism should be "multistranded." It should consider gender domination, political domination, and the domination of nature at the very heart of capitalist accumulation. Critique refers to boundary struggles that respond to contradictions generated by the entwinement of the foreground logics and background conditions of capitalist accumulation. In "Between Marketization and Social Protection: Resolving the Feminist Ambivalence," Fraser provides what in my view is a deepening of the analysis offered in "Marx's Hidden Abode."[34] While the latter is important for the point of departure of Fraser's critical theory, the former helps us think through the complex normativity that results from the dynamics of functional and functional-normative imbrication. Drawing from Karl Polanyi's work, she gives an account of the normative ambivalence that results from the mediating relation between ecology, economy, and politics. This account helps Fraser critically assess the ambivalence inherent in the very notion of emancipation expressed in the fate of social movements.

"Between Marketization and Social Protection" displays best Fraser's latent Hegelianism. In order to conceptualize the normative ambivalence of boundary struggles, Fraser further develops Polanyi's notion of a double movement between marketization and social protection into a triple movement that includes emancipation. This theoretical move is exemplary of Hegelian determinate negation as mediation and the ambivalence that follows from mediation. As I have shown elsewhere, for Hegel, negation is always of some concrete determination, whether a logical category, a philosophical position, or a historically specific identity or institution.[35] Negation, however, yields an alternative determination. It is never mere negativity or sheer destruction. It is an exclusion that sets or posits alternative boundaries and hence a relation of something and its now established other. Now any thing or identity is such because it has boundaries and maintains itself (determines itself) by asserting its boundaries. A boundary, however, is something that marks a limit. Marking a limit, Hegel emphasizes, is coextensively transgressing it. A boundary marks what something is on the basis of what it is not and hence establishes its opposite as intrinsic to it. Because any identity is both itself and its other, any concrete identity is subject to a logic of ambivalence. If understood as exempt from ambivalence, any given identity is but reified—an abstract, one-sided determination.

Fraser focuses on Polanyi's key concepts of "disembedded markets," "social protection," and the "double movement." Polanyi argues that nineteenth-century British capitalism developed through a "double movement" of marketization and social protection. The double movement articulates the relation between markets and society in terms of "embeddedness." Embedded markets are subject to extraeconomic norms such as "the just price" and "the fair wage." Disembedded markets, in contrast, are self-regulating, governed by supply and demand. For Polanyi, markets can never be truly disembedded from noneconomic background conditions such as "cultural understandings and solidarity relations." The crucial point is that markets undermine their own ecological and social conditions.[36] By turning land, labor, and money into commodities, marketization despoils nature and disintegrates communities that make it possible in the first place. Because marketization undermines itself, it leads to the self-protection of society in the form of measures like "protection of the soil and its cultivators, social security for labor through unionism and legislation, and central banking."[37]

Polanyi simplifies matters, Fraser argues, by romanticizing social protection and demonizing marketization. Social protection "shields from exposure" to the threat of a cold economy, while social protection provides security. Yet as the feminist movement has shown throughout the twentieth century, social institutions are "also loci of oppression," *and* "disembedding" contains an "emancipatory moment."[38] This points to an irreducible ambivalence that follows from the mediating force of marketization *and* social protection. Self-regulating markets should be understood in light of the ways in which they mediate their noneconomic conditions of possibility and vice-versa. The same can be said of social protection. In order to theorize the normative ambivalence that follows, Fraser introduces the notion of emancipation. While Polanyi doesn't use this concept, it allows Fraser to theorize in "Marx's Hidden Abode" what she calls "boundary struggles." In "Between Marketization and Social Protection," Fraser glosses emancipation as the critical perspective that "ranges across the boundaries that demarcate spheres, seeking to root out domination from *every* 'sphere.'"[39] It is ambivalent, however, because in doing so, it sometimes aligns with marketization (and its erosion of social institutions that reproduce forms of oppression) and sometimes with social protection (resisting the marketization of all areas of existence).

Polanyi's double movement, then, ought to be transformed into a triple movement in which "any two sides mediate the third." To neglect the mediating function *and* mediated character of each is to misunderstand it *and* the other two. Capitalist crises are therefore "three-sided conflicts." A critical account of capitalism "should treat each term as conceptually irreducible, normatively ambivalent, and inextricably entangled with the other two." This means that accounts of capitalist crises cannot assume the normative stability of functional aspects or the functional stability of norms since the very effectiveness of marketization, social protection, *and* emancipation generate both positive and negative meanings and effects. Each has a *telos* of its own and therefore has concrete possibilities of inversion through the interaction with the other two.[40] A critique of capitalism, then, must understand not only how emancipation is mediated by social protection and marketization but also how marketization and social protection are mediated by emancipation. For this reason, a critical account of capitalism requires "large-scale theorizing."[41] It requires an analysis of the mediating force of all three, not only in terms of their foreground working and its background conditions, but also in terms of the normative ambivalence of such imbrication.

An account of capitalism that affirms the ends of emancipation, rooting out domination wherever it occurs, must take into account the complexities of mediation and normative ambivalence. It remains critical when it "reckons with emancipation's inherent ambivalence."[42] As Fraser writes, "Only by appreciating this ambivalence, and by anticipating its potential unintended effects, can we undertake collective political reflection on how we might best resolve it."[43] This entails articulating the mediating intersection between multiple logics and sites of domination. Here we can appreciate the fundamental difference between Jaeggi's and Fraser's accounts, a difference that in my view stems from their radically different deployment of Hegelian motifs. Rather than yielding a metacriterion based on an experimental pluralism that bespeaks historical learning, Fraser's Hegelianism articulates the notion of a triple movement, which seeks to understand the complexities of mediation and the irreducible ambivalence of any alternative determination. Rather than laying out an ontology of social practices, Fraser's Hegelianism pays heed to the complex dynamics of neoliberal capitalism, thereby seeking to assess neoliberal institutions in their functional-normative complexities. In my view, then, Fraser's Hegelianism leads to a thoroughgoing conception of immanent critique, one that begins from the struggles of the age and that understands that metacritical concepts are not exempt from the very dynamics that they seek to clarify.[44]

3. CRITIQUE, CAPITALISM, COLONIALITY

In closing, I want to develop further what I see as deeply promising in Jaeggi's and Fraser's work. Their account of the entanglement of the functional and normative aspects of social reality and the consequences of this entanglement for critique is extremely illuminating. I want to develop their insights in a different direction, however, by considering alternatives to Fraser's account of multidimensionality.[45] For Fraser, multidimensionality follows from the mediating relation between the foreground logic of capitalist accumulation and its background conditions. This presses us to understand social struggles as boundary struggles, which draw from a complex normativity at the intersection of economic and noneconomic orders. While the conceptions of normativity and critique that become available are promising, they require deepening Fraser's rewriting of Marx's notion of primitive accumulation. In closing, then, I want to briefly suggest that a critique of capitalism along Fraserian lines entails a critique of coloniality.[46]

Recall that, for Fraser, reactualizing Marx's account of primitive accumulation involves moving from the foreground of exploitation to the background of expropriation. This means moving from the dynamics of exploitation to the dynamics of appropriation. It is a move, then, to an account of the dynamics of "violence and outright theft" that are *ongoing* conditions for capitalist accumulation. Indeed, for both Marx and Fraser, this move does not merely provide a genealogy of capitalism. It conceptualizes the ongoing logic of capitalist accumulation. For Fraser, moving to the backstory entails tracing the ways in which neoliberalism "(re)privatizes and (re)commodifies" social reproduction, pursues a new round of enclosures and shifts the boundary between the human and the nonhuman, and exploits shifting political conditions. I want to add that it requires tracing the institution of hierarchies—specifically, racial and gender hierarchies—fundamental to the functional-normative entwinement distinctive of capitalism. Doing so, however, requires placing the development of capitalism squarely within the history of an ongoing colonial project.

To be sure, Fraser mentions the significance of postcolonial critiques of imperialism for articulating political dynamics as background conditions of neoliberal capitalism. And in her recent essay, "Expropriation and Exploitation in Racialized Capitalism," she helpfully examines the ways in which race "emerges . . . as the mark that distinguishes free subjects of exploitation from dependent subjects of expropriation."[47] She argues that what is needed is an expanded view of capitalism as an institutionalized social order "but also" built on expropriation. Hence a critical analysis of capitalism must track the historically specific relations between expropriation and exploitation by "geography and demography."[48] She suggests, accordingly, the need to "disclose the mutually constitutive relations among historically specific logics of accumulation, epochal constellations of political subjectivation and the shifting dynamics of racialization in capitalist society."[49]

Fraser's amendment comes close to my own suggestion that what is needed is an account of coloniality. She argues that in order to clarify the persistent entanglement of capitalism and racial oppression, we must track the ways in which capitalism, as an institutionalized normative order, institutes the very distinction between "free" subjects of exploitation and unfree subjects of expropriation. It is the task of tracking the very institution of this distinction that calls for an account of coloniality. Following Aníbal Quijano's work, an account of coloniality traces racial "classification" to a colonial project that coextensively articulates as one pattern—capitalism—all forms of control of labor.[50] The interlocking character of a system of racial classification and capitalism is furthermore coextensive with Eurocentrism as a new mode of production and control of subjectivity and with the nation-state as a new system of collective authority, one that excludes populations racialized as inferior. Although much more needs to be said here, I suggest that situating the account of capitalism within an ongoing colonial legacy helps specify the operations of power at work in the very institution of a distinction between subjects of exploitation and subjects of expropriation.

The ability to track these operations of power does not move us beyond a critique of capitalism. On the contrary, it centers any such critique in its "multidimensionality," to speak with Fraser, delivering a more differentiated understanding of the entanglement of the functional and normative aspects of social reality. This centering furthermore attunes us to the irreducible ambivalence of any normative concept central to the theoretical and political task of critique. It provides awareness to not only the fraught terrain in which these concepts are deployed but their fraught histories and effects. Preserving the critical character of critical theory, then, requires transforming its theoretical assumptions in light of these strictures. It seeks to track not only the operations of power that account for the heterogeneous and complex ongoing development of capitalism but also the complexity of any critical account of capitalism.

NOTES

1. Karl Marx, "For a Ruthless Criticism of Everything Existing," in *The Marx-Engels Reader*, ed. Robert C. Tucker (New York: W. W. Norton, 1978), 15.

2. Nancy Fraser, "What's Critical about Critical Theory: The Case of Habermas and Gender," *New German Critique* 35 (1985): 97–131.
3. See Fraser, esp. 107.
4. Fraser argues that a theory is critical when it "frames its research program and its conceptual framework with an eye to the aims and activities of those oppositional social movements with which it has a partisan though not uncritical identification" (Fraser, 97).
5. See esp. Rahel Jaeggi, "Rethinking Ideology," in *New Waves in Political Philosophy*, ed. Boudewijn de Bruin and Christopher F. Zurn (New York: Palgrave Macmillan, 2009), 63–86; and Rahel Jaeggi, *Kritik von Lebensformen* (Frankfurt: Suhrkamp, 2014).
6. Consider, for instance, Adorno's own ambivalent relation to these concepts in *Dialectic of Enlightenment*, trans. Edmund Jephcott (Stanford: Stanford University Press, 2007), and *Negative Dialectics*, trans. E. B. Ashton (New York: Continuum, 1973).
7. See, for example, Amy Allen, *The End of Progress* (New York: Columbia University Press, 2016).
8. See my *Hegel's Theory of Intelligibility* (Chicago: University of Chicago Press, 2015).
9. Jaeggi, "Kriseninduzierte Transformationen," in *Kritik*, 342–55.
10. Jaeggi, "Towards an Immanent Critique of Forms of Life," *Raisons Politiques* 57 (2015): 18.
11. Jaeggi, *Kritik*, 202–3.
12. Such a history can be understood as a "learning process," as a "process of accumulated experiences."
13. See Jaeggi, *Kritik*, 288ff.
14. Jaeggi, 345.
15. It is interesting that Jaeggi does not refer to Brandom's work in this context, as their accounts of Hegel converge on many points. See Robert Brandom's *A Spirit of Trust* (work in progress, University of Pittsburgh, 2014). The manuscript can be found at http://www.pitt.edu/~brandom/spirit_of_trust_2014.html. Accessed November 23, 2017.
16. See Jaeggi, *Kritik*, 414.
17. Jaeggi, 410.
18. The very notion of contradiction, in Hegel, is grounded in the master category of negation. See *Hegel's Theory of Intelligibility*.
19. See Jaeggi, *Kritik*, 194–96, 227–30, 383. Jaeggi also writes, "It means that that practice can no longer fit into the normative self-conception and the connection of practices with interpretations of the world that accounts for those practices and interpretations. Put another way: It means that something is wrong with that connection" ("Critique of Forms of Life: Forms of Life as Instances of Problemsolving" [6th International Symposium on Justice, Pontifícia Universidade do Rio Grande do Sul, Porto Alegre, 2013], 22).
20. Problems as contradictions are "realizations . . . of tensions that were present in the situation itself" (Jaeggi, "Critique of Forms of Life," 17).
21. As Jaeggi writes, "They are not only dysfunctional but in their dysfunction they are simultaneously *constitutive* for the modality in which the inherently contradictory formation functions" (Jaeggi, 17).

22. Jaeggi, *Kritik*, 421.
23. Jaeggi, 422–23.
24. Jaeggi, 423.
25. Jaeggi, 445, 446.
26. Capitalism, Jaeggi argues, is an economic and social order that emerged in Europe as the result of a break with the feudal order during the eighteenth and nineteenth centuries, given high technological development and substantial concentration of capital. It is a social and economic order that developed out of that break by managing the contradictions of the feudal order. It is structured around the ownership of means of production, existence of free labor markets, accumulation of capital, and orientation toward profit. This characterization ignores the accounts of capitalism in, for example, decolonial thought from Enrique Dussel to Aníbal Quijano's writings.
27. Rahel Jaeggi, "What (If Anything) Is Wrong with Capitalism? Dysfunctionality, Exploitation and Alienation: Three Approaches to the Critique of Capitalism," *Southern Journal of Philosophy* 54, Spindel Supplement (2016): 44–65.
28. Nancy Fraser, "Behind Marx's Hidden Abode," *New Left Review* 86 (2014): 55–72.
29. Nancy Fraser, "Can Society Be Commodities All the Way Down? Polanyian Reflections on Capitalist Crisis," *Archive ouverte en Sciences de l'Homme et de la Société* (FMSH-WP-2012-18, 2012), 4.
30. Fraser, 56.
31. Fraser, 57ff.
32. Fraser, 68.
33. "This implies that, even as these 'non-economic' orders make commodity production possible, they are not reducible to that enabling function" (Fraser, 69).
34. Notwithstanding the fact that "Behind Marx" is a more recent text.
35. See my *Hegel's Theory of Intelligibility*.
36. Karl Polanyi, *The Great Transformation* (Boston: Beacon Press, 2001).
37. Polanyi, 211.
38. Nancy Fraser, "Between Marketization and Social Protection," in *Fortunes of Feminism: From State-Managed Capitalism to Neoliberal Crisis*, ed. Nancy Fraser (London: Verso, 2013), 227–42.
39. Nancy Fraser, *Fortunes of Feminism: From State-Managed Capitalism to Neoliberal Crisis* (London: Verso, 2013), 145.
40. Fraser, 145.
41. Fraser, 145.
42. Fraser, 241.
43. Fraser, 241.
44. For my criticism of Fraser, see Rocío Zambrana, "Paradoxes of Neoliberalism and the Tasks of Critical Theory," *Critical Horizons* 14 (2013): 93–119.
45. It is surprising to see that neither Jaeggi nor Fraser develop their accounts of multidimensionality by citing or engaging black feminism or other women of color feminisms, traditions that have elaborated "multidimensionality" ("interlocking systems of oppression," "intersectionality," etc.) powerfully for decades.
46. Here I am drawing from decolonial thought as elaborated by Aníbal Quijano in "Coloniality, Modernity/Rationality," *Cultural Studies* 2–3 (2007): 168–78, and other texts.

47. Nancy Fraser, "Expropriation and Exploitation in Racialized Capitalism," *Critical Historical Studies* 3 (2016): 10.
48. Unlike Jaeggi, Fraser here acknowledges the need to provide a genealogy of capitalism that predates the eighteenth-century developments that Jaeggi traced. See Fraser, 11.
49. Fraser, 11.
50. See Aníbal Quijano, "Colonialidad del Poder y Clasificación Social," in *Festschrift for Immanuel Wallerstein, Journal of World Systems Research* 11 (2000): 342–87.

CHAPTER 7

On the Politics of Forms of Life

Daniel Loick

In many public spaces in Frankfurt, a sticker can be found with the following exhortation: "Don't marry, be happy!" What sort of imperative are we dealing with here? Is it the advice of a marriage counselor? A stag party slogan fit for printing on a T-shirt? An allusion from pop culture?

On closer inspection, the eye catches the name of the initiative responsible for this intervention. The sticker comes from a feminist group that, with the motto of the "Care Revolution," takes up the critique of marriage and traditional love initiated in the 1960s and 1970s as well as the more recent discourse on polysexuality and polyamory. Marriage is still a patriarchal institution, the sticker can be interpreted as saying, that rests on the exploitation of female reproductive work and that makes those who enter into it unhappy. But how, one might ask, is the statement "Don't marry, be happy" to be classified according to a classical philosophical taxonomy? The statement is not concerned with a classical *ethical* command, because it is not directed at individual conduct; also not with a *political* demand in the conventional sense, because it is not directed at some state institution; nor with a *moral* prescription, because it does not impugn any injustice or inequality; and just as little with an *aesthetic* claim, because it refers to happiness rather than beauty. In the following chapter, it shall be shown that we are concerned here much more with a genuinely *political* speech act or, to be more precise, with the idea that the statement belongs to the genre of the *politics of forms of life*. The concept of a politics of forms of life is not only well suited to philosophically delineate a series of increasingly significant forms of political engagement. Aside from this, it has momentous implications for critical theory and its practice in the present that have often been overlooked.

First, the concept of the politics of forms of life will be terminologically fleshed out. To this end, two recent essays from the field of contemporary critical theory concerning the normativity of forms of life will be discussed—namely, Maeve Cooke's analysis of a postuniversal demand for recognition and Rahel Jaeggi's justification of the criticizability of forms of life. In the second section of this chapter, a justification shall be offered for why a politics of forms of life is not only analytically interesting but also desirable in the context of an emancipatory political practice. Three arguments will be addressed: the politics of forms of life (1) dispenses with a reductive economism, (2) makes the experience of moments of happiness possible for political actors, and (3) rehabilitates the category of credibility. In connection to this, the politics of forms of life will be defended against three pertinent criticisms: that of the liberal, the anticapitalist, and the radical democratic. I conclude with some remarks on the future of the politics of forms of life.

1. WHAT IS A "POLITICS OF FORMS OF LIFE"?

In her essay "Beyond Dignity and Difference," Maeve Cooke investigates the normative consequences of a series of projects that articulate a public demand for recognition, although they do not fit with a traditional notion of political action. Cooke names three examples: the international Slow Food movement, an initiative for the advancement of the Welsh language, and the Assembly for the Protection of Hijab. These three groups share the aim of "public recognition of the value of particular ethical conceptions, cultural traditions and religious beliefs and practices" without, however, being related to the value of political justice.[1] Cooke calls these demands "postuniversal" demands because while they do in fact aim at a potential universalization of one's own way of life, they do not do so by prescribing a moral law or a legal duty. According to Cooke, these groups extend an "invitation" whose acceptance is not compulsory but instead is able to be "encouraged by opening our eyes to new possibilities and perspectives."[2]

Cooke's essay is useful for making the genuinely political aspect of demands for recognition intelligible where they might not at all be understood intuitively as political. Indeed, she examines the previously mentioned initiatives exclusively in view of their struggle for recognition in public discourse—that is, in view of their effect on an external public. To be able to effectively invite a potentially interested audience, however, the relevant practice of each group must itself be actually lived. The Slow Food movement, to take one of Cooke's examples, can only articulate a demand for public recognition if it includes a demonstrative aspect, if it thus *exhibits* the culinary and ecological superiority of this form of gastronomy. This type of politics does not merely raise political claims; it constitutes a form of life that has a political character precisely *as* a form of life.

Rahel Jaeggi has worked out in detail the concept of a form of life and its philosophical implications in her major work, *The Critique of Forms of Life*. Jaeggi is the first to provide a sufficiently sound definition of what is entailed by a form of life. According to her definition, forms of life consist of "conceptions and habitualized ways of behaving with a normative character, which relate to the collective manner of living without being strictly codified nor constituting an institutional obligation."[3] A form of life consists conceptually then in these four essential characteristics: (1) it signifies not single practices but rather *a bundle of associated practices*; (2) it is related not to individual but to *collective* ways of life; (3) with its reference to *habit*, it contains a passive moment; and (4) it is implicitly *normative*. Even armed with this definition, forms of life are notoriously difficult to identify because there are so many disputed or borderline cases. It could however be said by way of approximation that forms of life constitute a dimension that is more existential or "deeper" than mere lifestyles, fashions, or habits but that they are not as strictly regulated as institutions or organizations.

In dialogue with Hegel, Dewey, and MacIntyre, Jaeggi conceives of forms of life as "attempts at problem solving." To criticize a form of life then entails examining whether it is an appropriate reaction to a preexisting crisis. For example, patriarchal marriage is no longer an appropriate form of life because it has proven itself to be incapable of organizing reproduction and intimacy in a way that is consistent with the freedom of women. It should therefore necessarily give way under changed societal conditions. As Cooke's work shows, demands for recognition are extended as an invitation rather than as legal or moral commandments or prohibitions; similarly, Jaeggi suggests that the critique of forms of life is not, in her words, "a matter for the police." Instead, new forms of life are "experiments" whose success or failure is apparent only in real practice rather than abstractly on the drawing board.

While Cooke's essay is concerned with the theoretical consequences of a politics that takes seriously postuniversal demands for recognition, she neglects the aspect pertaining to the form of life. This is precisely where Jaeggi concentrates, particularly on the philosophical problems raised by their normative evaluation. Jaeggi in turn courts danger by neglecting the genuinely *political* aspect of forms of life. Because she conceives of them primarily as historically situated strategies for solving problems, she must minimize the obviously confrontational, polemical, and transgressive aspect of many initiatives and projects. These initiatives are consciously and strategically concerned with developments in civil society, and they often link the formation of one's own form of life with a broader political engagement.

Connecting the concepts of "politics" and "forms of life" sounds contradictory only to modern ears. In his *Politics*, Aristotle saw the whole meaning of the polis explicitly in its facilitation of "the Good Life."[4] In his writings on the aesthetics of existence, Michel Foucault reminds us that in antiquity there existed a close relationship between an individual's way of leading his or her life and his or her practice of politics. Good governance of the polis is only possible if citizens are in a situation where they can first master themselves and their passions.[5] In modern times, however, this connection between politics and forms of life is broken. With the consolidation of the modern state and the corresponding separation between public and private, the assumption has been that politics is a public matter, while one's form of life is a private concern. Yet since the onset of modern times, there have been repeated attempts to form collectives and initiate projects that have understood their practices explicitly in terms of the politics of forms of life, thereby restoring the ancient connection between the conduct of life and the polis while opposing the liberal separation of the ethical from the political. To be counted among these projects are the early socialist utopias such as Charles Fourier's phalansteries, Gustav Landauer's evocation of anarchist rural communes, artist colonies like Monte Verita or Barkenhoff in Worpswede, the Parisian bohemians and dandies with whom Walter Benjamin sympathized, or the biopolitical utopias of the early Soviet Union with the infamous invocation of the "New Man," whose problems Leon Trotsky reflects—to name just a few. The practice as well as the political theorization of the form of life experienced a certain boom in the period of 1968 and the traditions of revolt extending from it. The following are, generally speaking, examples for this: in the 1960s and 1970s, groups like the rural or urban communes, autonomous schools and kindergartens, and artistic movements of the avant-garde such as Dada, Fluxus, and Situationism; in the 1980s, squat houses or factories and subsistence-oriented agricultural projects; in the 1990s, queer feminist experiments with polysexuality and polyamory, gay rights, and AIDS activism; and in the 2000s and 2010s, autonomously organized subeconomies such as local exchange trading systems, peer production, commoning, collaborative consumption, and the occupation and reappropriation of urban spaces or public camping on privately held land, as in the case of the Occupy protests.[6]

This list shows that the politics of forms of life is not, as Cooke's essay suggests, an eccentric exception to typical political action. It has always been a widely dispersed—and perhaps at present even one of the most important—forms of political engagement. At the same time, a politically reflexive, deliberate understanding of one's own form of life is not, as Jaeggi seems to suggest, an exception within the competitive search for experimental solutions to problems but has become a relevant societal factor since the second half of the twentieth century at the latest.

Viewing such forms of life as inherently *political* is due not only to their own self-interpretation but also to the Aristotelian determination of the irreducibly ethical character of the polis and of the political character of the form of life. A politics of forms of life is not a politics in the modern sense of the term (understood as focused upon the state), nor is it an ethics in the modern sense (understood as an individual matter of private concern). On the one hand, all the aforementioned groups, currents, and movements have expectations and utopias that are capable of generalization or even allow implementation only for the whole of society. On the other, they always contain another dimension that is not convertible into a universal vocabulary or government program without remainder. The political element of the politics of forms of life does not primarily consist in making demands on the state or society with leaflets, demonstrations, or parliamentary interventions (although they generally do that, as well), nor does the life-shaping aspect of this form of politics end with the acknowledgment that political engagement always implies a distinctive lifestyle or constitutes a subculture (although this is also the case). This becomes clear when we once again turn to the critique of marriage put forward by feminist groups: the slogan "Don't marry, be happy" is distinctive precisely through its interweaving of political and ethical aspects—it presents neither a demand on the state nor counsel on how to live one's life but rather seeks to guide personal practice that, as such, has a political meaning. Therefore, the politics of forms of life is concerned with politicizing the following question: *How do we want to live?*—that is to say, politicizing life itself.

2. THE POLITICS OF FORMS OF LIFE AS EMANCIPATORY PRACTICE

Not only is the politics of forms of life an important societal phenomenon whose theory thus far has been systematically misunderstood; its meaning is also important especially for an explicitly *critical* social theory and practice. In saying that, we of course do not mean that *all* politics of forms of life are emancipatory. There are also bourgeois, neoliberal, or fascist forms of life. In what follows, however, the concern will be with those projects and initiatives that, according to their own claims, aim at an emancipatory social transformation. The distinctiveness of this politics shall be demonstrated by three features: (1) the *overcoming of reductive economism*, (2) the *facilitation of experiences of happiness*, and (3) the *rediscovery of credibility as a political category.*

The latter two aspects stem from the first one, the rejection of economistic or reductive conceptions of the social totality. This can be made clear by means of a paradigmatic event: the throwing of tomatoes at the conference of delegates of the SDS (*Sozialistischen Deutschen Studentbund* / Union of German Socialist Students) in Frankfurt in 1968 by members of the *Aktionsrates zur Befreiung der Frau* (Protest League for the Emancipation of Women), which frequently is seen as the prelude to the second Women's Movement in Germany. Berlin-based activist and filmmaker Helke Sander justified the women's intervention on account of the continuation of a patriarchal division of labor within the SDS in which men were responsible for politics and women for the wash. She said in a speech that bore the title "The SDS: A Puffed-Up, Counterrevolutionary Pile of Dough," "We cannot free women of societal oppression individually. We cannot therefore wait till after the revolution, since a revolution that is only political and economic will not remove the oppression of private life which is apparent in all socialist countries."[7] That the situation of women had improved in neither the actually existing socialist countries nor the anticapitalist groups in the West led to a disavowal of both the orthodox Marxist base-superstructure schema and the talk of a main or fundamental contradiction from which all other mechanisms of oppression and control are deducible and compared to which these other mechanisms are of lesser importance. The significance of this attack upon a stubborn and persistent way of thinking is scarcely to be overestimated. Along with a critique of the traditional economism of the left, there was an intense pluralization of political attention; themes were suddenly brought into the focus of political interest that had previously been held by groups on the left as matters either of private concern or of lesser significance: the raising of children, welfare work, and sexuality.[8] The reverse side of the disappointment with the failed liberation of women in socialism is the insight that heterogeneous emancipatory trends have their own temporality. The politics of forms of life was first authorized by overcoming economism, at least to a certain extent. If socialism does not contain all that is good, it suggests that capitalism is not automatically the summation of everything bad.

This transformation of social theory has a specific ethical implication. The notion of an all-determining societal totality had repudiated the possibility of an authentic experience of happiness under capitalism. The affective recompense for one's political engagement would have to be postponed until after the revolution. This is not merely problematic for a theory of society on account of its negation of the specific experiences of many disadvantaged groups; it also produces an aesthetic and heroic understanding of politics according to which political agents should advocate for a fundamental transformation altruistically and completely independent of their concrete interests and needs. This heroic understanding of politics is surpassed by dispensing with a reductive notion of the social totality and by reorienting the theory of society in view of an analysis of heterogeneous emancipatory trends with an asynchronous temporality. The politics of forms of life renews within modernity the Aristotelian attempt to connect an ethically "good" practice of living one's life with the experience of happiness.

Philosophically speaking, there is a realignment from a *moral* critique to an *ethically perfectionist* one. The politics of forms of life is characterized by a self-interpretation and self-reflection that does not merely mobilize indignation, it makes use as well of a vocabulary that is rich in ethical conceptualization. By analyzing the manifestoes and self-interpretations of past political forms of life, it becomes apparent that the criticism of these societies is not only directed at their injustice, disorder, and perpetual crisis but also for being generally boring, depressing, narrow-minded, or banal. A particularly telling example is found in Trotsky's *Problems of Everyday Life*, where he announces that socialist life will be "richer, broader, more full of color and harmony"[9]—these categories would not at all be suitable to describe a political program that eschewed any reference to a form of life or that was disinterested with ethics. Regardless of whether the practices preferred by Trotsky are indeed in a position to fulfill the hopes placed in them, they certainly open a more comprehensive perspective on political engagement than is possible with the heroic fixation on the question of justice. They are, at least potentially, in a position to counteract the "impotence of the ought" that Hegel deployed against Kant and to serve as a sufficiently strong motivational basis for political action (being evaluated, of course, on how well it fulfills these promises).

Third, the rehabilitation of the category of reliability for political action is connected to the preceding ones. With the modern disjunction between good actions and happiness, the connection of an action to its consequences was also brought generally to a state of crisis. The total context of society is not only concerned that the agent's power to act is strictly circumscribed; it places every ostensibly successful action under suspicion of being merely ideology to the extent it is suitable for excusing or justifying the cohesion of the whole: "The smallest step towards their pleasures," as Adorno puts it succinctly in his *Minima Moralia*, "is one towards the hardening of their pains."[10]

From the perspective of the politics of forms of life, reservations such as those expressed by Adorno appear to be flimsy excuses. In contrast, the followers of these practices assume that alternative forms of communal living can be discussed, experimented with, and revised without first having to wait for a major breach. In the words of Herbert Marcuse, they work by "demonstrating and anticipating."[11] The concepts of "invitation" or of "experiment," as they are used by Cooke and Jaeggi and philosophically inspired by Hegel or Dewey, are from a political perspective closest to the classical anarchist theories of transformation that inverted the orthodox Marxist theory of revolution. Rather than the revolution serving as the precondition for a transformation of life, the revolution is made possible by a change in the arrangements of living—and therewith the preparation for and rehearsal of emancipatory practices. Already at the beginning of the twentieth century, Gustav Landauer wrote, "What we call socialism is a joyful life in a just economy. People today do not know, do not experience it with the true knowledge of partaking and engaging, with the knowledge that inspires envy and the lust for imitation, what that is: *joyful, beautiful life*. We have to show them."[12]

3. ON THE DEFENSE OF THE POLITICS OF FORMS OF LIFE

The flip side of this demonstrative and anticipating dimension of political forms of life is that it can have the opposite effect to what was initially desired: it can show what does not in fact work and what remains unjust or attenuated, and consequently certain alternative ideas can be fundamentally discredited. As with every other experiment, however, such failure proves not against the experimental process as such but only against the working hypothesis that underwrites that individual experiment. However, objecting to an isolated failure is to be differentiated from objecting to the experimental procedure as such—that is, objecting to the very idea of a politicization of forms of life as problematic. The politicization of forms of life should be defended against three of the most commonly voiced criticisms: (1) the *liberal* critique, (2) the *critique of capitalism*, and (3) the *radical democratic* critique.

According to political liberalism, represented by contemporary authors such as John Rawls, Ronald Dworkin, and Jürgen Habermas, the state should remain neutral or "agnostic" concerning questions of forms of life. The liberal state concedes to individuals a dimension of freedom for making decisions about how to lead their life without being bothered too much by governmental intrusion. This restraint is necessary because of the danger of paternalism, which begins as soon as individuals are inhibited from the autonomous realization of their own life goals; it begins then (as, for example, Trotsky demands) where the state seeks to "educate" its citizens or to institute a dictatorship of morals.[13] Aside from this historically not unfounded concern for maintaining a liberal dimension of freedom for the individual, there is an additional reason for desiring the ethical neutrality of the state in the furtherance of pluralism. Only by abstaining as much as possible from preferring a particular form of life for its citizens is it possible for the state to ensure the equitable coexistence of incompatible, particular conceptions and consequently a nonviolent plurality of forms of life. Only if the state does not prejudice a particular ethical conception is it able to fulfill its role as the institutional guarantor for, as Rawls would say, a "reasonable plurality of opinion."

Against the liberal separation of forms of life from politics, two arguments above all can be presented.[14] First, liberalism is in no way neutral concerning forms of life but rather implicitly privileges certain forms of life and excludes or denigrates others. It is unavoidable in the creation of civil norms that questions relating to forms of life are affected, as is obvious in the tax law concerning marriage, the laws of adoption, and so forth. In addition, liberalism is itself a "way of life" that feeds on the pattern of interpretation and body of knowledge unique to its lifeworld, cultural representations, and conventions of affectivity, which are in no way indeterminate but rather highly determined and determining.[15] Even the most audacious biopolitical strategies of the Soviet Union could not have expressed it more openly than the employee of a consulting firm who states in Carmen Losmann's documentary, *Work Hard Play Hard*, "We have to reprogram the employees' DNA!"[16]

The second argument against the liberal imperative of neutrality arises especially from within the perspective of subaltern, outsider, or outcast forms of life. Those who slip outside the frame of an acceptable form of life cannot choose as a matter of course to experience their type of life as political or not. This can be made clear in light of the public discourse surrounding gay and lesbian civil partnership: queer love is open to a constant politicization; it cannot so easily withdraw to a romanticized, private standpoint in contrast to heterosexual relationships. Questions of desire, of sexuality, or of the education of children no longer seem to be private matters—they are *immediately* political. Now if the liberal imperative of neutrality asks of such forms of life that they abstract from their concrete experiences, needs, and interests and then translate their terms into a vocabulary that is supposedly neutral in order to be able to contribute to public discourse, then on this point the liberal conception of political justice is self-contradictory. The preconditions that members of the community must satisfy in order to gain admittance into the public sphere are unequal. The political significance of the question of the form of life is therefore repudiated neither from the perspective of the state nor from that of the form of life itself. This does not imply, of course, that values such as autonomy in the conduct of life or a pluralism of forms of life have become obsolete and that there are no longer any objections to a dictatorship of a particular form of life—it means primarily that the politicization of the question of the form of life is in itself justified.

A second and veritably classical critique of the politics of forms of life argues that many political forms of life, especially in the context and tradition of 1968, have been incorporated into a post-Fordist capitalism or have even prepared the way for it. Luc Boltanski and Ève Chiapello have presented an especially influential version of this criticism in their book, *The New Spirit of Capitalism*.[17] The authors see precisely those values that constitute the peculiar ethical perfectionism of a politics of forms of life (a focus on human self-realization, authenticity, creativity, fantasy) as the expression of an "artistic critique" that has been articulated above all by students and those in the culture industry. This critique has replaced the "social critique" put forward by the labor movement and has subsequently been put in the service of an intense and especially perfidious form of exploitation. At first glance, the argument proposed by the authors has some persuasive power. Superficial analyses of developments in pop culture and mass media since the turn of the millennium have highlighted all the artifacts that document a complete loss of meaning for the symbols that formerly represented resistance. A sociological analysis of current labor relations appears to confirm this diagnosis: the increase in immaterial, affective, or cognitive labor can lead to an internalization of heteronomous goals. This then can lead to an ideological masking of existing power relations as well as an increase in psychological suffering—for example, through burnout, exhaustion, and depression.

Thus it is difficult to dismiss the fact that even emancipatory impulses are integrated and domesticated gradually, that they are able to have ambivalent or paradoxical effects. This was noted not least by the intellectual leading lights of the politics of forms of life themselves, with concepts such as Marcuse's "repressive tolerance" or the Situationist's "recuperation." However, the thesis of the necessary integration of rebellious impulses by capitalism implies a problematic reintroduction of a reductive or deterministic understanding of the totality of society. Those who claim that the contentious emancipation of 1968 and the following years have not "really" changed anything or who reduce it to being merely a forerunner of post-Fordist or postmodernist labor relations subscribe to the privileging or prioritization of a so-called base and consequently to the dethematization and trivialization of other relations of domination and oppression. If social analysis is instead based on the much more plausible image of society as an ensemble of relatively autonomous spheres or clusters of practices, which in fact influence one another but are never reducible to one another and never dissipate, the limits of the reductive anticapitalist perspective come into view. Progress in the overcoming of a single social grievance is not undermined because it fails to address *all* other grievances. The legal, political, economic, and cultural achievements of feminism, for example, are not less desirable for failing immediately to abolish capitalism. Therefore, it is Boltanski and Chiapello's critique that subscribes to the already superseded privilege of the economic sphere. Against this view, the same objections can be posed as the ones voiced by feminists to their orthodox Marxists opponents in the 1960s.

The third and final objection that is commonly made against the politics of forms of life is the radical democratic critique. It is especially Chantal Mouffe who in a number of texts has dealt with the theme of exodus, a theme that possesses some parallels to that of the politicization of forms of life.[18] In Mouffe's view, political strategies that abstain from a confrontation with existing political institutions and that are devoted instead to building their own counterinstitutions not only have abandoned the open stage where the public matter is negotiated, the *res publica*, but also fundamentally misconceive the principally agonistic character of the political. Ironically, then, the politicization of forms of life can have a depoliticizing effect if it is accompanied by a withdrawal into the private sphere and a reinterpretation of questions concerning society into questions concerning private matters. This tendency of privatization and individualization can occur for two main reasons, which conflict with each other: either because the form of life is so successful that it loses its general political character (this is the case when, for example, squatters' buildings are transformed into rented lofts), or, on the contrary, because the form of life is so strenuous that it is no longer attractive to its members, so they retire from politics altogether.[19] The political aspect is thus lost as much by rigidifying the demand for happiness into an absolute as by eliminating it altogether.

However, the radical democratic critique too is correct only to a

certain extent. First, rather than foreclosing possibilities, the earliest examples of a politicized form of life open new arenas for political debate. If, for example, a man wearing a dress or a woman with a beard can be understood as a political act, then opportunities for democratic disputation are increased and not reduced.[20] Redirecting the attention of political actors away from the state leads directly to a strengthening and invigoration of the individual. Second, an empirical and historical analysis of political forms of life shows that they are seldom concerned *exclusively* with the politicization of their own form of life. The thematization of a form of life generally accompanies other "classically" political concerns: those who mourn a friend who died of AIDS by participating in a die-in would presumably also publically oppose homophobia, and those who plant a vegetable garden in the city would also likely participate in demonstrations against GMOs. As with the preceding two criticisms, the radical democratic critique therefore points more to a pitfall, a challenge, or a temptation than a necessary tendency within the politics of forms of life.

4. FOR AN ARCHIVE OF POLITICAL FORMS OF LIFE

All forms of politics have specific challenges, dangers, or temptations: reformism may become corruption, revolution may become Stalinism, subversion may become spectacle. The mere fact that a politics of forms of life is not immune to these dangers is insufficient to discredit it. Rather, it is a reflection upon these dangers—how from the beginning this reflection is undertaken by those who subscribe to this politics—that is the precondition to learning from experience. Thus it is indispensable that the obscured knowledge of past forms of life is salvaged, that preceding reflection receives attention, and that the theoretical and practical achievements of political forms of life are prized. Such action would stand against the social status quo and the political philosophy that is adequate to it, political liberalism, but also against a current tendency of the global left to be dogmatic and totalitarian.

This task causes considerable problems for the social sciences in that the politics of forms of life often possess only a modest degree of institutionalization. The experience of those who live political forms of life is seldom recorded, and their accounts are not publicized. Add to that, the politically significant dimension of life is not thought to be political and consequently is ignored by a sociologically and politically informed theory. To the contrary, in this chapter it is shown that, from the standpoint of social theory, the politics of forms of life is an interesting phenomenon. First, on the analytical and theoretical level simply because it represents notoriously underinvestigated sociocultural practices that have become common in the past 150 years but that are likely to be overlooked if one gauges politics only by what is of concern to the state. Second, on the political-normative level, because it can provide significant impetus to many classical problems of emancipatory political action. It follows then first of all that work in the archive is worthwhile: perhaps from the ruins of the New Sensibility ideas will a new New Sensibility emerge.

This chapter is translated from German by Joel A. Feinberg.

NOTES

1. Maeve Cooke, "Beyond Dignity and Difference," *European Journal of Political Theory* 8, no. 1 (2009): 91.
2. Cooke, 92.
3. Rahel Jaeggi, *Kritik von Lebensformen* (Berlin: Suhrkamp, 2014), 77.
4. Aristotle, "Politics," in *The Complete Works of Aristotle: The Revised Oxford Translation, Vol.* 2, trans. B. Jowett, ed. Jonathan Barnes (1984; repr., Princeton: Princeton University Press, 1987), 1252b.
5. Cf. Michel Foucault, "The Ethics of the Concern for Self as a Practice of Freedom," in *Essential Works of Michel Foucault, 1954–1984, Vol. 1. Ethics: Subjectivity and Truth*, ed. Paul Rabinow (New York: New Press, 1997), 286ff.
6. For the classification of some of these as exodus practices, cf. Daniel Loick, "Exodus. Leben jenseits von Staat und Konsum? Einleitung," *WestEnd. Neue Zeitschrift für Sozialforschung* 11, no. 1 (2014), 61–66.
7. Helke Sander, "Der SDS—ein aufgeblasener, konterrevolutionärer Hefeteig," *Analyse und Kritik* 531 (2008).

8. An aspect of the critique undertaken by feminist women of their male associates aimed at making it possible to participate equally in the political struggle. Reproductive and welfare work should be made visible as such and be fairly shared. Of course, the thematization of forms of life, for women as for all members of the group, is the condition for maintaining the capacity to act politically. *Kommune 2* (Commune 2), a Berlin project in communal living, had undertaken an experiment in the linking together of political work and collective living between 1967 and 1968. Retrospectively, they formulated why it became impossible at a particular point in time for members of the group to separate politics from private life: one couldn't go to a political demonstration and then process what was experienced there isolated from the context of the bourgeois family structure. The establishment of collective structures for discussion made it possible to develop the necessary "ego strength" for the continuation of the difficult struggle. Commune 2 already made apparent that, as a condition for the ability to act, the experience of the collective is insufficient if it is purely a discursive practice. It must have a material character. It is a question not merely of effect, but of affect: the collective organization of living arrangements, eating, and personal care makes possible a more rational use of resources, and at the same time, the compassionate solidarity with one's associates produces a safe space in which revolutionary energies can renew themselves. Kommune 2, *Versuch der Revolutionierung des bürgerlichen Individuums. Kollektives Leben mit politischer Arbeit verbinden!* (Berlin: Oberbaum, 1969), chs. 1–2.
9. Leon Trotsky, *Problems of Everyday Life: And Other Writings on Culture and Science* (New York: Monad Press, 1973), 47.
10. Theodor Adorno, *Minima Moralia* (New York: Verso, 1974), 26.
11. Herbert Marcuse, *An Essay on Liberation* (Boston: Beacon Press, 1969).
12. Gustav Landauer, "Sozialistisches Beginnen," *Antipolitik* (Lich: Edition AV, 2010), 143. For a systematic interpretation of Landauer from the viewpoint of the politics of forms of life, see Eva von Redecker, "Topischer Sozialismus. Zur Exodus-Konzeption bei Gustav Landauer und Martin Buber," *WestEnd. Neue Zeitschrift für Sozialforschung* 11, no. 1 (2014): 93–108.
13. One of the most prolific theoreticians of the changes in the everyday life of the worker, Trotsky had correctly seen the need for constructing new forms of life. According to his view, the seizing of power was the easiest part of the revolution. But if the communists were to be successful, there would need to be alternatives in place for the everyday rituals of the czarists and the effectiveness of what he called the ideology of "vodka, the church, and the cinema." However, the Soviet politics of forms of life becomes problematic at the moment when Trotsky identifies the propaganda of the new forms of living together as "education." For education presupposes the existence of an educator who is assumed not to be in need of education herself—thus establishing a fundamental asymmetry in the politics of forms of life.
14. Compare the similar arguments put forward by Jaeggi, *Kritik*, 30–51.
15. As Lauren Berlant and Michael Warner have highlighted with precision in their text "Sex in Public"—an apt title because sexuality is never something private—the imagination of a hygienically purified citizenship is itself the direct expression of a form of life: national heterosexuality. "Sex in Public," *Critical Inquiry* 24, no. 2 (1998): 549.

16. For this reason, Herbert Marcuse considers socially transformative practices those that deal with forms of life. His concept of a New Sensibility was meant to represent this, which at present (i.e., the social forms that at that time when he was writing were anchored and highly contagious) constitutes a new type of humanity and anticipates in some fashion a psychic structure that is suitable for socialism: "Men who would speak a different language, have different gestures, follow different impulses; men who have developed an instinctual barrier against cruelty, brutality, ugliness"; Marcuse, *An Essay of Liberation*, 21. Marcuse's New Human should not be affectively implemented by a moral commandment; the New Sensibility owes from the first an alliance with the pleasure principle. Certainly, Trotsky would not have approved of Marcuse's examples: the New Sensibility is realized in "the erotic belligerency in the songs of protest; the sensuousness of long hair, of the body unsoiled by plastic cleanliness . . . in the psychedelic search" (36–37); he even goes so far as to stylize the miniskirt as an antiauthoritarian protest against the "apparatchiks" (26). Yet both are comparable—the version of a politics of the form of life from 1923 and the one from 1969—in that they do not separate politics from the promise of happiness.
17. Luc Boltanski and Ève Chiapello, *The New Spirit of Capitalism*, trans. Gregory Elliott (New York: Verso, 2006).
18. See, for example, Chantal Mouffe, *Exodus und Stellungskrieg: Die Zukunft radikaler Politik* (Vienna: Turia + Kant, 2005).
19. The politics of forms of life oftentimes appears to fall apart on account of the overburdening of personal relationships. Shortly after the failure of Commune 2, their members reflect on the effects of resorting to psychoanalytic instruments for diagnosing and treating their own subjectivity. According to the *Experiment in Revolutionizing the Bourgeois Individual* (*Versuch der Revolutionierung des bürgelichen Individuums*), the "repressive" politicization of the psyche became a problem: "The misuse made of scraps pulled from psychoanalytic texts only intensified the inquisitorial atmosphere in which no one wanted to divulge anything about their personal problems. The penetration with which some of the members attempted to unravel their individual rationalizations was already treated ironically at the time as a form of 'psycho-terror'" (18). At other moments, the communards noted the persistence of "a bourgeois atmosphere redolent of gossip and intrigue" (21). Other symptoms of the erosion of political forms of life through the exhaustion of intimate relationships include excessive demands and emotional overload, personalizing and moralizing conflicts, or mistaking the development of dependencies and needs in personal relationships.
20. Michel Foucault has justified the view that the private is the political (a formulation shared with the feminist movement) in terms of a theory of power: because the social field is on the whole pervaded by power relations, it is also shot through with practices of resistance. Foucault said in an interview, "Power relations exist between husband and wife, between those who know and those who are ignorant, between parents and children, in the family. In society there are thousands upon thousands of relations of power, and consequently, linkages of power and therefore little confrontations and micro-battles. . . . We are in conflict everywhere—at every moment, there is the revolt of the child who sticks

his finger in his nose at the dinner table to upset his parents"; Michel Foucault, "*Pouvoir et Savior*," in *Dits et écrits: 1954–1988. III, 1976–1979* (Paris: Gallimard, 1994), 406–7. While this example may strike some as humorous or banal, it can clarify the political dynamism of micropolitical interventions. Major changes can begin with making a scene at a dinner party or with illegitimately taking a seat in the front part of the bus.

CHAPTER 8

Forms of Life, Progress, and Social Struggle

On Rahel Jaeggi's Critical Theory

Robin Celikates

In his critique of Hegel, the young Marx writes, "It is clear that the arm of criticism cannot replace the criticism of arms. Material force can only be overthrown by material force" ("Die Waffe der Kritik kann allerdings die Kritik der Waffen nicht ersetzen, die materielle Gewalt muß gestürzt werden durch materielle Gewalt").[1] If Marx is right, for critique to become or be a force of subversion and social transformation, something else has to happen. At times, however, critical theorists and philosophers tend to ascribe a subversive force to critique itself, uncoupling it from the social struggles and social structures to which, according to Max Horkheimer—another founding figure of critical theory—it has to be linked in a "dynamic unity" in order to be "not merely an expression of the concrete historical situation but also a force within it to stimulate change."[2] If such an uncoupling of critique from social struggles and from the social conditions under which such struggles unfold—from "material force(s)"—occurs, this can not only lead to a pacified and one-sided conception of how social transformation is to take place in the future but also have distorting effects on how we think of social transformations that have happened in the past and of the obstacles they had to confront. The general aim of this chapter is to argue that this risk is increased by thinking of social transformations in terms of progress and learning processes. How far this general claim applies to Rahel Jaeggi's project in *Kritik von Lebensformen* is a second question this chapter raises without providing a definite answer. For this reason, while I develop some of the following considerations in direct response to that project—mostly in the form of requests for further clarification and elaboration rather than objections—most of my remarks will be more directly related to how the notion of progress is used in recent philosophical discussions that are both distinct from and connected to Jaeggi's approach. These more indirect considerations will mainly serve to raise the question of whether these are challenges that Jaeggi's account of progress has to face, and if that is the case, how her account would respond to them.

* * *

Let me start with a few general comments on Jaeggi's project in *Kritik von Lebensformen*, an immensely rich and complex book of almost five hundred pages to which my brief remarks cannot do justice. I find myself in fundamental agreement with many of Jaeggi's methodological and theoretical commitments and claims, especially with her claim that critical theory has been—from its very beginning—engaged in an immanent critique of forms of life; that it should continue to do so today, notwithstanding widespread Kantian hesitations; and that this requires developing an encompassing social philosophy that includes a specific kind of (moderately holistic) social ontology.[3] It is not enough to approach forms of life from a purely diagnostic or normative perspective; rather, we have to understand their ontological structure and how they make up the social world we inhabit in order to develop the right kind of critique.

Now the concept "forms of life" is of course a complex one, and using the term triggers Aristotelian, Hegelian, Wittgensteinian, and Cavellian intuitions that are all but easily compatible.[4] Against this background, Jaeggi's conceptual work on how to understand forms of life is highly welcome. As she understands them, forms of life are "forms of human coexistence shaped by culture" that encompass "ensembles of practices and orientations" as well as their "institutional manifestations and materializations."[5] She also speaks of "complex bundles (or ensembles) of social practices geared to solving problems that are in turn shaped by historical contexts and are normatively constituted" (58). These bundles can take on different "aggregate states" (74–75)—they can be very dynamic or relatively inert, without, however, dissolving into an unstructured flux or congealing into impenetrable and closed totalities.

The following comments will be structured around three concepts that play an important but in some ways ambivalent role in her approach—namely, the concepts of structure, struggle, and progress. After commenting on the role of structure in Jaeggi's account in the first section, I will turn to the relation between struggle and progress in the second section, but what I have to say there is in a way only indirectly applicable to Jaeggi's account—or rather, it is unclear to me in how far the questions I raise in the second section with regard to another prominent account of progress are applicable to Jaeggi's approach.

1. STRUCTURE

As Jaeggi of course acknowledges, forms of life have material conditions; they are not freestanding but always embedded in larger social contexts and structures (see, e.g., 121–22). But how exactly are we to understand this embeddedness? Can we fully account for it in the vocabulary of practice theory, as Jaeggi suggests, or do we also need other concepts, such as "structure" or maybe even "system," to theorize the material conditions and environments that provide the larger contexts into which forms of life are embedded? This question seems especially pressing as these larger contexts often systematically—that is, in noncontingent ways—prestructure the ways in which forms of life function and allow for reflection on their own functioning as well as for revision and development in light of this reflection. Another way to put this point is to say that, from the point of view of a critical theory of society, not all forms of life seem to be "located" on the same ontological or explanatory level; some appear as more basic, in ontological or explanatory terms, because they structure and format the conditions under which other forms of life are functioning and reproduced, criticized, and transformed.

Insofar as capitalism is a form of life—and Jaeggi's account provides strong reasons in favor of regarding it not only as an economic system but also as a form of life (see 69, 90)[6]—it seems clear that other forms of life such as the family or the academic form of life (107) are, if not directly determined, at least significantly and systematically shaped by their embeddedness in capitalist socioeconomic structures (as academics, we—some more than others—are confronted with the struggle to adapt to external pressures motivated by a neoliberal "spirit of capitalism" on a daily basis). To point to this need for explanatory and maybe even ontological hierarchization or differentiation does not necessarily involve calling for reestablishing crude base-superstructure dichotomies or misguided notions of unidirectional determination.

According to Jaeggi, the bundles of practices that make up forms of life contain "sedimentary elements," components that, through processes of "sedimentation" (121), have become, to a certain extent, inaccessible, implicit, or intransparent. They can take on aggregate states that range from more fluid to nearly fixed. In addition, Jaeggi emphasizes that "social practices and forms of life are 'materialized' in institutions and, even more 'materially,' in architecture, tools, bodies, material structures which (though themselves the results of actions) make us act. Therefore, they set limits to what we can do as well as enable us to do things in a certain way. Thus, practices and forms of life are givens as well as being created. And they can develop a certain dynamic of their own."[7] In other words, what the idea of structure is often taken to refer to—social patterns emerging out of practices but developing a dynamic of their own that is to a certain extent independent of actual practices and in turn shapes these practices—is built into her notion of social practice, insofar as practices also consist of interlocking patterns, not just individual actions. In this view, it seems that practices can get sedimented and aggregated in ways that build up structure-like patterns without, however, ceasing to be practices. This raises the question of whether the practice-theoretical approach can fully account for the fact that some forms of life—those that seem to be located on a structural, or structurally more "fundamental," level—are astonishingly stable and "sticky" (the main example, being, of course, capitalism, despite its recurring crises). Are these structures, their resilience, their tendency to develop a logic of their own, their path dependency, and their ability to shape and enlist practices in top-down ways not pointing beyond the practice-theoretical vocabulary that conceives of the emergence and reproduction of structures exclusively in terms of practices? Might that vocabulary not have to be supplemented with (rather than replaced by) a more structuralist or systems-theoretical perspective?[8]

Furthermore, taking structure seriously might be seen as challenging an overly strong interpretation of the second of the three preconditions of criticizability Jaeggi identifies in order to show that forms of life can be objects of critique: for something to be a potential object of critique, it has to be (1) subject to change at all, (2) a result of human action of some sorts, and (3) linked to a claim to validity and involve norms of some kind. These conditions are pretty straightforward, but a problem arises when Jaeggi further specifies the second condition by claiming that "it must be possible to blame or praise someone for the way things are—in other words, it must be possible to hold someone responsible for them."[9] Although she goes on to say that "it is not always easy to figure out whom to hold accountable when things go wrong," it is unclear whether this is always the right question to ask with regard to large-scale social structures. Who is to be blamed or held accountable for neoliberal capitalism, the post-Fordist transformation of labor relations, or the specific logic of the culture industry? Although there will in many cases be some names that come to mind, the emergence and reproduction of these more structural features of forms of life are not (primarily) reproduced via the intentions and actions of individual agents and therefore follow structural dynamics that the social sciences describe in terms of systemic logics, path dependence, and lock-in effects that are relatively independent of individual intentions and actions. Although these structures are of course still in some mediated way the result of human action, it is precisely their structural character that renders questions of (individual) responsibility and blame moot.

It seems that these more structural features of forms of life are also relevant for the tasks of critical theory as Jaeggi understands it: instead of giving ethical advice, telling people how to live, or identifying the contours of a good or just society, critical theory seeks to identify structural obstacles to processes that would allow people to ask these questions themselves and to collectively look for answers. From this perspective, what matters is precisely the fact that capitalism shapes forms of life in ways that make it very difficult to imagine how these forms of life could be reorganized so as to make genuine collective learning processes probable or even possible—but for this fact to come into view, we might have to complement practice theory with other theoretical resources from the history of critical theory (think, e.g., of how the objective dimension of "reification" was theorized from Lukács via Adorno to Habermas or of Althusser's notion of state apparatuses, neither as independent of nor as reducible to practices). While I agree that the notion of "aggregate states" is a very useful one and might go some way in capturing what is right in systems-theoretical approaches and thus in answering this question, the social-theoretical vocabulary needed to analyze, explain, and criticize the resistance and resilience of structures or systems against attempts to criticize or transform them might have to be richer and more complex.

2. STRUGGLE AND PROGRESS

Jaeggi's approach does provide not only an analysis of what forms of life are but also an account of how forms of life change, how they are transformed. While forms of life are primarily understood as instances of problem solving, their transformation is primarily analyzed in terms of learning processes. As I will try to show in this section, however, there are good reasons to wonder whether the categories of problem solving and of learning processes are really adequate.

To begin with, I agree with Jaeggi's claim that comparing an analysis in terms of problems and problem solving with the alternative approach based on the idea of needs and their satisfaction (202–3) shows the superiority of her approach, and this framework captures an important aspect of our social reality and the functionality or dysfunctionality of social institutions, but it is unclear to me whether this is really the whole story. It seems difficult to understand some social systems or forms of life in terms of problem solving in the first place. Let me put aside the complex case of capitalism for the moment. Arguably, the apartheid system—in some respects surely a form of life—has *not* been an attempt to solve the problem of social cooperation under the specific circumstances of South Africa, and its overthrow was not the result of a collective learning process in which white oppressors gradually came to realize that there are more rational ways of solving social problems or that "blockages of experience" stand in the way of the further development of their society. Nor am I sure whether the bourgeois family is best understood as a superior problem-solving mechanism rather than, say, an adaptation of patriarchal power relations to changing social circumstances. What are the historical and theoretical foundations for understanding a form of life through one lens rather than through the other—or does a more complex picture have to combine both perspectives? These questions are directly connected to Jaeggi's understanding of progress in terms of learning processes.

How strong is the notion of progress that is built into the idea of a social learning process? How much of a philosophy of history does it contain? Admittedly, Jaeggi's understanding of progress is formal, deflated, open, plural, nonteleological, and process oriented and as such already responds to the most prominent objections against strong notions of progress.[10] At the same time, however, Jaeggi insists that forms of life should be understood both as outcomes of learning processes and as enablers of further—progressive—learning processes: "The success of forms of life can be measured by the extent to which they meet the demands of problem-solving. They can be rational or irrational, appropriate or inappropriate; they can succeed or fail in their problem-solving process, without that process necessarily having to be conscious or intentional."[11] This raises a variety of questions—for example, about the criteria for such assessments and about how and by whom they are applied. In societies rife with conflicts not only about first-order problems but also about the procedures and agencies tackling problems, how questions such as who gets to determine what solutions to which problems are to be assessed in which ways and from which perspective are to be answered is far from evident (this also points to a limit of proceduralization).

Furthermore, in linking the dynamic of the processes in and through which forms of life are transformed to the idea of a learning process, Jaeggi invokes the notion of progress in the sense of a "progressive development . . . induced by crisis-ridden transformations" (317; see also 295–96).[12] But how do we resist being drawn into a vulgar Hegelianism that claims that "progress is what has led to US"—a problematic and self-congratulatory version of what Amy Allen calls "progress as fact" in contrast to "progress as imperative"[13]—and how do we avoid the pacifying and one-sided reinterpretation of often complex and violent processes of social transformation as learning processes that such a perspective surely does not necessarily succumb to but might very well encourage or provide little theoretical resources to discourage?

In what follows, I will briefly turn to a slightly different account of social transformation in terms of progress, problem solving, and learning processes—the one recently developed by Elizabeth Anderson—and look at the particular story it tells about the abolition of slavery. My questions will concern how this account presents critique and its subversive force as enabling progress and how the developments that are interpreted as progress are seen as following from the subversive yet "subtle" force of critique, a critique that, as we will see, is all too often uncoupled from any recognizably "material force" (both in the sense of the forces at play in specific historical constellations and the force enacted by movements that seek to transform these constellations). Of course, accounts of progress as the ones developed by Jaeggi and Anderson avoid the naïveté and triumphalism of other prominent stories of progress, as they are told, for example, in the works of Peter Singer or Steven Pinker,[14] but they still run the risk that the notion of progress itself can function as an epistemological obstacle (in Gaston Bachelard's sense), blocking our insight into the complex ways in which social transformations actually occur and slavery and other practices and institutions continue to shape our present.

In what follows, I point to some of the epistemic, theoretical, empirical, and political risks of employing the notion of progress as more or less linear learning processes of which a more or less local "we" is the subject.[15] The primary risk I am interested in is that of collapsing a complex and muddled history into a potentially self-congratulatory form of Whig history that one-sidedly construes social and political developments as learning processes and these learning processes as consisting in the change of attitudes and beliefs for the better in response to critique and argumentative claim making.[16] Taking this risk seriously involves asking, What does the idea of progress—and our corresponding self-understanding—blind us to?

It may be surprising that this risk also afflicts theories that account for progress in terms of social struggles and that position themselves on the "nonideal" side of current methodological debates in political and social theory. By focusing on Anderson's approach, I aim to illustrate how this risk can materialize in a theoretical environment where one might not suspect it because the account has been built—to a certain extent against the prevailing post-Rawlsian consensus—to avoid the pitfalls of overidealization. As Anderson puts it, the problem with overly abstract and ideal theories is that they violate what she calls "the representation principle": "Sound political theories must be capable of representing normatively relevant political facts. If they can't represent certain injustices, then they can't help us identify them. If they can't represent the causes of certain injustices, then they can't help us identify solutions."[17] In this sense, the critique I will provide is an internal and not an external critique, as it takes as its starting point the methodological commitments and self-understanding of the approach it criticizes and argues that, in certain respects, Anderson's work exhibits the same shortcoming she diagnoses in others—namely, a failure to represent normatively relevant facts about the historical processes she takes as exemplifying progress. I will end with the question of how far these shortcomings might also afflict Jaeggi's employment of the notion of progress, a question that is more difficult to answer as her approach operates on a higher level of generality and formality—progress as a social-philosophical category—and does not (yet) rely on reconstructing specific historical transformations in terms of learning processes and progress (although she follows Anderson in citing the abolition of slavery as an exemplary case).

In a series of recent papers, Anderson asks the following question: How do we know when a change in moral beliefs and attitudes is good—that is, a case of learning?[18] As her starting point and case study, she takes what she characterizes as a remarkable transformation of moral consciousness: the development from a "worldwide consensus" in 1700 that slavery was an OK practice (which was, she claims, only opposed by isolated individuals), subsequently destabilized by conscience-driven mid-eighteenth-century Quakers and then replaced by the abolitionist movement, which ushered in today's antislavery consensus. It seems obvious to Anderson that this is a case of moral progress, and of course it is (although that story might be more complicated as well, as we will see). But how and why can we speak of moral progress here without just begging the question in favor of our moral beliefs and practices and indulging in excessive self-congratulation (that is Anderson's question)? And what are the risks of doing so beyond the danger of self-congratulation (that is my question)? In order to answer the first question (she does not address the second one), Anderson—in ways similar to but also markedly different from Jaeggi—turns to John Dewey and tries to extract a pragmatist or pragmatico-experimentalist account of moral progress from his writings.[19] In an interesting variation on the fate of the master in Hegel's *Phenomenology of Spirit* (again following Dewey and picking up a claim at the center of so-called standpoint epistemology[20]), Anderson identifies a structural obstacle to the smooth move from identifying a problem relevant from the point of view of social coordination and cooperation to an intelligent form of norm updating and revision—namely, the fact that the powerful (those in control of norm change) are more biased in their own case than other people, that they suffer from specific forms of epistemic limitation *because* of their privilege—essentially because they are isolated from the kinds of experiences that spur critical moral reflection in the messy day-to-day reality of the less fortunate who cannot afford that type of ignorance (including about how power relations actually work). To counter this form of cognitive decay and subsequent moral stagnation (the analogue of the master's downfall in Hegel), there is thus a social need (a "need," or functional requirement, ascribable to society as a whole) for subversive and critical practices that can correct these biases by informing the powerful of the existing problems that risk to undermine social cooperation and coordination. Although the associated forms of contentious politics can reach from petitions and teach-ins via campaigns and demonstrations to occupations and riots, they all aim at disrupting established routines and habits in order to generate serious moral reflection on the part of the powerful, thereby (hopefully? if all goes well?) paving the way for moral learning processes and moral progress. Or so Anderson argues.

Anderson's account, however, runs into a series of difficulties. To see in more detail what goes wrong here, take Anderson's own preferred example: "how contention over slavery not just in pure moral argument but in deed—through testimony, petitions, lawsuits, political campaigns, demonstrations, dramas, subversion, and rebellion—can transform moral consciousness through processes that count as moral learning."[21] Now I obviously do not deny that some kind of progress has happened in cases such as this one, but how did it occur and how should we understand it?

A first problem with Anderson's approach consists in its limited focus that leaves out normatively relevant facts. Indeed, Anderson's account of British abolitionism in terms of moral progress can be seen as exemplifying the risks of Whig history with regard to how a story is told and backed up by "facts." History (writing) is Whiggish insofar as it construes historical development as the result of a development that, more or less inevitably, drives forward progress toward the present (a time, in comparison with the past, of greater enlightenment, freedom, human rights, etc.). Without engaging in the usual triumphalism of Pinker and others, Anderson's narrative still stands in danger of being too progress oriented, moralizing, and hero centered, largely ignoring social and political contexts and structures, continuities and discontinuities, dead ends, breaks, and, indeed, the heterogeneity of forms of struggle itself—historical "facts," that is, that would come into view as relevant if the story was told from a different angle.

To start with, take Anderson's claim that what we have today is an almost universal antislavery consensus. How does this sit with the fact that according to the United Nations, roughly twenty-seven to thirty million people today are caught in the slave trade industry, especially in India, China, and Thailand but also in Russia and the UK?[22] And what about mass incarceration and penal labor in the US, which, while maybe not themselves cases of slavery, bear certain structural resemblances to it?[23] To insist that slavery is nowhere legal and that this is why we can speak of progress is not particularly helpful—indeed it can be seen as positively ideological in the sense of masking crucial facts about our historical situation. After all, what counts (not only empirically but, one would think, also normatively—that is, even from the point of view of moral progress) is that it is an existing albeit changing social institution or practice that reproduces itself and remains highly profitable in ways that we profit from but do not want to be confronted with—whether it continues to exist openly as slavery or under the cover of the law is of secondary importance (of course it is of some importance, but we should get our priorities in describing the situation right). So why is this situation tolerated? It seems unlikely that this is an issue reducible to lack of information, moral sensibility, or problem-solving capacities or to slow learning processes,[24] but claiming that moral progress has made slavery an "unthinkable" institution certainly does not help to identify any answers to this question as it prevents the question itself from being asked in the right terms.

Turning to history proper, Anderson's hymn to abolitionism—which takes center stage in her account of the overcoming of slavery—also disregards its political "fate" or "function": in order to enforce the newly adopted goal of "abolition," Great Britain's rulers gladly took up the pacifists' cause as part of a new way of waging war and advancing colonial ambitions especially in the "scramble for Africa" (hence Robin Blackburn's label "Gunboat Abolitionism").[25] One of the chief justifications for the colonization of Africa was the suppression of the slave trade, all the while Great Britain continued to profit from its central role in a slavery-based Atlantic economy. In this context it is also worth remembering that abolition paid off financially, but not for the slaves, of course, as it was the British slave owners who were compensated with (what was then) 20,000,000 GBP for the loss of their "property."[26] Abolitionism was, in that sense, far from being a radical social or political project (or the motor of a somewhat freestanding learning process).

Another problematic assumption or implication of Anderson's argument is that slavery was ended, and even only seen as problematic, thanks to the efforts of the abolitionists (which, of course, were for the most part white Anglo-Saxons)—there is little room for the moral outlook, the agency, and the practices of the resistance of slaves themselves in this framework. As is well documented, however, slave resistance included significant and widespread forms of passive resistance, sabotage, escape, and flight.[27] Anderson thus risks reproducing a Eurocentric narrative in which not even the Haitian Revolution is accorded a prominent role, despite the discussions it has more recently triggered.[28] The reality of abolitionism and of the struggle against slavery is thus decidedly more complex than Anderson's philosophical reconstruction in terms of moral progress and social learning processes suggests.

This is connected to a second, more general and theoretically relevant problem that concerns the focus on morality, more concretely the idea that the problems with slavery were the wrong moral beliefs that sustained it and that therefore a change in moral consciousness was the way to overcome it. Such a moralizing perspective not only fails to account for the significance of structural (e.g., demographic, economic, and geopolitical) factors in the "success" of British abolitionism and the demise of slavery as it was practiced in that time in general. It also seems to misunderstand the basis of slavery and how it was challenged: neither was slavery upheld nor was it abolished exclusively or primarily for moral reasons.

Essentially, Anderson's story suggests, people understood that slavery gets in the way of economic development and rational social organization and problem solving and turns out to be incompatible with considered moral convictions. This analysis raises a fundamental question: Does it really make historical sense to say that it was the (perceived) decline in slavery's problem-solving capacity and the exposure of the public to morally relevant facts ("slavery is bad") that turned out to be the relevant factors in overcoming slavery?

The historical point this raises is linked to a more general problem: contrary to what Anderson seems to suggest, radical contentious politics often does not primarily aim at cognitively improving the powerful—at subverting only their moral belief system, assisting the slow learners, as it were.[29] Epistemic improvements or learning processes may of course be by-products of radical politics, but they are rarely its primary aim. Rather, contentious politics often aims at unseating the powerful, subverting the social and political relations that sustain them, again not necessarily by convincing them to step down (they rarely do) but by throwing them out or by changing the rules of the game (again, think of the Haitian Revolution). Instead of aiming at moral persuasion—convincing the other side that they should revise their moral beliefs—the struggles in question will more likely take other forms (and have historically taken other forms) such as various forms of disruptive disobedience, sabotage, threats of large-scale violence, armed struggle, and so on, all of which involve an irreducible element of "material force." Although it should be clear that this is not a normative claim and that engaging in persuasion can be strategically and not only normatively warranted, radical change in social and political power relations might involve, but is not reducible to, seeking to initiate learning processes.

What Anderson—and to a certain extent maybe Jaeggi as well—underestimates is the systemic and structural character of the context into which the practices and belief systems—or forms of life—they focus on are embedded. Their accounts ultimately seem to leave little room both for the "material forces" at play in the situation as well as for the "force" it might take to effectively challenge and transform it. Shifting patterns and relations of power and interest, however, play at least as important a role as "moral change," so that revolutionary transformation is usually not reducible to processes of collective learning.

These limitations lead me to call the model of moral progress through moralized (or moralizing) social struggle that Anderson proposes "Victorian": it seems to assume that the problem is less with power structures and more with the moral attitudes and sensibilities of those in power and that those attitudes and sensibilities can be progressively modified without substantially modifying the underlying structures (while acknowledging that the modification of these structures can be a long-term outcome of attitudinal change). This, however, is both a very limited and a potentially naïve model: it is limited in that it reduces social transformation to moral progress of a very specific kind, and it tends to be naïve in that it underestimates the obstacles to moral progress and social transformation and provides an irenic and pacifying view of the methods it takes to effect change.[30]

What is wrong with this picture is thus not the idea that struggles play a crucial role for historical change but rather how the struggles in question are understood, how they are uncoupled from "material force." Anderson leaves little room for the (after all empirically likely) possibility that what are in truth processes of strategic adaptation to changing circumstances and outcomes of often violent struggles that had to be forced onto the opposing party have been redescribed (and rationalized) as moral learning processes and as moral progress (to which at some later point they may very well amount). Such a redescription opens up not only psychologically welcome possibilities for self-congratulation but, as we have seen in the case of abolitionism, also room for political maneuvering. That the categories of "progress" and "learning process" have this ideological potential should guard us against using them in politically and socially decontextualized ways. Obviously that does not mean that I am denying the claim that progress or learning processes have taken place or that moral considerations and attitudes (sometimes even notions of moral progress!) play a role in motivating the struggles in question and thereby in triggering social transformations[31]—rather, I am pointing to the twin risks of ignoring the blind spots generated by the notion of moral progress and the problematic—moralized, pacified—understanding of social struggle and its obstacles it seems to imply.

So to repeat, of course overcoming systems of oppression and exploitation such as slavery or colonialism are instances of progress that can also lead to social learning processes, and of course opposition to them has often been driven by moral indignation and revolt—but if we use the categories of progress and learning processes, we have to be very careful not to distort both these systems and the process of overcoming them. These systems were not well-intended but flawed attempts at problem solving or cooperation; they were systems of oppression and exploitation. They were not experimental attempts of a community to solve the problem of altruism-failures or of coordination; they were imposed by some groups on others and sustained by extreme violence, and if we use the language of refinement or learning to describe the processes in which they were overcome (insofar as they were overcome), we underestimate that these are not simply cumulative learning processes but that they often involve structural shifts (e.g., in the economy), radical breaks, and material force as well as violent struggles (Marx's "critique of arms").[32]

In her complex account laid out in the book, Jaeggi makes it clear that she does not understand progress and the learning processes associated with it solely in terms of moral improvement. Her approach follows a more social-theoretical orientation and starts from the crises and contradictions that affect the practices and institutions that make up forms of life and that might trigger conflicts that spur societies into developing better practices and institutions—that is, into "learning." She thus embeds moral progress in larger and multidimensional processes of social change. The question still remains, however, whether Jaeggi's account—which shares the focus on moral change, problem solving, and learning while rightly insisting that how change came about is a dimension integral to its evaluation—can avoid the difficulties talk of progress and learning processes leads to in Anderson's case. Alternatively, critical theorists might be seen as better off thinking of complex and muddled processes of social transformation in ways that avoid the theoretical vocabulary of progress and learning and its seemingly inevitable Whiggish implications—but that, of course, is a challenge of its own.[33]

NOTES

1. Karl Marx, "Zur Kritik der Hegelschen Rechtsphilosophie. Einleitung," in *Marx-Engels-Werke*, vol. 1 (1843–44; repr., Berlin: Dietz, 1976), 385; Karl Marx, "Contribution to the Critique of Hegel's *Philosophy of Right*: Introduction," in *The Marx-Engels Reader*, ed. R. C. Tucker (New York: Norton, 1978), 60.
2. Max Horkheimer, "Traditional and Critical Theory," in *Critical Theory* (1937; repr., New York: Seabury, 1972), 215.
3. The latter claim is more fully developed in a joint publication: Rahel Jaeggi and Robin Celikates, *Sozialphilosophie: Eine Einführung* (München: Beck, 2017).
4. See, for example, the contributions to the special issue "Politiques des formes de vie" of *Raisons Politiques* 57 (2015).

5. Rahel Jaeggi, *Kritik von Lebensformen* (Berlin: Suhrkamp, 2014), 20–21; further references to this book are given in parentheses.
6. See Rahel Jaeggi, "What (If Anthing) Is Wrong with Capitalism? Dysfunctionality, Exploitation and Alienation: Three Approaches to the Critique of Capitalism," *Southern Journal of Philosophy* 54, Spindel Supplement (2016): 44–65.
7. Rahel Jaeggi, "Towards an Immanent Critique of Forms of Life," *Raisons Politiques* 57 (2015): 18.
8. This question of course echoes Jürgen Habermas's claims in *The Theory of Communicative Action* and the debate surrounding the distinction between lifeworld and system, but it neither depends on the specificities of Habermas's theory nor necessarily involves the dualism of lifeworld and system that has been rightly criticized.
9. Jaeggi, "Towards an Immanent Critique of Forms of Life," 19; see also 139–41/93–94.
10. See Amy Allen, *The End of Progress: Decolonizing the Normative Foundations of Critical Theory* (New York: Columbia University Press, 2016).
11. Jaeggi, "Towards an Immanent Critique of Forms of Life," 25–26; see also 315–19/192–95 in the book.
12. See also the more fully developed discussion in Rahel Jaeggi, "The Dialectics of Progress" (unpublished manuscript, 2016), Word file.
13. See Allen, *The End of Progress*.
14. Peter Singer, *The Expanding Circle: Ethics, Evolution, and Moral Progress* (1981; repr., Princeton: Princeton University Press, 2011); Steven Pinker, *The Better Angels of Our Nature: Why Violence Has Declined* (London: Penguin, 2012).
15. For another recent example of a story of progress and learning of which the "we" of humanity is the direct subject, see Leif Wenar, "Is Humanity Getting Better?," http://opinionator.blogs.nytimes.com/2016/02/15/is-humanity-getting-better.
16. As Charles Larmore asks, "Is not the notion of progress basically an instrument of self-congratulation?"; see Charles Larmore, "History & Truth," *Daedalus* 133 (2004): 3, 47.
17. Elizabeth Anderson, "Toward a Non-ideal, Relational Methodology for Political Philosophy: Comments on Schwartzman's *Challenging Liberalism*," *Hypatia* 24 (2009): 4, 130–31, 132.
18. See Elizabeth Anderson, "The Social Epistemology of Morality: Learning from the Forgotten History of the Abolition of Slavery," in *The Epistemic Life of Groups: Essays in Collective Epistemology*, ed. Miranda Fricker and Michael Brady (Oxford: Oxford University Press, 2016), 75–94; Elizabeth Anderson, *Social Movements, Experiments in Living, and Moral Progress: Case Studies from Britain's Abolition of Slavery* (Lawrence: University of Kansas, 2014); and the discussion at http://peasoup.typepad.com/peasoup/2013/07/featured-philosopher-elizabeth-anderson.html.
19. See Anderson, *Social Movements*, sec. 2.
20. See, for example, Alison Wylie, "Why Standpoint Matters," in *Science and Other Cultures*, ed. Robert Figueroa and Sandra Harding (London: Routledge, 2003), 26–48.
21. "Featured Philosopher: Elizabeth Anderson," *Pea Soup*, http://peasoup.typepad.com/peasoup/2013/07/featured-philosopher-elizabeth-anderson.html. Accessed October 2, 2016.

22. See, for example, Kevin Bales, *Understanding Global Slavery: A Reader* (Berkeley: University of California Press, 2005), and the reports collected on http://www.theguardian.com/global-development/series/modern-day-slavery-in-focus. Accessed October 2, 2016.
23. See, for example, Michelle Alexander, *The New Jim Crow: Mass Incarceration in the Age of Colorblindness* (New York: New Press, 2010); Whitney Benns, "American Slavery, Reinvented," September 21, 2015, available at http://www.theatlantic.com/business/archive/2015/09/prison-labor-in-america/406177/. Accessed October 2, 2016.
24. See also Amartya Sen, "Poverty and the Tolerance of the Intolerable," London School of Economics and Political Science, January 22, 2014, available at http://www.lse.ac.uk/publicEvents/events/2014/01/20140122t1830vOT.aspx. Accessed October 2, 2016.
25. See, for example, Robin Blackburn, "Gunboat Abolitionism," *New Left Review* 87 (2014): 143–52.
26. Nicholas Draper, *The Price of Emancipation: Slave-Ownership, Compensation and British Society at the End of Slavery* (Cambridge: Cambridge University Press, 2010).
27. See only the now classic 1942 (!) article by Raymond A. Bauer and Alice H. Bauer, "Day to Day Resistance to Slavery," in *Rebellions, Resistance, and Runaways within the Slave South*, ed. Paul Finkelman (New York: Garland, 1989), 84–115.
28. See, for example, Susan Buck-Morss, *Hegel, Haiti and Universal History* (Pittsburgh: University of Pittsburgh Press, 2009); Jeannette Ehrmann, "Constituting a Critique of Racism: Haiti and the Revolution of Human Rights," *Zeitschrift für Menschenrechte* 9 (2015): 1, 26–40.
29. Anderson does, of course, acknowledge that moral arguments may not be enough if they fall on deaf ears. The more dramatic forms of contention that then have to come into play, however, are still described by her as, essentially, forms of moral claim-making aimed at changing the slaveholders' minds. Consider the following claim, which is in line with her more abstract model of social norm change: "We can model the epistemic value of different modes of contention in terms of their potential for inducing error-correction, counteracting bias, clearing up confusion, taking up morally relevant information, making people receptive to admitting mistakes, drawing logical conclusions, and other epistemic improvements" (Anderson, "The Social Epistemology of Morality," 93).
30. To be sure, Anderson is sometimes more careful here and criticizes those "dominant Western historical narratives" according to which "the West has forever been an autodidact, arriving at the true principles of morality through its own self-sufficient reasoning, figuring out for itself when it has failed to apply them, self-correcting its course, and taking the lead in teaching these principles to the rest of the benighted world" (Anderson, 76). This critical point, however, does not seem to affect the substance of her account.
31. See Joshua Cohen, "The Arc of the Moral Universe," *Philosophy & Public Affairs* 26 (1997): 2, 91–134, esp. 130.
32. Against this maybe overly realistic view, Kantians might object that revolutions are won on the battlefield of ideas once they manage to convince the "impartial spectator"—that might be true as far as it goes, but it presupposes that a revolution

has taken place, and this revolution will first have to take place in the streets and squares. Learning processes have to follow in order to really talk of progress, but they have a different dynamic and temporality.

33. Along these lines, one could also argue that there is at least a misleading dichotomy involved in Axel Honneth's claim, in his recent *Die Idee des Sozialismus* (Berlin: Suhrkamp, 2015), that "not rebelling subjectivities but objective improvements, not collective movements, but institutional achievements should be regarded as the social bearer of those normative claims which socialism articulates in modern societies" (117; this passage does not appear in the English translation, *The Idea of Socialism*, Cambridge: Polity, 2017, pp. 73–74).

CHAPTER 9

Progress, Normativity, and the Dynamics of Social Change

An Exchange between Rahel Jaeggi and Amy Allen

Conducted by Eva von Redecker

EVA VON REDECKER: I would like to say a quick word to open up the conversation. I think that by moving the notion of progress to the center of your work, both of you accomplish something very interesting in that you transpose an elaborate and well-rehearsed debate in critical theory regarding the foundations of normativity away from the question of critique and into the history of social change and politics. This is what I find really exciting about this whole thematic field. Whether in problematizing the notion of progress, as Amy does, or in revisiting it in Rahel's way, the shift from a mere reflection of critique to one of historical development immediately makes the debate more substantial.

The approaches each of you offer could easily be construed as a direct clash—progress, for and against—but I am not so interested in pretending that your positions are even congruent enough to be exact opposites regarding the same question. I think it is more interesting to figure out the constellation in which they stand to each other. I hope we can probe this issue, which can be clustered around roughly three concerns: the conceptual role progress plays in critical theory, your respective versions of negativism, and how your views on progress are informed by different accounts of social change. To start us off on your separate takes on progress, I want to begin with a question that might seem a bit playful, but might move us to the important details. I'd like to ask Amy why she thinks that some residual notion of progress, despite her many critiques of it, is, at the end of the day, indispensable for critical theory. I also want to hear from Rahel about why she thinks we cannot simply work with an unmodified notion of progress. Why, for example, can we not take up Hegelian world history or historical materialism?

This conversation took place on July 16, 2016, in Kreuzberg, Berlin. It has been transcribed and edited for publication.—Ed.

EVR: Let's begin with Amy. Why do you think that at least a residual notion of progress needs to remain in play?

AMY ALLEN: I think I would have to start to answer that question by drawing on the distinction I make between backward-looking progress and forward-looking progress.[1] The idea is that the concept of progress has at least two sides: the backward-looking side is the one we employ when we read history as a story of progress in some sense, which could mean in terms of historical learning processes or social evolution or a more full-blown Enlightenment conception of the betterment of humankind. That's what I call progress as a "fact," which is in scare quotes because this is obviously a normatively laden notion. I borrow that term from Thomas McCarthy, who wrote about what he called "the facts of global modernity" and argued in *Race, Empire, and the Idea of Human Development* that we can't deny certain kinds of claims about progress as a historical fact.[2] So that's the backward-looking conception of progress. The forward-looking conception of progress is the one that we employ when we want to make our politics progressive—when we talk about the goal that we want to achieve, whether that is thought of in terms of a good society or achieving some sort of social ideal or, more negatively, as alleviating some forms of domination or existing conditions of oppression or suffering. The only sense in which I would say the notion of progress is indispensable for critical theory is this more forward-looking sense. I accept the idea that when we engage in the project of critique, we are critiquing existing social relations in light of some kind of conception of the better, whether that is framed positively in terms of some ideal we are trying to achieve or more negatively (as I would favor framing it) as trying to overcome or transform existing relations of domination. I still think this approach appeals to some kind of forward-looking notion of progress understood as a moral imperative or goal that we're striving to achieve. That's the sense in which I think critical theory needs or necessarily employs a notion of progress: progress toward some kind of improvement or even away from some negative state of suffering or domination. But the backward-looking conception of progress—namely, as a historical "fact"—we can and should do without.

EVR: I think we should definitely get to what you think is problematic about that backward-looking story, but I first want to hear why Rahel, in a certain way, also thinks that a straightforward notion of history as progress won't do and why we need to rethink the concept of progress. Or, to take a different starting point than critical theory, why do you find the notion of progress as it is employed in analytic philosophy's debates on moral progress not satisfactory either?

RAHEL JAEGGI: What I'm doing with respect to progress right now, and I only have entered this conversation in the last year, is something that is an outcome of what I've tried to develop in my book *The Critique of Forms of Life*.[3] There, progress appears only at the very end. It might actually be a very weak idea of progress, but let's face it: if we talk about something like a learning process or the process of overcoming problems, and if we talk about it in a way that includes some kind of an accumulation of experience in a Hegelian way, this is what people would call "progress." But I hadn't yet started working on that conception of progress, and it was something that just sat in the background of my book.

Why didn't I go for a straightforward idea of progress? I was not looking for progress as either an ideal or a fact. Instead, I was interested in establishing criteria for criticizing where we are now. These criteria would look at the developmental process itself instead of looking at what we want to achieve—at normative ideals, things we know as a matter of fact, or what we as philosophers know (that certain values or principles should be in place in order to establish a good society). In one understanding, progress would be something that gets us close to this kind of ideal. That is exactly what I didn't want to do when spelling out a mode of critique and a way of criticizing our form of life. My starting point was to look for criteria that would somehow be self-standing, where the process itself would give us the criteria for whether a certain form of life is irrational or not or good or distorted in a certain way.

To come to the point, I think we should not accept a teleological notion of progress. This should not come as a surprise: a lot of people think that whatever we think of progress, it shouldn't be teleological. But why shouldn't we think of it this way? It seems to be the easiest way to talk about progress, if you talk about it at all: to think of it as something that is defined by some kind of a goal that we could get further from or closer to. But in a negative mode, we have to start from the assumption that we don't know what the good life or the good society is or the principles by which we should organize social life. In this respect I'm inspired by an Adornian negativity: we shouldn't spell out the good or utopia. I'm also influenced by Marx's antiutopianism, so I'm always a bit nervous when people say that critical theory needs utopia in the end, where all will be good and kids will be laughing and playing and things like this. There is a kitschy tendency in utopian thinking. At any rate, I'm looking for a notion of progress that is not teleological. The other issue, of course, is fallibilism. We don't know yet what progress is, and we have to figure it out while we are doing it.

There are not many people who would advocate a strong teleological notion of progress anymore. The interesting part of the debate is whether or not we can find something like "progress as a fact" at all. Among those who deny that (not Amy, though), their reservations even undermine the assessment of why we might hold on to certain elements and certain ideals as better than others. One of the interesting things in the contemporary debate about moral progress—and this is why I engage with the issue—is that scholars start with these obvious or, at first sight, local instances of progress that would be very hard to deny. I'm not sure whether these hold, but it was a starting point for me to think about social change and ask how, in those few instances of fortuitous development, we got from here to there. This is actually the discussion I am more interested in than the question of progress itself. I'm interested in the debate about social change and its idealism. I think there's a notable tendency toward idealism in that part of the contemporary philosophical discussion that is not critical about progress. But even some of the radical critiques of the notion of progress seem to be no less idealistic and no less stuck in a frame of mind in which you do not investigate historical conditions and do not try to figure out the material side of social change that might lead to another world.

EVR: I think that defines the task well. Before we go into more detail about the negativistic turn and the material side of social change, I want to linger a moment longer on the first question: How central to critical theory is progress? Maybe we can define the task of the concept a bit closer and then weigh its importance and dangers. It seems to me that in your work, Rahel, despite saying you started off by looking at local, nearly indisputable instances of progress, a stronger notion of progress—of what Amy calls "historical progress" and not merely "progress in history"—does play a role. After that, obviously, Amy, I want to hear about the possible pitfalls of such a conception and why critical theory might lose more than it gains by maintaining a substantial notion of progress.

RJ: Simply put, my take is that in critical theory, we have, more or less, three alternatives. The first is Kantianism or some sort of freestanding morality in which we are positively able to spell out what the good is. This need not be Kantianism; it could also be an Aristotelian notion of the good. For critical theory, however, it has mostly been Kantianism: a freestanding morality or normativity for which you don't need a notion of progress or social change. Most Kantians have a notion of progress, and most Kantians in critical theory are optimistic about being able to spell out what the "better" would be. However, they don't need to elaborate on the change itself because, from a normative point of view, it doesn't really matter how it comes about, or whether history has a tendency, or whether there are moments in history that destabilize institutions so that some sort of change emerges. The second alternative is some kind of Nietzscheanism or, as it is for contemporary critical theory, Foucauldianism, which (and I'll put this very cautiously) tends not to be able to rebut the relativism with which it is constantly confronted, or at least they have no strong, genuine idea of how to react to these problems. The third alternative is a version of Hegelianism or Marxism and some kind of immanent criticism of institutions. Here, of course, the Hegelian and the Marxist options are different, as different as the Nietzschean and the Foucauldian and versions of Kantianism might be.

I suspect that in the end, both Foucauldianism and Nietzscheanism need to resort to some sort of Kantian, freestanding morality. Even if they bracket their moral position in a fruitful way or accept certain notions of equality or freedom as historical and not founded philosophically in normativity, I still think they very much rely on the Kantian position as a result of rejecting the Hegelian-Marxist one. I think of the Hegelian-Marxist position as one in which normativity comes about in and through history, which is an idea that most people think is crazy, especially if history and normativity are understood in their strong Hegelian senses. It is a normative history and a normativity acquired historically. For Marx, it is different because the present does not represent rationality but irrationality. Yet even that irrationality is in a certain way justified within historical materialism. The possibility of change for the better resides in the inverted version of social institutions that capitalism brought about. Here, the normativity is neither relativistic nor freestanding. That is what I find attractive, apart from the notion of progress, as a critical theorist. Even if this suggests that history has a telos in the end, and even if it's a crazy story that everything that's going on is somehow a progressive move toward a rational outcome and should be embraced for normative reasons, the other story would conceive of social change or history as a series of unrelated events. That seems like a mistake to me.

Instead, we need to discern a social dynamic in history in which institutions and practices are related to what has been wrong with and undermined in previous institutions. I find this idea very compelling, and I don't think we can do without it. We can't conceive of history as unrelated events. Even if you were to advocate a negative teleology and see history as declining, you would still have an idea of how things relate to each other and how new institutions come out of old ones. I don't think this is easy to understand or conceptualize. Of course, we shouldn't do it the way Hegel and Marx did it, but as critical theorists, we have to come up with a way to conceive of how existing social institutions play a role in new ones.

EVR: I love how you say that the notion of history that is theoretically attractive is at the same time crazy. According to you, Amy, it is not its craziness that is the problem but rather that such a notion is dangerous or holds political baggage, and this gives you reasons to move away from it. These would also be reasons not to embrace what Rahel calls "the third strand of critical theory," but presumably, you would sort the options differently to begin with?

AA: Yes, I was very excited to hear that there are three options for critical theory, actually, Rahel, because last time we spoke about this, you told me there were only two!

RJ: Well, number one is not really critical theory!

AA: I thought it was because your second option collapses into the first. That's what we talked about previously. I think this is progress of a sort! Now there are three options on the table! But I think it's interesting that Rahel inverted their temporal order. I think there is a way in which one could understand this debate as unfolding in an interesting kind of dialectic, whereby the Nietzschean-Foucauldian third position actually represents a kind of "determinate negation" of the first two, in the sense of the term invoked by Horkheimer and Adorno in the *Dialectic of Enlightenment*.[4] I'll come back to the three options, but I also want to say, in response to Rahel's worry about idealism, that for me, the question about progress emerges in a different way. For me, it is closely bound up with the question of normativity and what I would characterize as a metaethical question about how we can ground the first-order normative judgments that we employ as critical theorists. So there is a sense in which my concern with the question of progress is really not at all about the question of the dynamics of historical change. This is not really something I've thought through, primarily because I'm most concerned about how some sort of idea of progress or normativity in and through history is used in some forms of critical theory to ground normativity. It may be that in my work on progress, I am guilty of some form of idealism because my focus is on this latter question. That's OK with me because it's an important question. It doesn't give you a complete critical theory, but it is a question that has exercised a lot of energy and imagination in critical theory over the last thirty-five years at least.

To the main question, I would sort the options for critical theory in a slightly different way with respect to the question of how to ground normativity. I would employ more or less the same categories: Kantian, left Hegelian or Hegelian-Marxist, and some sort of genealogical alternative. Perhaps controversially, I would put Adorno in the last category and not with the Marxists, although, of course, he's complicated.

The Kantian account attempts to grasp normativity as a freestanding account of practical reason or a constructivist concept of normativity. It doesn't need a notion of progress, but there is one that falls out of it: once you have your transhistorical, universal conception of practical reason, you can talk about progress—historical or otherwise—with respect to what those standards generate.

RJ: Yes. Progress might be an outcome, but it is not an irreducible part of this philosophical account.

AA: I think we both have questions about whether the freestanding account of progress really counts as critical theory in the strict sense. I would say that in the Hegelian-Marxist account, in its classical and in some contemporary formulations (and there is also a question whether this criticism would apply to Rahel's account), there is an attempt to derive an account of normativity that can be transhistorical or "global," if you want to use Philip Kitcher's terminology, from an account of history as a progressive historical learning progress.[5] The best example of this is Axel Honneth's "The Normativity of Ethical Life," in which he discusses how to develop immanent criteria out of a historically specific, situated understanding of how norms are embedded in forms of life.[6] But the hard question is, how do we avoid conventionalism? Honneth wants to address that question by developing some sort of transhistorical, stronger conception of normativity. Here we can speak of the problem of the idea of progress. In a way, that's where my book, *The End of Progress*, starts—namely, with two problems of that particular story of progress.

One is a more conceptual problem that can be articulated in a politically neutral way: the problem of self-congratulation. To say that I won't appeal to any transhistorical, suprahistorical, or context-transcendent standards to make large historical claims about progress but instead derive them immanently in a way that will allow me to draw those broader conclusions is a little like trying to pull a rabbit out of a hat. I think there is a worry that naturally arises that this reading of history either implicitly helps itself to standards that are transhistorical or context-transcendent in a strong sense or that it really, in the end, can't escape conventionalism. So the worry is that either there is a metaphysical standard in the background enabling the transhistorical judgment or progress really amounts to telling a story about history that makes us feel better and happy about where we've ended up. That's the self-congratulation worry.

Second, there is the more political worry about discourses of progress. This could be thought of as a specific version of a self-congratulatory story that has been told many times throughout the history of the Enlightenment in which European modernity, or Euro-American moderns, have congratulated themselves on their own history and have read their history as a story of progress and development. That particular story is one that is very closely bound with colonialism, neocolonialism, and the civilizing mission—all these very problematic political positions. The stories of the cognitive or normative developmental superiority of European modernity were (and in many cases still are) used to justify certain kinds of pernicious political arrangements that undergirded colonialism and neocolonialism. That is obviously a very strong charge, and it is not like the concept of progress per se necessarily entails this kind of judgment, but conceptions of progress that position European modernity as the outcome of a learning process do, I think, entail that judgment. Unfortunately, in some critical theory, especially in Habermas's theory of modernity and also in some way in Honneth's work, which revives and extends that line of Habermas's thinking, both the conceptual and the political problems are at play.

This brings me to the Nietzschean-Foucauldian or genealogical alternative for critical theory. One difficulty I have about the way Rahel characterized it (and she probably wants to protest the way I characterized the Hegelian alternative) is that it is more than reading history as a series of unrelated events. Alternatively, if that's part of it, it is for very specific methodological reasons that I think are important. This is the sense in which I'm not kidding when I say that one could view this as a kind of determinate negation of these kinds of Hegelian views. It's true that there are Kantian and Hegelian elements in this view—Kantian in the sense that, properly understood, my view and the Foucauldian view hang onto some kinds of first-order Kantian normative commitments, such as freedom as autonomy. That is an ideal in the name of which I work.

There's also a very Hegelian (or left-Hegelian) historicizing move in this genealogical account in which rationality and normativity are seen as thoroughly embedded in history. However, there is a fundamental and transformative break with each of these ways of thinking about normativity, and I think that involves two things. First, it is not a reading of history in terms of decline and fall but rather a far more ambivalent telling of history as stories of progress and regress at the same time, with neither one really overriding the other. Seeing it in this way, we try to understand both the domination and the promise of the norms and practices that have been handed down to us. Second, reading history as a series of unrelated events is a very specific methodological move that is designed to allow us to get more critical distance on a modernity that is itself structured in terms of a historical consciousness. In other words, it accepts the basic Hegelian idea that something like a historical consciousness is part of the legacy of modernity and then reads history as a series of unrelated events that come one after another in order to get us to see that as a specific historical a priori or form of life. There's an extrareflexive historicization of historicity in this account. I find that aspect of the account very interesting and consider it one that demonstrates that the genealogical account is in fact a distinct alternative—one that starts from a transformative reading of the Hegelian position.

RJ: I want to react to Amy's idea that the three versions of critical theory might tell a progressive story of determinate negation. One could say that it starts as left Hegelianism, and at a certain point, that doesn't work anymore. It is clear that the grand narratives don't work anymore and no one believes in that kind of Marxism or Hegelianism these days. In that case, there would be two remaining options: the freestanding normativity of Kantianism, which Habermas did embrace at a certain point, or the genealogies of Nietzsche and Foucault. Both might be seen as reactions to the problem that Hegelianism and Marxism ran into, but that would not be a very dialectical resolution. Alternatively, we might say regarding critical theory, and especially with respect to your placement of Adorno in the camp of Nietzsche and Foucault, that the interesting thing about the first Frankfurt generation is that these three options were already simultaneously present. I'm not so sure about Kantianism, but of course you can find in the *Dialectic of Enlightenment* both left Hegelianism and Nietzscheanism. Maybe critical theory is an interesting mix of these, and maybe we do not have to choose.

But to your remarks, I could have said that whatever the position of Adorno and early Horkheimer, who seemed much closer to left Hegelianism and Marxism than Adorno, the most interesting and fruitful question is the way in which the first generation of critical theorists understood, analyzed, and criticized fascism. The notion of regression is present everywhere in their analysis. For them, it's not simply that fascism is something morally evil, bad, or that doesn't live up to the standards of the categorical imperative. Of course, all of this is true. But they thought about it and analyzed it as a moment of regression. If you talk about regression, you hold on to the notion of progress. It is not spelled out teleologically or presupposed factually, but it is implied in the conceptual logic. Analyzing fascism in terms of regression speaks to me, and I consider it much more fruitful than most other approaches because—and I guess that could be said for genealogy as well—this analysis is not only evaluative but also informative.

Let's think of what is going on today, when an attempt to do some sort of ideology critique of fundamentalism is actually not popular. Most people are stuck in the idea that there is something morally evil going on. There are people who think of it as a regression and that we moderns should not accept it. But that is not the kind of fine-grained analysis or dialectical analysis of regression that we're talking about in critical theory in relation to progress and regression. For me, the reason to think about progress here would be that we need a notion of regression, which is a much more attractive notion to me because it is a clue to historical dynamics.

To return again to your remarks, I did not accuse you or genealogy of anything as such. I don't think I've made up my mind about the prospects of coming up with an interesting account of what the dynamics of social change would be in relation to these three options. My claim is more modest: if those are indeed the alternatives, it makes sense to attempt again to work with the third option and develop a modest and pragmatic idea of the philosophy of history. We lose a lot if we cannot come up with a social theory that sees history as more than unrelated events. It is from within an understanding of an emancipatory or meaningful succession of historical moments that we can judge trajectories of transformation. We are then able to say that certain developments don't make sense at all and that some are entangled in the dialectical dynamics of the reaction to and the overcoming of problems. Therefore, I am not so much saying that Hegelian-Marxism is the only way, but I am instead attempting to outline what we lose in some (perhaps too easy) critiques of philosophy of history—namely, the whole conceptual grasp of social change and how we might redeem some of those features.

Maybe this opens up another area of discussion regarding your concerns about progress. If we were right about historical progress, would we then also be right to be self-congratulatory? Not that it would ever be commendable to be self-congratulatory, but I want to slightly disentangle a tendency to argue via guilt by association on the side of progress-skepticism. That our Western modernity, and German politics in particular, have committed real atrocities and still considered them progressive, or even justified them as measures required for progress's sake is beyond question. But maybe we get further by saying that those were not progressive. Just like socialism, progress might not even have happened yet, but that doesn't imply that it was impossible or that we lacked the criteria to identify it.

EVR: One thing you both share is the conviction that we should presuppose neither a definite goal nor an external framework for assessing change. But you each suggest a different mechanism for how to approach our present and what led up to it. In Rahel's case, the mechanism is something like nonregressive problem solving, and she's already elaborated on what one can do with the notion of regression. In a certain way, that concept is more indispensable to her than the notion of progress. I think in Amy's case, it is a problematizing genealogy, which she defines and designs as a very specific type of genealogy that is also richer than one might have thought genealogy was. I'd like to ask you, Amy, how problematizing genealogy, or what you call "historicizing historicity," can do some of the work Rahel suggests we should do via the notion of regression without presupposing that there is something valuable in the present that we shouldn't let go of or fall back behind.

AA: I'm not sure I would say that it is supposed to work without presupposing something valuable in the present.

EVR: That would raise the next question: What is it that you presuppose? It seems to be a fairly narrow idea of freedom: freedom from domination. Is that what you would see as indispensable or as something that we have already partly achieved?

AA: It presupposes at least that much. There may be other things. I am fairly sure of and explicit about the fact that there is some conception of freedom as autonomy that, as I've argued in my earlier work, is part of the genealogical account, and it is explicitly coming out of some kind of Kantian and Enlightenment lineage that transforms this idea. But it's not a Kantian conception of rational autonomy.

EVR: So you accept the content of Kant's idea but not his justification?

AA: No, I think the idea also is transformed. In some of my earlier work, I talk about how I think Foucault is transforming this Kantian idea of autonomy from some kind of submission to laws to an idea of understanding or he's coming to see that what we take to be necessary is in fact contingent.[7] But the process of coming to see that is a kind of autonomy. It isn't simply a process of binding ourselves to moral laws. You might say that it has the form of Kantian autonomy with different content. I understand it as a kind of radically transformative taking up of a certain Kantian conception of autonomy. Furthermore, I'm interested in the way that Foucault, for example, positions himself as an inheritor of the Enlightenment tradition and the way in which that notion of inheritance is understood in the Derridean sense of placing oneself in this tradition while radically transforming it. Certainly the notion of freedom is in the background. Explicitly, in my account, the work that problematizing genealogy allows us to do is to free ourselves up in relation to the present and to be in a position to see autonomy as what Foucault would call a "historical a priori," or what Adorno would call "second nature." I'm not sure I would even say this is necessary for transforming it. I think there could be transformations that happen for other reasons.

RJ: But do you consider genealogy necessary for transforming autonomy progressively?

AA: When engaging in the work of critique, it is necessary first to free ourselves from our relationships to the institutions and features of our historical a priori that set the conditions of possibility for thinking and acting for us. I think the idea of the historical a priori is very close to the idea of forms of life, and I'd like to talk about that. I see them as being more or less the same. But again, Foucault situates that idea within this resolutely nonprogressive but also nonregressive reading of history. I would frame my interest in the question of progress and history in their relation to normativity, and I see that as different from a question of how to understand how social changes happen. I think the Foucauldian reading of history has a very specific point with respect to critique that enables us to engage in the work of critique by freeing ourselves up in relation to, as he put it, "what thought silently thinks" and thus allowing it to think otherwise.[8] That might be different than thinking about historical transformation in order to gain a better understanding of the causal mechanisms that enable them to happen or set forth conditions to make historical transformations more or less likely. I wouldn't want to draw an overly sharp distinction there, but I think it's a different angle, and the question I'm interested in with respect to history is what the point of thinking about history is for critique and for critical philosophy. How should we think about history so that we can engage in the work of critique most effectively? I think we should think of history neither progressively, as a story of learning processes, nor regressively, as a decline and fall, but both progressively and regressively at the same time. This is what enables us to problematize most effectively our own present, taken-for-granted, and apparently natural features of our form of life, if you'd like to use that terminology.

EVR: In a way this distancing helps not by its connection to the site of social change but by providing a clearer view when trying to assess those dynamics, which we do as critics and political actors. Although you highlight that power and rationality are entangled, you seem not to consider them amalgamated in a completely indissoluble way: by distancing ourselves or bracketing our form of life, we might attain something like a clearer picture of how exactly they are entangled.

AA: I don't know, but I'd like to stick with the point about social change. Sometimes it may be the case that social transformations happen as a result of people gaining distance or engaging in some kind of critical work, whether that's in the form of written theoretical treatises or just engaging in more critical reflections in their own lives. I suspect that it is very rarely the case that the more critical theoretical work is inducing social change and in fact is more often coming in later and trying to understand what has already happened. Certainly there are cases in social movements in which activists employ critical vocabularies and theoretical positions, but often the dynamics work the other way: the critic enters after the fact and tries to figure out what happened. That's why I'm trying to be careful about the causal element. If you think about the way people engage in a work of individual or collective self-transformation, it's often prompted by a kind of critical reflection on who they are and what they want to be, whether individually or as a community. But again, sometimes transformations happen, and individuals are left trying to figure out what happened and what they think of it. They get swept up in the tide of events or were busy thinking other things, and then they look back and say, "How do I make sense of this transformation?" That's why I'm trying to separate the causal question from a more normative question but not to insist on a strict separation; I just see them as different questions.

Considering questions of rationality and power, I would say that I'm skeptical of the possibility of ever really disentangling ourselves from power relations, or from the weight of social and historical circumstance if you don't want to use what sounds like a very pessimistic language of power to talk about it. However, it is true that freeing ourselves up in relation to our historical a priori is something like trying to get some distance from that entanglement while recognizing that we can't really get outside of it, and we're always going to be trying to engage in that process of negotiation.

EVR: Doesn't that description lend itself to a stronger claim about the conditions of progress? Perhaps as long as we keep our historical past in a language that is self-congratulatory, we enter encounters in a way that forecloses progress as an imperative, as you understand it to happen. This is kind of a proviso: to make any encounter—because I think, for you, the social dynamics come more from encounters between different contexts—happen in an open and progressive way, the parties who are engaged need to undergo this self-distancing. I think it is quite categorical, so I want to sharpen the point a bit.

AA: That's true. I would say that telling a certain kind of self-congratulatory story—for example, one about European modernity as an instance of moral and political progress—is an impediment to making progress in a certain sense. That particular self-congratulatory story needs to be undone. Again, it is a local or contextual claim because it is only true for people who are situated within and are the beneficiaries of Euromodernity. It seems to me that the worry about this story is the way in which it is bound up with colonial domination—in the sense that it both serves as the justification for a set of colonial relations and falls out of a colonial sensibility. The stories about progress and the Enlightenment are rooted in this experience that Europeans—people like Adam Smith, Hume, and so on—read reports from the colonies about what the lives of indigenous people were like. These stories led them to develop a stadial model of progress. They thought, "Those people must be more primitive than we are, and there must be a progressive story that goes from how we used to be to how we are now." The stadial model is not only a justification of colonialism but also a reaction to an encounter with indigenous peoples; it was immediately set up as a relationship of superiority by Europeans who heard these stories in which Europeans served as inheritors of that primitive condition. That story is one that I discuss in my book and take from the sociologist Gurminder Bhambra, who has done interesting work on the developments of these stadial readings of history and how they come to infect a lot of social theory.[9] The problems with that story are such that, as individuals who are situated in positions of power in this global, postcolonial context, it is very important for us to try to work against and undercut them. Otherwise, in intercultural debates about political norms, we are implicitly (or sometimes explicitly) positioning ourselves as superior to traditional, nonmodern "others" who haven't learned something that we have learned.

EVR: So you are saying that if you are situated in that History (with a capital *H*), then you have to distance yourself from that framework?

AA: That's right.

EVR: I think for Rahel, it is not important to presuppose this particular story of European modernity having somehow led to all the values we need and cling to. That's not where the notion of progress or regression stands and falls. But if there were nothing someone could be self-congratulatory about, then your account, Rahel, would not generate any directionality at all, right? Because you could not even say what nonregression would be or what one should not fall back behind. Or do you think that you could orient your outlook from any given context?

RJ: I don't know. This raises a problem for me. I think what I'm doing is much less substantial. It is not about historic modernity as an overarching learning process (which, by the way, would immediately pose the paradox of how and when we entered the realm of developed morals). It is more about whether we can establish normative criteria for emancipation on the basis of whether this is or is not a learning process or a process of accumulating experiences, a term I like better than "learning process" because experience is a richer notion. It doesn't work in English, but in German we use the word *Erfahrungsprozess*. Actually, I think of what I'm doing as something that would work in a pluralist way. The idea that "they" are in some former stage from where we are now is something that would not be applied as a criterion of whatever cultural situation or stage. No matter how far a group is from our ideas of freedom, autonomy, or self-determination, or however one would measure that kind of distance—this distance itself is not the criterion to impose. The focus on past experiences should enable us to analyze the dynamics of change in terms of our learning blockages or absences thereof from within whichever given context. I think that's what Amy's description is grasping, because of course the self-congratulatory version of modernity is a learning blockage. This is exactly the fantasy that the *Dialectic of Enlightenment* undermines. Analysis of this sort rids us of this all-too-optimistic, delusionary idea of what we as moderns are. This is the aspect of postcolonial thinking that I believe is a crucial contribution to critical theory. Your book is important because it reminds us that this skepticism and undermining of self-congratulatory ideas has always been a part of critical theory, and nowadays postcolonial studies has largely taken on the role of formulating it. In the end, what you're describing and doing is getting rid of learning blockages and trying to free us from a narrative that doesn't allow us to see the dialectics of our progresses in the plural.

What's in the background of my approach, and why I think it's interesting to talk about social change, is that progress is somehow a change within change. My idea (and again, I didn't invent it) is that history is a crisis-driven dynamic of problem solving. I like the idea of problem solving because it enables us to come up with a more pragmatic, or pragmatic-dialectical, version of what's going on. The main idea, though, is that crises trigger change, and progress is something that takes place within these changes and these dynamics. There are two things that I take from Marx: first, the well-known formulation that we make our own history, but not under circumstances of our choosing, and second, with respect to revolutions and social dynamics, that there is an active and a passive element. This is the kind of thing I'm interested in: the rational and the not-so-rational dynamics, or the agent-related and the not-so-agent-related side of change. I would like to figure out how change is triggered by human agents—sometimes in reaction to problems that needed to be overcome or that people tried to overcome. But sometimes certain events, circumstances, or innovations take precedence, and new experiences emerge. Then again, there is a dynamic in which unknown, new experiences that somehow interrupt a course of history or a certain historical way of living are reintegrated into a narrative and a form of life. We need to understand the untidy situations in which drastic change is brought about by, for example, technical innovations, which is what I was talking about in the Constellations lecture.[10]

The invention of the typewriter has done something for the emancipation of women, certainly, and so has the pill. At the same time, those who invented the pill and the typewriter didn't do so because they wanted to liberate women. These side effects were unknown and unintended. This kind of plot, in which there are unintended consequences and at the same time social conflicts and social actors who take up certain problems and turn them into crises that are partly of our own making, has to do with our normative self-understanding. Crises in human history are not like natural disasters. They are things that unfold into crises, like poverty, famously, or the problem of the rabble in Hegel.[11] This is not just about people starving; it's about people who have normative claims on society that they think are not fulfilled. This is the kind of dynamic I'm interested in. I haven't written a book on progress as Amy has, but in the end, I don't even know if there is such a thing as progress. Do I have to hold onto some real-life empirical progress? I don't know.

EVR: I'm actually totally convinced that you have written a book on progress and that this is one dimension of your *Critique of Forms of Life*. But in listening to you elaborate your approach, it occurred to me that the way I posed the question presupposed that you needed the framework in order to assess what should be sublated in advance. But you could probably say that if we describe problems richly enough, then in some sense, the description of the problem generates the criteria of what might count as surpassing the problem. I can now begin to see how that doesn't presuppose the backward-looking account of progress. Of course there always lurks the Foucauldian or even Benjaminian worry that the way in which the problem is described leads to the situation in which what everyone takes to be a solution is nevertheless what we might want to call "a regression"—for example, that the problem of immigration in Germany today is framed in terms of "how many refugees we should accept." Would you share that worry? Or do you have any inbuilt warranties against it, perhaps combining the assessment of learning with genealogical distancing?

RJ: There would be no warranty, clearly, because there is no presupposed telos. I start from the situation of crisis and disorientation—or as you say, by describing problems from scratch. And of course not all remedies of disorientation are progressive; many formulations of problems and solutions are ideological. To me the best way to spell out our shared intuition that indeed they are often wrong—as in the presupposition that a nation decides sovereignly to whom to grant asylum and generally considers this a burden—comes from examining which developments feed into that framework. I think that in this instance, as with many others, one can make a good case that it is an impoverished process, or one that failed to integrate all aspects of past experience, or one that is less rich and complex than it could be if one compares it with what we might have learned. That is different from a stadial teleology. It is a freestanding process driven by determinate negation in which you don't need to know what the overall direction of the movement is. As Adorno says in a famous citation, "Progress would transform itself into the resistance to the perpetual danger of relapse. Progress is this resistance at all stages, not their steady ascent."[12] I wouldn't even think of Hegel as someone who has this kind of overarching teleology. I would say that freedom is more a principle of development than a substantial value that comes at the end and that we realize more and more. It's more the principle that undermines the institutions that establish unfreedom of a certain kind. We could argue about Hegel on this point, but this idea of freestanding determinate negation doesn't actually need to claim that there's already something progressive in history. On the other hand, I wouldn't deny that there are instances of local progress. We wouldn't live without certain things.

AA: That's actually a point of agreement between us, I think. Something like what you're calling a "freestanding determinate negation" is what I had in mind when I jokingly referred to the Nietzschean-Foucauldian account as a determinate negation: there is no goal to which it aims, and yet it is working through, in some sense, these earlier views and trying to solve problems you might say are internal to them. That's obviously talking about theoretical positions and not about actual norms or practices, but it's a similar principle. I wanted to say something about learning processes too. Just as I am more or less happy to stick with a forward-looking conception of progress as what it is we're trying to bring about when we engage in some kind of critical work that aims toward social transformation, I would also be willing to countenance some kind of understanding of a learning process. But within the particular context and invocation of certain types of progress, and even in critical theory, I think we need to think in terms of the phrase that's popular in postcolonial literature: "learning to unlearn." That is a kind of problem-driven learning process, but one that involves thoroughly problematizing the backward-looking account of history as a story about progress. I think that's a place where we might agree.

One question I have for you, Rahel, is that you said, off the cuff, that your account is not substantial and local, but because it is freestanding, maybe it ends up being too Kantian in a problematic way. However, I had the opposite thought: How do you see yourself avoiding the problem of relativism? We haven't talked about this yet. I have a story that I try to tell in *The End of Progress* about how I'm interested in metaethical or normative questions about progress as they have been employed in critical theory. How are questions about progress used to justify our present normative view that we then employ when we engage in critique? Those stories trade heavily on the backward-looking account of progress that I think is problematic. I think the Kantian story, which could be seen as an alternative to this more Hegelian progressive historical learning process account, is problematic for other reasons that we probably agree on—namely, it gives too freestanding an account that is not embedded enough in history and is therefore not true to the methodological aims or starting points of critical theory. The structure of the argument in my book in terms of the normativity question is then a sort of process of elimination.

I think that we agree on the three options. My strategy is to work through the first two and say that I don't think these will work, for various reasons, and the more genealogical story is the one we're left with. But then, of course, this still leaves the worry about relativism or conventionalism. Conventionalism is perhaps better, if we're talking about norms that are generated in a socially embedded way in forms of life, as this is not an individual relativism but a cultural relativism or conventionalism. I want to know your response to this conventionalism or relativism worry. You say that we would not want to impose the things we use to solve our problems on other people who have different problems or other ways of solving them. I think that intuition is right, and I agree with the desire, if we're going to make judgments about progress, to make them local and contextual. That's what I call "progress in history" as opposed to historical progress. But I don't know how you avoid the problem of relativism or conventionalism. My strategy is to say that giving up on the notion of progress on a metanormative level doesn't mean that we have to collapse into relativism because relativism is a first-order normative position. One can be a contextualist about normativity and still believe in certain normative principles, just as one can be an epistemological contextualist and still believe in truth. In other words, one can be a contextualist about normativity and think that it is generated locally, contingently, historically, and so on and still hold onto first-order normative principles that are nonrelativistic and that may even be universalistic in scope. That's my attempt at a solution, briefly, but I'd love to know what yours is.

I'd like to say one last thing about problems. Eva was trying to pose them as a kind of wedge between us or a question on which we might differ. But when reading *Critique of Forms of Life*, it struck me that your account of problem solving through Dewey is very close to how I see problematization working in Foucault in a really interesting way. Foucault also has this idea that problematization has both a nominal and a verbal sense. Things become problematic at a certain point. He didn't use the language of "crisis," but he does talk about things becoming problems for us at a certain point, and that's what he wants to uncover. At the same time, he also wants to problematize things and shed light on problems that not everyone sees as problems or understands to be problematic or that we need to understand in a different way. There's a back and forth between those two registers in Foucault's account that is also part of your presentation of Dewey. I guess it is the part about problem solving where the Foucauldian is going to get nervous. But the idea of problems and problematizations is a really interesting connection between our two projects.

RJ: You're right to ask how I avoid relativism and conventionalism. I would say that I try to do so by coming up with a formal criterion. We don't judge the outcome of a form of life. Nor do we judge what its inhabitants are doing in a substantial way or what norms and practices or embodied and evaluative practices they are coming up with. What we do judge is the process: How did this come about? Judging the process is somehow bracketing the substance or the content of the form of life while at the same time highlighting that the process in the background of the crisis matters. This rests on a dynamic notion of form of life, one that is not stable, because all of them go through some form of dynamic. This dynamic is judged as a process using the criterion of whether there are certain kinds of learning blockages, of which ideology would be one version. However, there are others, such as certain institutions or mechanisms, that don't allow you to experience certain things. This move is an attempt to come up with a context-transcendent criterion that is at the same time not freestanding universalism. It is about the dynamic itself. It should avoid conventionalism because in a certain sense, the frame or context itself is fundamental. Through relativism you can only see whether certain things are right or wrong when you take into account this framework of their thought or way of living. The idea is to go beyond the framework without standing outside of it.

Again I think about Hegel, not in his theory of an ethical life or in a way that commits me to defending him all the way down, but in that his philosophy of history seems to give us conceptual tools to evaluate the framework itself or to go beyond the framework and to see that the framework has evolved and has a certain "right." A certain "right" can simultaneously mean that at some point and given a certain specific situation this framework might suggest the wrong moves. To come up with a concrete example, it might not be regressive to wear a veil under certain circumstances when you are attacked as a Muslim woman in the Western world. It might not only be an act of resistance, which it certainly sometimes is; it might also be the right move to raise consciousness or to politicize an issue. It might also be wrong, but this depends not on whether the veil itself is a sign of domination or not, but on what kind of constellation it is in, and what kind of outcome occurs as a result of a certain kind of regressive tendency. The move back to certain kinds of neobourgeois family values in some recent Western middle-class milieus might be more of a regression than what is mentioned above. The idea is that it always depends, and every Foucauldian would say it always depends on the situation whether something is an act of resistance.

EVR: Maybe, since you're agreeing too much, I can drive the wedge a bit further. I think Rahel's notion that a problematic form of life ultimately points one in the right direction is stronger than what we have discussed so far. For Amy, we are driven to go beyond given forms of life because they occlude something. Rahel has something like practical contradictions at the core of her account. I think we can see this difference beautifully in Adorno's view of interpretation. You both see interpretation as contextual and say that we need to interpret problems and that their solutions depend on how we describe them. In support of that you, Amy, quote Adorno as saying, "Interpretation . . . is criticism of phenomena that have been brought to a standstill; it consists in revealing the dynamism stored up in them, so that what appears as second nature can be seen to have a history."[13] I would say, Amy, that in your genealogical approach, you're making clear that "what appears as second nature can be seen to be history." I think Rahel pursues a much stronger reading than the one that you give to the line in your book, focusing on the "dynamism stored up." Because Rahel has this idea that if you get rid of the learning blockage, you not only get to something that you didn't see before, to what "thought has silently thought," but actually you already get a direction. The dynamism is really there, and it propels you in the right direction. That is quite a strong Hegelian investment on the ontological or social-theoretical level. I don't think you could agree with that, Amy.

AA: No.

EVR: Good!

AA: I think that often we don't know what we get. I would be much more cautious about that.

EVR: If we stay with the "propelling" element, I'd like to ask each of you what you see as the motor of dynamism. You, Amy, have the passage where you say, with Adorno and Foucault, that unreason, or the nonidentical, something that escapes the current frame, moves us.[14] I think you, Rahel, would have a different frame of what brings us forward—for example, contradictions. Maybe you could say a bit more about your respective investments in historical materialism, which is perhaps the biggest difference between *Critique of Forms of Life* and *The End of Progress*. What is it that resists in reality and moves us forward?

AA: I would only say that it "moves us forward" in a very limited sense. This is a bit confusing. Could we say something like, "So, yes, it's right that I try to say that there's a figure—that I try to read in a very nonsubstantial way—that one can find in the idea of unreason in Foucault or the nonidentical in Adorno." Whether it actually enables us to move forward in a directional sense is a totally open question. One of the things I find attractive about Foucault's understanding of history, and maybe this is related to the dynamics of historical change, is its complete open-endedness. He is quite rightly, in my view—but not entirely consistently, if one reads his overly optimistic writings on the Iranian revolution, for example—making the case that we just don't know what progress is, and so we have to think about the future in an open-ended way. I think that is compatible with the idea of trying to make things better, or to solve problems, if you want to use that language. "Minimize the relations of domination" is, I think, the language Foucault would use, or "respond to suffering," if we want to talk about it in a more Adornian way. But we can't know what the direction of that would be, which is why Foucault says in his "What Is Enlightenment?" that the work of critique has to always be ongoing.[15] I doubt that we would disagree on that point; it's actually pretty obvious, in a way, that if we reject some sort of strong, positive utopianism, then we accept that the work of critique has to be ongoing. That's related to this caution or skepticism about saying too much about the direction of social change, which is set free by this process. What the outcome of the critique is going to be, though, I think we just cannot know.

EVR: It's interesting that by pointing to nondomination, you put more substantial content on the normative side of the directionality than Rahel does. Earlier we spoke of freedom, and I think that if Rahel is committed to the view that the contradictions in crises point us in the right direction, then in some sense she has a thinner idea of progress because she's not even committed to saying it's always about domination or freedom. But there's a much thicker notion of history or context or social practice assumed in her account.

RJ: Yes, I feel bad about it. I don't refer to domination or freedom as the basic principle. Amy can at least say that she has some idea of nondomination and a world with less suffering. It seems to be such an impoverished account of progress to say that it's just some way of accumulating experiences. It's not that I don't have strong commitments and ideas, but with respect to this philosophical project, I actually tend to be much more restricted. It might be that in this very narrow or thin formulation of progress there's a thicker notion of experience that seems to rely on an idea of richness or completeness of experience that is more normatively laden than it appears to be. The idea of rationality at stake here seems to be more utopian or seems to do a lot of work that is not as thin and as processional as I want it to be.

Returning to Eva's question of what it is that triggers or makes us leave in a certain situation, for me this is crisis and contradiction on the objective side. This also means that, with respect to normative foundations, or the normative foundations of critical theory in particular, a lot of work is done by the idea that there are crises. It's not that critical theorists would disturb this totally beautiful (but under certain criteria wrong) form of life, or would try to intervene in something like a peaceful island where people are unconscious, or would meet a romantic and naïve person and tell them to strive for modernity. That's not the kind of critique we are doing. When I said that progress is change within change, I meant it in the same way that I would say critique is a certain movement within a crisis that is already ongoing. It's a certain way to trigger and intervene in a moment of crisis. For me, this work has an objective side, which is also a material side. My conceptual intervention within critical theory is meant to balance out an ultrastrong focus on the constructivist approach to whatever could count as a problem.

I want to move the discussion back slightly toward this historical materialist idea of crisis or contradiction. I'm very aware that contradiction doesn't do all the work. One of the problems with the Marxist idea of contradiction is that everyone thought that contradiction had a logical status, which means that you don't need to criticize something because it's wrong on its own terms and doesn't even need human agency to collapse. This is not the kind of contradiction I have in mind, but I am at least flirting with the idea that there's something that cannot be denied when it comes to crises.

In a psychoanalytic analogy, one would say that of course you can have different interpretations of a symptom, but there's something that the symptom shows. If within the process of psychoanalysis the therapist doesn't somehow try to find the right cause for the symptom, or if she denies certain aspects of it, then she might not have a correct or deep enough insight into the situation. She would not be able to name the problems in terms of a diagnosis that would apply to the patient. At the same time, it's an interactive process in which those who criticize certain crises or symptoms and diagnose certain problems do so by diagnosing them and triggering something within a patient that will then prove the analyst right or not. This is where crisis and contradiction come in. In contradiction, there's more to it. It's something that contradiction has (this is determinate negation), and the potential for its possible solution is somehow written into the problem's description. This is the stronger notion of normativity that comes with this idea of contradiction.

AA: I don't disagree with most of what you said, although I might phrase it differently. But the language of contradiction does seem strong. Not only is there the worry that it's objective and logical and does not need agency, but I think it also very strongly implies—though you say that you don't want to hold onto a teleological reading—a kind of teleological directionality.

I think the place where our views are really close is in the relationship between the critic and the objective conditions, if you will. I like the way that Foucault characterizes critique as "following lines of fragility in the present."[16] The idea is that the lines are there, and the critic traces them, and one has to have the combination of these two aspects of critique. It's not as if the critic is just coming in from the outside. The lines of fragility and fracture are there, but there is work done by tracing them and by opening up the space within the present that happens as a result of that work. That sounds quite similar to some of the ways that you're using the notion of crisis, though maybe not exhaustively.

EVR: I'm excited that you've already started to talk about psychoanalysis because I was hoping we might get to conclude on that topic. I was wondering what analogous psychoanalytic formulations we might find for your respective approaches. Perhaps for Rahel, progress is this vivid and unblocked appropriation of experience: a model of nondenial, enrichment, and development. Amy's account might be put in this way: for any such development to take place, there needs to occur a decentering of narcissism, so that one sees the crisis of others and not just the crisis one is in. That's why you seem to say that we need to outgrow our form of life, just as we might grow beyond primary narcissism in psychoanalytic terms. I don't know if you agree with that characterization.

AA: I like it!

EVR: Would you, Rahel, consider it a necessary element for the appropriation of the world that one sees more than one's own crisis?

RJ: To me, this resonates with the idea of impoverished experience, if the problem is a distorted process of experience, a distorted learning experience, or an incomplete *Erfahrungsprozess* (a process of accumulating experiences). There is then the Adornian idea that a strong kind of irrationality is in play if we cannot even encounter "the other" in the world. What I think is interesting is that you said, Amy, that you are much more skeptical because no matter what we come up with, we don't know whether it will lead to emancipatory or progressive results. I would totally agree. It just came to mind why, in the end, I am more interested in regression than progress. I would hold onto the notion of regression, but I see it as the counterpart, but not the flipside, of progress. It's not as if we get a full-blown notion of progress as soon as we have an idea of regression. This runs parallel to something that people very often say about negativity: it is a "trick" of sorts because you only know what's good if you know what's bad. I don't think that's true. For progress and regression, it's not true either. The relationship between them is different, more complex, and more tentative. I would say that my idea of progress is based on a retrospective dialectics. It's not something that you could or would even try to have a forward-looking account of, such as an answer to the question of why this step that we do or this kind of problem solving attempt we're engaged in might be progressive. We just want to make sure that it is not regressive. Again, it might turn out later that we haven't seen a whole lot of aspects that would have convinced us that what we thought of as nonregressive was actually regressive. Whether it's progress or not is something you can only see in retrospect because you never know what will happen. This is the experiential side: you start experiments. Problem solving is a pragmatic aspect of this. You come up with a certain solution, and you don't know the effects or even what you're driven by in coming up with a certain solution.

AA: I would agree. The content that I give in my own account of what would constitute "forward-looking progress" is not fully worked out in *The End of Progress* but is something I discuss in another recent paper, "Emancipation without Utopia."[17] The core idea is that what would constitute progress in a forward-looking sense is minimizing relationships of domination and transforming them into nondominating, mobile, reversible, and unstable power relations. It's a very negativistic conception of forward-looking progress. I don't think I'd want to talk about that in terms of preventing regressions. I would agree, though, that whether or not any change that we try to instill turns out to be progressive, even in that negativistic sense, could only be determined after the fact.

I want to come back to psychoanalysis quickly. There's a lot to say, but one thing that strikes me in relation to negativism and the idea of minimizing domination is that there's an interesting analog on the individual level in psychoanalysis. This is not true for everyone who engages in psychoanalysis, but the psychoanalyst Joel Whitebook said to me while we were talking about my work on progress not long ago that he thinks that psychoanalysis is antiutopian in principle. He was referring to Freud's famous line that the goal of psychoanalysis is to turn "hysterical misery to common unhappiness."[18] I think that's very much like the idea of transforming relationships of domination into mobile, reversible power relationships. To me these ideas are very similar.

EVR: But don't we want more?

AA: Yes. But what about the dream?! When I was in Brazil talking about that paper on emancipation, a student in the audience asked, "What about the dream?"

This dialogue first appeared in the *Graduate Faculty Philosophy Journal*, volume 37, number 2 (2016), 225–51. It is reprinted here with permission of the journal's editors and the authors.

NOTES

1. See Amy Allen, "Critical Theory and the Idea of Progress," in *The End of Progress: Decolonizing the Normative Foundations of Critical Theory* (New York: Columbia University Press, 2015), 1–36.
2. See Thomas McCarthy, *Race, Empire, and the Idea of Human Development* (Cambridge: Cambridge University Press, 2009).
3. See Rahel Jaeggi, *The Critique of Forms of Life* (Cambridge: Harvard University Press, forthcoming); Rahel Jaeggi, *Kritik von Lebensformen* (Berlin: Suhrkamp, 2013).
4. See Max Horkheimer and Theodor W. Adorno, *Dialectic of Enlightenment: Philosophical Fragments*, trans. Edmund Jephcott, ed. Gunzelin Schmid Noerr (Stanford: Stanford University Press, 2002).

5. See Philip Kitcher, *The Ethical Project* (Cambridge: Harvard University Press, 2011).
6. See Axel Honneth, "The Normativity of Ethical Life," trans. Felix Koch, *Philosophy and Social Criticism* 48, no. 8 (2014): 817–26.
7. Amy Allen, *The Politics of Our Selves* (New York: Columbia University Press, 2008), 45–48.
8. Michel Foucault, *The Use of Pleasure*, vol. 2 of *The History of Sexuality*, trans. Robert Hurley (New York: Vintage Books, 1985), 9.
9. See, for example, Gurminder K. Bhambra, *Rethinking Modernity: Postcolonialism and the Sociological Imagination* (New York: Palgrave MacMillan, 2007).
10. Rahel Jaeggi, "Critical Theory and Philosophies of History" (presentation, Constellations Conference: Post-Colonialism, Critical Theory, and Democracy, New York, April 15, 2016).
11. G. W. F. Hegel, *Elements of the Philosophy of Right*, trans. H. B. Nisbet, ed. Allen W. Wood (Cambridge: Cambridge University Press, 1991), §242, 267.
12. Theodor W. Adorno, "Progress," in *Critical Models: Interventions and Catch-Words*, trans. Henry W. Pickford (New York: Columbia University Press, 2005), 160.
13. Theodor W. Adorno, "On Interpretation: The Concept of Progress (I)," lecture 15 of *History and Freedom: Lectures, 1964–1965*, trans. Rodney Livingstone, ed. Rolf Tiedemann (Cambridge: Polity, 2006), 135; cited in Allen, *The End of Progress*, 195.
14. Allen, *The End of Progress*, 194.
15. See Michel Foucault, "What Is Enlightenment?," in *The Foucault Reader*, trans. and ed. Paul Rabinow (New York: Pantheon, 1984), 32–50.
16. See Michel Foucault, "Critical Theory/Intellectual History," trans. Jeremy Harding, in *Critique and Power: Recasting the Foucault/Habermas Debate*, ed. Michael Kelly (Cambridge: MIT Press, 1994), 109–37.
17. See Amy Allen, "Emancipation without Utopia: Subjection, Modernity, and the Normative Claims of Feminist Critical Theory," *Hypatia: A Journal of Feminist Philosophy* 30, no. 3 (2015): 513–29.
18. Sigmund Freud and Joseph Breuer, *Studies on Hysteria*, in vol. 2 of *The Standard Edition of the Complete Psychological Works of Sigmund Freud*, trans. and ed. James Strachey (London: Hogarth Press, 1955), 305.

CHAPTER 10

Reply to My Critics

Rahel Jaeggi

It has been a great honor for me to have my work discussed by scholars as outstanding as those who have contributed to the symposium and this book. This is an occasion any philosopher could only wish for, and I feel hugely indebted to all who created it. This said, I am immensely grateful to the volume's editors in particular, because they gave me the chance to answer to the wonderful chapters written for this collection more thoroughly than initial time constraints would have permitted. Demanding as this task was, answering to the inspiring comments and critiques formed a welcome incentive for me to strengthen and refine my approach.

Since many of the points in question overlap, my reply will be organized along the lines of the topics discussed.

1. PROGRESS AND ITS DISCONTENTS (AMY ALLEN, ROBIN CELIKATES)

The first topic is the question of progress, progressive social change, and the putative unavoidability of progress, issues that Amy Allen and Robin Celikates have addressed in their chapters and comments.

Since progress and regression and the attempt to come up with a plausible version of progressive social change will be discussed in an upcoming project and are topics that my book *Critique of Forms of Life* already points to, I will first say a few words about why I am interested in the subject at all and why I defend some concept of progress notwithstanding the obvious difficulties that go along with it.

Interestingly enough, I very much agree with Amy Allen's characterization of progress in the following respect: the idea of progress and some normative idea of history (or even of logics in history) have been at the core of Frankfurt School–type critical theory. Yet we disagree on how to evaluate this observation. For Amy this is a part of the tradition's heritage that we should get rid of in order to overcome the Eurocentric bias that has prevented critical theory from forming alliances with postcolonial theory and some of the most important social movements of our time. For me, to the contrary, notwithstanding the relevance of this observation, I am committed to the view that some notion of progress and its opposite, regression, are *indispensable* for a critical theory in the tradition of left-Hegelian critique—exactly because of its interest in emancipation.

In my view, this is true with respect to two related questions.

The first concerns the *normative foundations* of critical theory. For a critical theory that wants neither to build on a freestanding normativity nor to be in some way contextualistic or relativistic with respect to its normative foundations, some notion of progressive social change seems indispensable. I am in agreement here with David S. Owen, who states that it is (only) "by adopting an historical framework that can distinguish between progressive and regressive social change, critical theory can rationally ground its normative orientation while avoiding both foundationalism and relativism."[1]

This is to say, when the chickens come home to roost, there are not so many theoretical alternatives for a critical theory. While so many critiques of society build on some kind of Kantianism (or, as it is, Rawlsianism), and while so many critiques of society go, in contrast, for the second, contextualistic or relativistic option, I think that it is worth defending the third option, a strong version of immanent criticism unique to critical theory from its very beginning. This is, as I agree with Amy, linked to some normative understanding of history. As I will argue later, I hold this position not out of some nostalgia for traditional critical theory but because of its advantages vis-à-vis other frameworks of social critique. (It also helps us avoid the odd combination of theoretical skepticism and practical and political moralism that some brands of Foucauldianism have developed.)

The second feature then occurs on the level of *social analysis*. Critical theory should be interested in *how social change comes about*. It is, in my view, a fundamental feature of critical theories (beginning with Hegel and Marx) to come up with an account of social transformations, even if this can no longer be (and in Western Marxism, never was) an orthodox version of historical materialism and even if it should no longer rely on strong teleological logics of history. To employ the concepts of progress and regress then gives us a normatively laden narrative of history and social transformation that draws a connection between the *erosion* of social institutions and practices and its overcoming. After all, this was exactly what Marx had to offer against utopian socialism or various anarchist movements: instead of a moralizing or romantic backward-looking critique of capitalism, he spelled out the crisis-driven *dynamic* of capitalism, thereby raising the problem of how this very dynamic might have "bred" the potentials for its overcoming.

Of course, we no longer buy into the historical determinism that is evoked here. But still, the fact that this kind of thinking about social and historical transformations has been abandoned in some strands of contemporary critical theory and replaced with an all-too-strong focus on normative justification might lead to a situation in which we lose the social theoretical skills and resources needed and therewith one of critical theory's most specific and fruitful dimensions—namely, the intertwinement of social analysis and critique. To engage in a discussion about progress is thus a welcome chance to get back to these issues, including the question of how material, social, and normative developments interact in order to provoke social change.

I don't want to be misunderstood here: I am not claiming that recovering this idea of normativity in history and spelling out the notion of progressive social change are easy tasks or that we just have to buy into this notion in its long-established Hegel-Marxian version. I am only saying that this is a key issue for laying the philosophical and conceptual groundwork for engaging and eventually reconstructing these dimensions of critical theory.

As Adorno's and Horkheimer's analyses of fascism, anti-Semitism, and various modes of contemporary social life in terms of *regression* teach us, it makes a difference whether we *judge* fascism as an instance of a *moral wrong* or even something that is morally evil or *analyze* it in terms of *regression*. Moral wrongness or evil is a *purely normative judgment* on the cruel and inhuman institutions and practices—deeds that constitute, for example, a fascist regime. But even if they are indisputably true, and even if Adorno himself certainly also employed categories like cruelty or inhumaneness, these judgments are in a certain sense *less informative* than the comprehensive analysis that the take on fascism as a mode of regression has to offer. To analyze fascism (or, to take a less obvious and contemporary example, certain cases of populism and fundamentalism) not only as a moral evil but also as an instance of regression is an *attempt in understanding*; instead of being timeless, the category employed has a sociological and historical index. Not only do we then understand *that* certain institutions are a moral disaster; we also understand how the state of affairs in question came about. And moreover, to understand how this wrongness *came about* is, in this setting, intertwined with understanding why it is *wrong*. As for our contemporary situation, we are certainly in need of a renewed understanding of these regressive tendencies and a vocabulary that can cover them. Thus it is less a matter of smug self-satisfaction about "where we are," the Whiggish complacency with the status quo of the Western liberal world that leads (me) to reconstructing some notion of progress; it is rather the need to understand and judge instances of regression that are so omnipresent and obvious in the contemporary situation.

It is obvious now in which way my take on progress and "learning processes" in history is radically different from Amy Allen's. While for Amy the idea of a learning process is the emblem of colonialism and ethnocentrism, for me it is the starting point for a materialistic and dialectical *departure from moralism*. My main point is that without an analysis that enables us to understand why and how a certain instance of wrong came about (which, again, requires some notion of progress/regress), we will not be able to adequately hold our judgments of wrong apart from an unhelpful and dangerous moralism. It might then be useful to reverse the burden of proof. As against incurring the "risk" of using the concept of progress that Robin Celikates invokes, I in turn want to address the risks of avoiding it. I have in mind here the risk of ending up in some kind of moralism, the risk of being evasive or being parasitically dependent on well-established normative frameworks without establishing an alternative one, and finally, the risk of an inverted Eurocentrism, an asymmetry with respect to other cultures that is sometimes the effect of arguments based solely on "guilt by association."

From the perspective of emancipation, even if we shouldn't pretend to be "in the same boat" with those whose perspectives and experiences have been neglected by colonialist and imperialist perspectives, Habermas's early insight that "a process of emancipation only knows of those involved" ("ein Emanzipationsprozess kennt nur Beteiligte") still seems to be true, with which I mean emancipation is a result of critique and self-critique. While not taking for granted "our own" form of life and while not even being so sure that, under alienating conditions, it is actually "our own," there is no way out of constantly evaluating and criticizing our and others' way of life. The asymmetry produced by colonialist ideology shouldn't be replaced by an asymmetry caused by the restriction of analysis and judgment in order to avoid ethnocentrism and "Whig history." As Uma Narayan rightfully holds, "refusing to judge" doesn't solve the problem since it can easily turn into yet another "western gesture that confirms the moral inequality of the Third World cultures by shielding them from moral and political evaluations that 'western' contexts and practices are subject to." The real task then would turn out to be, again in Narayan's words, "to distinguish misrepresentation and 'cultural imperialism' from normatively justifiable criticisms"[2]—thus, in my words, to engage in the project of critique and emancipation, a project that can't refrain from judging upon forms of life. The distinction between "*our* form of life" and the "others' forms of life" might then turn out to be less helpful than it seems to be at first sight, which is exactly what my project aims at—it is as against the liberal tendency to refrain from judgment with respect to ethical matters or matters of the good life as well as the relativist impulse.

Yet if my approach is *affirmative to the notion of progress*, it is driven by the conviction that we need to *reconstruct* the idea of progress in the end in somewhat a "deflationary" way in order to reintroduce it into contemporary critical theory in a nonteleological and non-Eurocentric manner. With respect to the danger of "Whig history" then (discussed by Celikates), I should emphasize that neither am I claiming (or even dealing with the claim) that history is actually moving toward progress nor is my interest in reconstructing a notion of progress motivated by the idea of progress as a positive goal—a point of reference that informs our utopian hopes and directs our emancipatory efforts. So using Amy's helpful distinction, I am interested in neither progress *as a fact* nor progress *as an imperative*. What I am interested in is *progress and regress* as categories or conceptual tools, as *analytical and evaluative criteria* within social philosophy. (And for me the whole point in progress and regression as categories lies in the fact that the analytic and the evaluative element here are intertwined.)

The solution (that I have arrived at in my *Critique of Life Forms* but only tentatively spelled out with respect to progress) is then not only deflationary but also somehow *formal*: The rationality (of some kind) as well as the normative implications of forms of life arises from the fact that they *are instances of problem solving*. As such, they can succeed or fail. They can be rational or irrational, appropriate or inappropriate. The general result of my project can thus be formulated as follows: Forms of life succeed when they can be understood as the result of successful processes of learning and when they enable further learning. And the task of a critique of forms of life is to ask the metaquestion regarding the *criteria* whereby one can recognize whether a certain kind of dynamic, a crisis-driven social dynamic, can be seen as a process of learning and an accumulation of experience. This means we should establish criteria for the very quality of social dynamics of transformation. Blockages of experience and hindrances, caused, for example, by ideologies and an impoverishment of experience, then serve as criteria for a critique of forms of life or, as it is, as criteria for instances of regression. It wouldn't be wrong to translate this result in the somehow simpler formula: forms of life are good, rational, appropriate in that they are *not regressive, but progressive*, the result as well as the starting point for progressive social change.

This *formal account* of the dynamics of progress and regression—the dynamics of erosion of institutions and practices as a result of the immanent contradictions and crises they run into and produce—is *less substantial* from the beginning (in contrast to, for example, Axel Honneth's account) but at the same time *context transcendent* in its aim. It is, so to say, a robust but not substantial concept. It leads to the possibility of figuring out a variety of historical dynamics—thus it doesn't work on the level of a unified world history but on the level of sorting out different strands that in the next step have to be analyzed from the perspective of their interdependency. (In short, it is more in line with global history than with a unified and teleological world history.)

It is more than obvious that there is quite a lot left to say. A theory of *progressive social change* has yet to be developed and argued for. And the idea of an accumulative process of experience is, as we will see later, in the midst of a heavily disputed terrain. Still, what is disputable here is different from a substantial claim about the course of history that could even turn out to be a Whig history (as Robin Celikates fears).

2. THEORIES OF SOCIAL CHANGE AND THE ROLE FOR SOCIAL STRUGGLES (CELIKATES, ALLEN)

Robin Celikates certainly shares my interest in (theories of) social change. Still, with respect to the notion of progress, he asks whether the recent debate on moral progress and the attempt to look at processes of social transformation from the perspective of progress are not prone to lead to a "pacified and one-sided conception of how social transformation is to take place in the future," which may also be having "distorting effects on how we think of social transformations that have happened in the past and of the obstacles they had to confront." And as Amy Allen has pointed out in the discussion, the question remains whether there is enough room for social agents in my discussion of social change.

Now I entirely agree with Robin Celikates that we shouldn't uncouple our "critique from social struggles and from the social conditions under which such struggles unfold" and, as it is, that we should take "material force(s)" into account in our analysis. But I don't see why the risk should be increased by "thinking of social transformations in terms of progress and learning processes." It is only increased if we think of social transformations in the wrong terms.

As against incurring the danger of conceiving of social change in an all-too-idealistic way, downplaying the material forces and the ambivalences that go along with the processes described (as Celikates accuses Anderson of), it is exactly my intention to spell out that even the most obvious examples of moral progress have occurred not in a smooth and easygoing way but rather a messy and contested one. The idea that I am developing in "'Resistance to the Perpetual Danger of Relapse': Moral Progress and Social Change" (this volume) is that changes are a result of crises and mismatches with respect to material circumstances and changing attitudes with respect to normative questions.

My project thus emphasizes a more materialistic view where it is not moral consciousness alone that changes when we find instances of moral progress, arguing against an endogenous understanding of moral progress while at the same time avoiding deterministic functionalism. As I hold, we need to give an account that understands both the independence of each dynamic and the way in which they interact in order to broaden the picture and give a full and rich account of the various dynamics that come together in order to enable change (for the better). This is why (besides the aforementioned fact that I haven't been talking about empirical progress) I can't help but think that Celikates's comparison between Anderson's and my account doesn't fit that well. Whatever one thinks of Anderson's position (that I myself find pathbreaking and interesting in various ways), the basis for a comparison here seems to be weak and not specific enough.

Putting this aside, there is still a difference between our positions: If I am interested in recovering a somewhat pragmatist-materialistic account, I am also arguing that an emphasis on social struggle alone—the emphasis that Robin suggests—is still an all-too-voluntarist understanding of social change and progress. So if I agree with Robin on the matter of the "material" side and complexity of social change, nevertheless, in my account, social struggles are only one dimension of this material side, the other being the crises that a given situation has run into. When uncoupled, neither dimension can stand on its own feet when it comes to its emancipatory character.

This is not an alternative altogether since we need both social struggles and social crisis to understand social change. Still, in my recent work, I certainly lean toward spelling out the "objective" side—that is, the side of the immanent "crises" of social formations that lead to social change. To me, evoking social struggles alone seems to be too deflationary a way to draw on the "material force" that Marx had in mind, a force that, as I want to argue, is yet again inherently related to an account of a historical dynamics of crises. The (somehow omnipresent) reference to social struggles alone then does not replace the issues of understanding progress, history, and progressive social change but needs to be supplemented by them.

Karl Marx offered a description of the task of critical theory that enjoys wide popularity among its contemporary proponents: the task of a critical theory, according to Marx, is to be part of the "self-clarification (critical philosophy) to be gained by the present time of its struggles and desires."[3] Critical theory then is "partisan" in the sense, formulated by the early Max Horkheimer, that critical theory is the "intellectual side of the historical process of proletarian emancipation."[4]

Now however attractive it may be to interpret Marx's dictum in a contemporary, deflated way as stating that the task of a critical theory is to take sides with existing social struggles, it is a well-known fact that even for the young Marx, the relationship between theory and practice was more complex (and not altogether unproblematic).

Marx could still rely on two presuppositions when situating the relationship between theoretical reflection and social struggles: The first assumption was that one could concentrate on only a single historical movement—namely, class struggle—that would become increasingly focused on the confrontation between two classes (capital and labor, the bourgeoisie as the owners of the means of production and the proletariat). The second, connected certainty was that these same social forces driving the struggles in focus were undoubtedly progressive and had a clear emancipatory direction.

But why would they be emancipatory? For Marx this was not only a matter of freestanding normative evaluation, as in those social struggles that serve certain emancipatory goals—freedom and equality, let's say—are instances of progressive and emancipatory changes. Deeply anchored in an ultimately Hegelian foundation (in the philosophy of history), the relationship can be sketched very roughly as follows: the "conflicts of the age" not only occur at a particular historical time; in Hegel's terms, their time has come. They implement "what was ripe for development."[5] They are the result of a specific large-scale historical development—in Marxist terms, of the development of the forces of production, of the social conflicts and contradictions to which the latter give rise, which find expression in the class struggle. However we understand the relationship between the development of the forces of production and class struggles and between the revolutionary potential and the condition of its realization, in detail, it is certain that although the dynamic described here depends on the volition and actions of social actors, it is not based on those factors alone. As Marx puts it already before developing his complex "materialistic philosophy of history," "Revolutions require a passive element, a material basis."[6]

Now of course one can interpret these relationships (and try to make the tensions looming here productive) in different ways or criticize them in favor of a more agonistic conception. One can also—as many contemporary versions of critical theory tend to do—subject the original program of the philosophy of history to "metaphysical debunking" and take one's orientation from social movements that are actually virulent.

However, one then faces different sorts of problems, problems that have probably become more acute in recent years and decades. Today we are not only confronted with a multiplication of social struggles and a plurality of lines of conflict that do not always converge; we also more and more frequently encounter situations that, although marked by social misery, injustice, and suffering, do not give rise to corresponding social movements or do give rise to movements but none that could be regarded as emancipatory.

If a critical theory does not want to fall back on freestanding normative standards in response to this and if, conversely, one does not want to justify partisanship for social struggles in a decisionistic or merely standpoint-theoretical way, then an approach that takes its orientation from the immanent crises of the current situation and the observed social formations recommends itself as a fruitful alternative.[7]

With this we are back to Marx. The active dimension, as I take it, is the occurrence of social struggles, dissidence, and conflict; the passive dimension, as I take it, is the set of preconditions for revolutionary social change that Marx conceives of as crises and contradictions within the deep structure of a social, economic, and political order. It is where these two dimensions intertwine—this is what I take from Marx—that the chance for social change and, consequently, for progressive social change evolves. So from this we can derive criteria for the progressive and, as it stands, emancipatory character of the movements in question by analyzing whether and how they are adequate, as against inadequate or regressive, reactions to the crises, contradictions, and tensions in question.

It is this insight—the insight into the double aspect of social revolutions and social transformation and change—that I take to be the most productive side of Marx's theory of revolution.[8] But then taking this as my starting point leads me to the idea of accumulation and learning processes.

3. LEARNING PROCESSES (MAX PENSKY, CELIKATES)

The biggest misunderstanding now (even if it is certainly me who is to blame for it) is that my reference to "learning processes" should be an indication for a reformist instead of a revolutionary program, as Pensky takes it, or an indication for a "pacified" version of social change, as Celikates suspects (not specifically regarding my approach but with respect to all those who are using the terms "progress" and "learning process"). Max Pensky and Robin Celikates seem to share the assumption that "learning processes" always go smoothly and are a matter of someone (or even the group in power) being persuaded and effortlessly led in the right direction.

Now this is an interesting misunderstanding (probably also based on varying experiences with respect to learning). Without a doubt, I have to clarify my understanding of learning processes—that is, of *dialectical* learning processes. My understanding here is that learning processes never go smoothly. As a result of a crisis-driven dynamics, they are conflictual and threatening—and, as I will argue, they don't leave the institutions and practices in question intact but might end up overcoming and destroying them.

So within this basically Hegelian, dialectical, and even Marxist framework, "accumulative learning process" ("ein sich anreichernder Erfahrungsprozess") is the overarching name for social transformations that can be radical or less radical, revolutionary or reformist (in case this distinction makes sense to us any more at all). There is no reason revolutions themselves shouldn't be considered as results of a learning process in this sense. The premise that goes with this (and has solid Marxist foundations) is that even revolutions are results of an accumulative process driven by logic that is not the logic of pure, unrelated, and unpredictable events. Of course, *this* is certainly a disputable premise—but the dispute that we then enter has nothing to do with the alternative between reform and revolution, radical or less radical, violent or peaceful change.

What I have in mind is a somewhat materialistic as well as pragmatist version of what Hegel develops as "Erfahrungsprozess" in his *Phenomenology of Spirit*. In *Critique of Forms of Life*, I have sometimes used the concept of "Erfahrungsprozess" (experiential process or the process of experience) instead of learning process—which might be more accurate (besides the obvious translation problem with respect to "Erfahrungsprozess"). "Learning process" might then not have been a happy terminological choice, if only because it invokes unwelcome memories of one's school days.

What seems to be misleading here is (1) the cognitive bias, (2) the individualistic and intentionalistic bias, and (3) the "harmonistic bias" of the concept of learning processes.

As for the *cognitive bias*, it might be worth mentioning that the idea of learning (as it should be effective in my approach) is inspired by Dewey's idea of education and learning. Learning (as I take it) is a *practical matter* here. It is a process in which we overcome obstacles with respect to our capacities to deal with the world. It is not only inspired by practical problems and our desire to cope with the world; the process itself is not merely cognitive but a complex mix of practical and reflective moments in an experimental process of trial and error. One learns as one is involved in a complex situation that one has to deal with.

As for the *individualistic and intentionalistic bias*, what I have in mind when I claim that "forms of life" can (and should) undergo learning processes is, of course, not an individual but a *collective learning process*. With all due respect for the immensely complicated social ontological issues involved, it is the social formation itself here that undergoes a learning process. This is a (moderately) holistic claim. It is not individuals and then an aggregation of individuals who have "learned" something; it is the form of life itself that has. Using Dewey's concept of "learn environment," I have referred to this complicated matter as "learning learn environment" in order to grasp the nonindividualistic but also, to a certain extent, the nonintentional character of the concept. "Learning" here doesn't mean that someone/some entity has faced a lack of knowledge with respect to something and in relation to which one then accomplished a learning process in order to meet the desideratum or, as it is, to "solve the problem." Rather, saying that a form of life has *undergone* (the passive mode is more apt here) a learning process doesn't refer to more than the fact that (in retrospect) it has changed as a result of having faced problems and dealt with them in an accumulative manner. In practice-theoretical terms then, it is important here to conceive of them in terms of emergence and resilience rather than in terms of intention and action (alone).

Conceiving of learning processes as a practical and collective matter, it should be obvious then that these learning processes are not processes on the level of individual insights or individual moral betterment. It is the collective experience of a certain social formation then that (reflected upon mostly in retrospect) gives way to a changed attitude toward and a changed set of social practices and institutions that reflect the failures and erosions of the practices and institutions that have been overcome. On the level that I have in mind, learning processes are multifactorial social processes that emerge out of experiences of failure and a dynamic of crisis.

Which finally leads to the alleged peacefulness or *the "harmonistic bias" of an understanding of social change as a learning process.* Neither the concepts of "problems" and "problem solving" nor the idea of learning (as a result of successfully solving a problem) are meant to indicate that these developments proceed without conflict. And even further, problem solving is not in itself a good thing. It is just a way of proceeding after a period of crisis and the erosion of social practices and institutions. It merely indicates a stabilization of modes of social cooperation and social reproduction; it is not, as such, already a *good* solution.

If in my terminology (and my theoretical framework) forms of life figure as instances of problem solving, this does not imply that they are "good," and it doesn't imply that they have arrived at normatively acceptable solutions. That a problem has been "solved" doesn't imply that it is a solution that everyone has agreed upon or that the terms of cooperation are fair. Neither does it imply that the solution is ethically satisfactory for everyone involved. And, of course, it doesn't imply that the solution is stable. To the contrary, the idea of forms of life as problem-solving entities means to grasp the conflict-prone dynamic, and it intends to grasp the "material" aspect—namely, the way human beings organize their social, cultural, political, and economic lives is related to (or guided by) problems in the sense of tasks and shaped by problems in the sense of crises. We have, then, a conflictual dynamic in more than one sense.

As Rocío Zambrana puts it nicely, to speak of forms of life as instances of problem solving is to speak of a social formation in terms of its history rather than an anthropological ground or "need." It is also to speak of forms of life not in terms of "values and orientation" but in terms of dealing with the material necessities involved in the reproduction of social life. In other words, it also emphasizes the *reactive* side of forms of how we live.

Apartheid in this sense (and on the abstract level I'm arguing on) certainly is a way of problem solving, as is slavery, as is feudalism, as is capitalism. (That we might not share the understanding of the "problem" here and might even detest the solution doesn't affect this claim.) So if Robin resolutely states that the apartheid regime (or chattel slavery) can for sure not be seen as an instance of problem solving and a result of learning processes, this is actually not in line with my use of these concepts.

A form of life then can be criticized along the lines of whether it has or has not been a result of a successful or adequate learning process or, the other way around, whether it is or is not marked by systematic blockages of experience. To go through a crisis-driven "learning process" in a certain way—that is, in an accumulative process or, put negatively, in a mode that is not regressive and not characterized by certain blockages of experience—is the normative standard for evaluating forms of life, a standard that empirically is not met very often, a standard that forms of life can live up to or fulfill, and a standard that it can be measured against. (*This*, of course, might be up for debate.) What one then might develop is an account in which the critique of capitalism uses these criteria in order to criticize capitalism as a form of life. (And in order to be clear on this, I would never hold that contemporary capitalism is the result of a successful and accumulative learning process. If I would be engaged in such an analysis, I would rather spell out the moments of regression and learning blockages involved.)

I am now in a position to clarify the implication that actually *is* at stake in my account and, as I said, is debatable: however conflictual and crisis prone the dynamic understanding of social transformations suggested, it *does* indeed think of the dynamic as a "productive" one. The new set of social practices and institutions that evolve in processes of social change are a reaction to the erosion and crises the prior ones have run into as a result of the unsuccessful attempt to give an answer to the problems that arose in the former framework. The main point here is the continuity within discontinuity (and the other way around) that is thus indicated. No matter whether this process evolves in the mode of a radical rupture or revolution or in a "reformist" of evolutionary way, as a determinate answer to a determinate problem, the "solution" (whether it leads to improving or overcoming the set of institutions in question) doesn't come out of the blue but is connected to the respective failures of the situation that has been overcome. Here I suggest taking on what I think of as the most important lesson from the Hegelian and Marxian conception of social change: the dialectical concept of determinate negation. According to this understanding, even the most radical revolution or breakdown of an existing social order contains this element of continuity and of an accumulative process—the new society "developing in the womb of the old," as Marx famously had it.

I will get back to my understanding of negativity (that Pensky as well as Zambrana raise) later. But let me first mention a second way in which the charges Max Pensky comes up with when he accuses me of unsuccessfully navigating between a reformist and a revolutionary position don't seem to be well placed. He illustrates the alternative beautifully with heroines and a debate from the (left-wing) past: the debate between Bernstein's reformist-evolutionary approach and Luxemburg's activist-revolutionary position. In Pensky's view, my position is unsuccessfully situated "somewhere in between" the evolutionary reformist and the revolutionary activist path. Following Pensky though, "this goal may be neither possible nor desirable."

As much as I like Pensky's Luxemburg/Bernstein setting, I don't think that the difference that Max Pensky attributes to these two historical figures is even located at the level on which my approach is situated. If the disagreement between Luxemburg and Bernstein is about reform versus revolution, a trust in an evolutionary process versus the striving for revolutionary action, my approach is located on a methodological metalevel that neither addresses these alternatives nor precludes one of them.

From this point of view, Bernstein and Luxemburg have more in common than Pensky allows for. After all, they both go for some version of historical materialism, and they both buy into some idea of deep structural historical transformations that are the preconditions for revolutionary as well as reformist change. If a dialectical account of social change is marked out by the idea that changes evolve dialectically and according to the principle of determinate negation, then we will have a "discontinuity within continuity." Luxemburg and Bernstein diverge upon the question of where the continuity ends and the discontinuity starts—that is, whether history has or has not reached a certain stage in which the "qualitative leap" of a revolution is still necessary—and they disagree about the radicalness of the change involved. But even Bernstein wouldn't deny, on the conceptual level, that revolutions sometimes take place and have taken place and thus that at specific historical periods and under specific social circumstances, transformations will proceed in a revolutionary instead of an evolutionary-reformist way—and how could he? But even if, on the other hand, Luxemburg has an activist or voluntaristic element built into her theory of revolution, this disagreement is located on a concrete, empirical level—that is, on their respective analyses of capitalism and on their respective diagnosis of the dynamics of capitalism in the concrete historical situation. (As we know, tragically enough they were both wrong, even if one can say that Luxemburg's "socialism or barbarism" came closer to the actual historical events than Bernstein's predictions.) These matters can't be and won't be solved or even predetermined on a methodological or conceptual level alone. It is with respect to the concrete analysis of capitalism that the decisive difference comes up—and this is an analysis that I don't even begin to engage with.

4. NEGATIVITY, DETERMINATE NEGATION, AND DIALECTICS (PENSKY, ROCÍO ZAMBRANA)

I will get back now to the question of Hegel's theory of negativity and determinate negation that I mentioned in passing, since both Pensky and Zambrana disagree with my use and understanding of it, even if on different grounds.

Let me start with Pensky's reproach that the marriage between pragmatism and Hegelianism he sees at work in my book leads to a "loss of the negative": "Jaeggi's conception of immanent critique errs in effacing the work of negation implied in the claim of the contradictory character of forms of life. This loss (not negation) of the negative seems to me to lie behind and to make possible Jaeggi's distinctive combination of dialectical criticism with the pragmatic belief in the meliorist, progressive capacity of forms of life to learn from, rather than collapse under, their own self-negations."

Again, the source of the misunderstanding seems to lie in the understanding of learning processes, as discussed earlier. In my understanding, learning processes are not to be equated with a belief in the "meliorist, progressive capacities of forms of life," a smooth process of getting better. Rather it is through collapses and crises that this learning process, understood as dialectical, takes place. Even if, getting back to the distinction between normal and radical epistemological crisis, some processes go more smoothly than others, in my understanding "collapsing" and "learning" are not in contradiction. Learning here means to go through threatening crises and to work out contradictions such that the present state of affairs is eventually transformed. "Transformation" here actually means (or at least can mean) that a former form of life is left behind. The erosion and the eventual collapse of a certain set of institutions and practices, motivated by its internal contradictions, leads to its overcoming.

Why would we talk about "learning" here and why would we translate the Hegelian concept of "experience," as developed in the *Phenomenology of Spirit*, to "learning" if this seems to be so misleading? What I want to grasp is the idea of an *accumulative process*. To employ the concept of "learning" then doesn't imply a denial of the potentially disruptive character of the "experience" that a form of life or a set of institutions have undergone. It only highlights the accumulative character of the process that has led to the erosion and eventual collapse. And it emphasizes the idea that the transformation to take place—the form of the new set of practices and institutions that will eventually replace the previous ones—will be shaped by the character of the erosions. It will, even if not following a strong and deterministic logic, be the "determinate result" of a determinate problem. It is, thus, the aspect of accumulation (which in turn is a way to get a hold of what is relevant in Hegel's "determinate negation"), not the supposed smoothness or peacefulness of the transition, that is at stake here.

At the bottom of our disagreement now lies the very understanding of negativity. Pensky accuses me of not adequately distinguishing between two different versions of negativity and contradiction, a difference that he applies to the difference between Marx and Hegel: "The clear difference is between Hegel's larger claim that the contradictory elements of a moment of ethical life are *compatible, even necessary* given the conceptual core of that form, and Marx's view of ideology as legible only from the perspective of its impending real collapse."

Pensky is right when he points out that for Hegel, negativity and contradiction are in some respect rather modes of being than modes of transformation or destruction, as with respect to the "contradictory mode of being" of a child or the contradictory mode of being of a modern family that is supposed to set its younger members free at some point. And clearly, dialectical transformation (and the destruction of the old) is in some respect a sign of the "liveliness" of a social institution, a sign of its functioning well (as in the process of the younger generation outgrowing the family of origins) rather than of its dysfunctionality (even if I find the reference to transitional states as childhood as a "contradictory" situation not really intuitive). It would be wrong though to ascribe this mode of dialectical transformation to Hegel and another, more radical one to Marx, as Pensky does. Pensky is right in holding that the instances of *Sittlichkeit* (ethical life) as portrayed in the *Philosophy of Right* are for Hegel (already) rational. Thus they would only be characterized by those "healthy" contradictions and processes that are somehow constitutive of the form or life itself rather than an immanent source of its destruction. But I have my doubts already with respect to the status of the civil society. Max Pensky seems to have an overly optimistic view here, whereas I ascribe a perspective to Hegel that emphasizes the destructive tendencies of civil societies and their inherent tensions, conflicts, and potentially unstable tendencies, threats that are different from the instability of a family that reproduces itself. But leaving this aside, Hegel knows of both the "harmonious" or constructive view of transformation, negativity, and contradiction and the destructive one that leads to radical transformation and overcoming of the form of life in question. To ascribe the latter ones to Marx alone would not only be an all-too-conservative reading of Hegel. It would also leave Hegel's *philosophy of history* out of the picture—and its vital and fundamental role for Marx's materialist version of it. While the *philosophy of rights* spells out the rationality of modernity and its social and political institutions (whatever we think of this enterprise), it is his philosophy of history in which Hegel gives us an account of the dynamics of history, an account of how this form of life came about. Here we see forms of life emerging and disappearing due to contradictions that rely on self-imposed (normative) standards. Think of the ancient mode of living that is destroyed by the principle of individuality (symbolized in Socrates) that it has itself brought about. In this case, the form of life doesn't only reproduce itself but enters a radical process of transformation (as does, in Marx, feudalism, which is destroyed in order to make place for capitalism). So we find both versions of contradictions and change in Hegel as well as in Marx. It is an interesting question how these two relate to each other. But neither a Hegelian dialectic nor my pragmatist version of it excludes the radical and destructive mode of negativity that Max evokes and holds against me.

Of course, this holds only as long as the destruction has a constructive side, but here we are back with the topic of accumulation and continuity in discontinuity. So even if one shouldn't attribute the two versions of contradiction (the "soft" and the "hard" one) to Hegel on the one side and Marx on the other, as an analytical point, it is important to be clear about these different ways in which negativity comes into the picture in order to parse out where the negativity requires radical change (hence learning can be dangerously adaptive if it is not ready to go for radical transformations) and where it doesn't (and learning is "normal").

One might of course criticize the leveling down or evening out of the respective differences that I seem to do, since in my account, "problem" and "crisis" are used more or less equivocally where the distinction seems to be just gradual. The question of how to get a hold of the qualitative difference between these moments that eventually evolves is certainly not an easy one. But even more pressing with respect to the plausibility of an accumulation account of social change is the question of how to conceive of the moments of disruption, contingency, and innovation that are part of historical transformations, as we know of them. The idea of accumulation itself is thus a debatable aspect. Does history actually follow the path of determinate negation and dialectical sublation? Are the crises we are faced with entirely of the sort where a strong dialectical concept of "contradiction" can apply?

The point in question can be put in terms of a distinction that Alasdair MacIntyre works with. He distinguishes between the ongoing "normal" dynamics of societies and cultures in which problems of various kinds come up and are solved without the need to transcend the framework in question. Analogous to Kuhn's "normal science," we are faced here with the kind of "normal" problem-solving dynamics without which a social formation wouldn't work at all. The second kind of crises MacIntyre refers to as "epistemological crises." Epistemological crises are not crises in epistemology but crises that transcend the very framework in which they have come up. There is no solution to the problem within an established framework; only by transcending it will a solution be presented. This is what we know of as paradigm changes or (scientific) revolutions.

Now what is at stake here is not only the supposed radicality of the transformation in question. Within a dialectical understanding of social change, the crucial question would be whether it is possible to arrive at an understanding of "rational paradigm changes"—that is, a mode of change and an understanding of it that can take into account the contingencies and the innovative moments as well as its inherent logic and the fact that revolutions don't come out of the blue. On this methodological level (that shouldn't be confused with the political level), we are not talking about a shallow middle way between reform and revolution. What is rather at stake is a more important and deeper issue: whether we succeed in theorizing paradigm changes as a result of neither unconnected and totally contingent radical innovations and events nor strict and deterministic logics of history.

In my framework, the notion of a learning process is a somewhat "debunked" version of stronger accounts of the "historical process," the reason for this debunking being that it allows for cautiously "building" up a newly reconstructed understanding of these processes, bringing together pragmatist ideas as well as some ideas of MacIntyre into a basically Hegelian framework. The reason for doing this is a methodological one, since I am convinced that there is something to be gained by a materialist and dialectic understanding of history while holding that serious systematic and reconstructive attempts have to be made in order to work with these ideas in contemporary critical theory.

There is another decisive question that Max brings up that is not easy to answer. If the accumulative dynamics of contradiction (whether we are well-advised to call it "learning" or not) leads to the demise of a particular constellation and a respective form of life, who then is left over to learn? Who is the *subject* or bearer of this experience? If there are destruction and demise, is there even continuity in place that justifies the idea of an accumulated experience? I can't claim here that my answer is already sufficient. If we don't want to evoke a somehow reified (and anyway unconvincing) version of "Geist" (spirit) as a macrosubject capable of learning here, the answer will be complicated.

The first steps toward a compelling answer though would be the following: As I have said earlier, the "subject" of experience has not completely vanished by being transformed. There is continuity since the new social order is not completely new but linked to the old one by way of "sublation." From an observer perspective, the new is a result of the old that contains elements of the old, not in terms of reminiscences but in terms of a continuity of the problem, in terms of it being the subject of the process; it is a process, after all, and not a series of unrelated events, so it can be individuated as a process—identical and nonidentical with itself as a change over time. We as observers might be able to see the continuity or to come up with and understand the dialectical narrative that constructs the continuity, but what about the "subjective" side of this experience? That is, what about the forms of life and the individuals "inhabiting" the forms of life that have now become uninhabitable and have gone down or even died out? Who is it then who would reflectively "know himself" as the continuation of the former form of life? Who, again, is the "bearer" of the experience described? Here we certainly need to say more about the media—language, concepts, institutions, buildings, streets, customs, narratives, and art—in which this reflection takes place if we don't want to fall back to an implausible analogy with the subject. And we should be careful not to fall into naïve metaphysics of the (collective) subject as unitary self-presence here.

When Max accuses me of pursuing a *functionalist strategy*, I again see a misunderstanding at work in his interpretation of the role of the functional. For him dialectical contradictions and (normative) dysfunctions are an alternative that he connects to Hegel/Marx on the one side and pragmatism or functionalism on the other. For me, to the contrary, the idea that where forms of life fail, they do so on functional as well as normative grounds is genuinely Hegelian. The concept of a normative-functional failure, crisis, or deficit that I apply is meant to grasp the particular kind of normativity that is at work here. To be sure, it is not easy to figure out in which way Hegel would have a normative critique of society, not only because the normativity part, as far as it doesn't conform to a Kantian-constructivist idea of normativity, is likely to be obscured but also because a superficial ("lazy," as Terry Pinkard calls it) reading of Hegel denies him a critical stance at all. The idea that normative and functional failures play a crucial role in understanding Hegel's approach to normativity (or since I don't necessarily claim to be true to Hegel in a philological sense, in order to develop a Hegel-inspired approach that shows us a way out of a freestanding conception of norms and even paths the way for a materialistic understanding if it) allows for foregrounding the crucial claim that transformations in normative orders are grounded in the materiality of forms of life and thus can and must be understood historically.

In my reading then, the deficit of bourgeois society—the crisis-prone dialectic that it undergoes—is a good example of a failure on normative as well as functional terms. If it fails, it fails on normative terms since it is not the (functional) fact of poverty as such that counts here but a deficit that can only come into view with respect to bourgeois societies' self-understanding as societies in which the individual gains his subsistence as well as honor through partaking in the labor-mediated mode of social cooperation that distinguishes these societies from their predecessors. On the other hand, this failure to live up to its self-understanding is not a moral issue alone. It is also the case that the mode in which it functions is violated by this failure, and this again will lead to instabilities of various sorts (in the long run). But yet again, this does not mean that civil society is prone to collapse on merely functional terms (as some again lazy reading of Marx would suspect). It is here that the intertwinement between the normative and the functional aspect comes to the fore.

Of course, it is not easy to spell this out without falling back into the simpler assumption that civil society is crisis prone because it produces anger on the side of the "rabble," which then causes rebellion. My intuition here is that the intertwinement is working on an even deeper level. The task here is somehow similar to the thesis defended by Joshua Cohen in his celebrated article "The Arc of the Moral Universe," where he makes the (very Hegelian) claim for ethical explanations, the claim, that is, that ethical grounds play a role in the demise of institutions like slavery.

I certainly agree that more philosophical work needs to be done in order to argue more convincingly for this claim. But however complicated it might be to spell out and defend this normative-functional approach, bringing in functional criteria here does exactly not serve the role that Pensky attributes it to. It is rather (and again) a slightly materialist tendency that informs my efforts: normativity is not the freestanding enterprise that Kantians would want it to be.

Now what is it that Rocío Zambrana finds fault with after giving an extremely insightful account of my approach throughout her chapter?

> Jaeggi's articulation of the entwinement of the functional and the normative is extremely insightful, yet her understanding of Hegelian contradiction and determinate negation neutralizes the critical purchase of her account. She remains squarely within classical readings of Hegel based on a conception of history as progressive and contradiction as the motor of progress. To be sure, Jaeggi works hard to rewrite the modality of Hegelian dialectics (necessity is not ontological but rather practical) and to dispel the specter of dialectical closure (learning processes are fallible, provisional, and pluralistic). However, her rewriting of contradiction and determinate negation does not allow her to fully develop the implications of her own account of the entwinement of the functional and the normative. The inversions of both norm and reality imply a *thwarting* of the goal at work within the entwinement of the normative

> and the functional that complicates any conception of historical learning.

212 I'm not so sure whether I understand the point in question. Let me try to spell out what I get here. It is, as I take it, the remaining optimism about the rationality of the supposed logics of history. That is, instead of really giving way to an open-ended history, radical contradictions, and the possibility that a contradiction actually might lead to nowhere, my account does not seem to take seriously enough the deeply ambivalent character of the transformations at stake. In my account, contradictions point to a *deficit* of the respective practice and the respective norm. As for the inversion of norm and reality, in my account, it goes like this: Let's say that capitalism applies to the norms of freedom and equality while at the same time exploiting workers and creating conditions of extreme inequality. In my (ideology-theoretical) view, this is not only some kind of a lip service, a norm evoked but not applied that eventually will or at least might be realized. It is a practical contradiction—the fact that in this case norms and reality do not coincide has systematic reasons that are connected to the very structure of the social formation in question itself. This assumed we do have to understand two further facts about the discrepancy between the natural-rights norms that guide the Western version of capitalist bourgeois societies and its brutal reality. First, it would be wrong to assume that the norms are simply *not realized* in this case. To the contrary, capitalism wouldn't even work without instituting freedom and equality in a certain way; the capitalist labor market, for example, relies on the assumption that the respective contract partners are free and equal. But of course it is the actual realization of the norms in question that leads to their inversion: capitalist exploitation is exploitation under the assumption of freedom and equality. These norms are inverted because they are realized. Second, if this does not make the norms in question completely obsolete, it does not leave them intact either. It is not just that reality; the practices and institutions in question "don't live up" to the norms. The fact that freedom and equality are factors in capitalist exploitation shows us a deficit with respect to the norms themselves (norms of whom we then can say have an ideological function). I wouldn't be opposed to seeing

this as a "thwarting" of the goal at work. What then is the difference to Rocío? My interpretation probably still has some kind of continuity in place. Even if, in my account, the ideas of freedom and equality have to transform themselves along the line of a more material understanding of equality and a social understanding of freedom (and even if, let's say, we had to "learn" that they can be realized only through a social revolution and in socialism), this analysis is still based on working out some potential implied in these norms, while Zambrana goes for an even more radical take on the inversion or thwartedness that has occurred and therefore for an even more openness of the outcome. While I still take it that the "inversion" in place leads to something—that is, while the idea and practice of socialist freedom would be a result of, again, an accumulative process that reflects the shortcomings of the former situation and the ideological character of the norms—Zambrana thinks of these results as ambivalent through and through. And while in my account it should still be possible to distinguish between learning and blockage, for Zambrana, blockage is not the fallibility of a solution at a later moment but intrinsic to the solution itself. If then any resolution equally entails a problem considered from another perspective, we will not be able to identify accumulative processes and hence we cannot claim "progress." Things are complicated, of course: faced with a variety of practices and a variety of dynamics that I take as independent and dependent from each other—that is, as interwoven in various ways—progress or learning in one respect might lead to blockages and regression in another. Still I want to argue that even in order to identify ambivalences, we cannot avoid establishing criteria. To diagnose "ambivalences" as such doesn't tell us much unless we are in a position to tell regressive from progressive moments apart, as difficult and messy as this might be. And while the measure for success (hence accumulation) certainly becomes problematic once we allow for both sides (norms as well as reality) to change within the process in question, I react to this difficulty by establishing a somewhat freestanding—and in some ways formal—account. Whether a "progressive" (nonideological) or accumulative social process is taking place is not something that we could judge according to substantial criteria (some goal that has to be reached). We should have a look at the process itself.

In this respect Rocío's interpretation of my position is somehow misleading. It is not that "more opportunities for collective self-determination" would serve as a definite criterion for me, as Rocío takes it. After all, capitalist societies can be said to be more dynamic, more open-ended, and even more pluralistic than some other socio-economical formations, a social order that is famous for learning by going through and reacting to various crises. In this sense "capitalism learns all too well"—but this is not learning in my specific sense.

Rocío also slightly overestimates or rather misplaces the role of pluralism for my idea of a critique of forms of life when she says that (according to me) a critical theory of forms of life should be "grounded in an 'experimental pluralism' since openness to other forms of life makes possible learning."

While it might be the case that openness to other forms of life enables learning, my approach is certainly not "grounded" in this idea of pluralism. Pluralism does not play such a fundamental role, even if Zambrana is right that (among other obstacles) the incapability to confront other forms of life in an adequate way should figure as a learning blockage. (But then what interests me more is the reason for this incapability, the modes of regression or the modes of ideological closure that lead to the need to avoid exposure to alternative forms of life.)

Actually I'm quite critical of the ever-so-often repeated phrase that modern societies are marked by the "fact of pluralism." I'm not sure that capitalist societies are actually as "plural" as liberal theorists assume. And for sure the starting point of my project was to not buy into the "fact of pluralism" in a way that prevents the critical assessment of forms of life (or, as it is, "comprehensive doctrines"). The final remarks of my book on "experimental pluralism" actually take up the pluralism issue where I left it in the introduction: seen as so many ways to figure out how we can and should live, this kind of pluralism is not the starting point for refraining from judgment but the other way around. Thus my proposal for criticizing forms of life does not neglect pluralism (and certainly doesn't defend a monolithic ideology of social homogeneity); it is compatible with the "fact of pluralism." But it certainly gives it another twist.

Now Rocío elaborates her thesis in terms of a comparison between Nancy Fraser's and my accounts of capitalism, where Fraser's account is supposed to make a case for Zambrana's understanding of negativity and ambivalence. I have had conversations about capitalism with Nancy for quite a while now (to the point that we are turning them into a book), and I am very much in line with Nancy with respect to the need for a renewed critique of capitalism in terms of a crisis critique. I myself think of the differences between Nancy and me primarily in terms of complementary accounts. She develops a theory of (contemporary) capitalism while I work out bits and pieces of the normative and socio-ontological questions involved. I think of Nancy's masterful way to spell out the unintended side effects within neoliberalism as an attempt that is grounded in identifying contradictions on the deeper, structural level of capitalism as a social order, contradictions and functional disorders that seem to be more than ambivalent. Still, there is an issue that Rocío has detected with great sensibility and insight: in the end these contradictions, as much as they are on the "objective side," become visible as political conflicts, which is another way of saying, here dialectics work without being grounded in a philosophy of history. This issue certainly needs to be discussed—but let me (in line with what I said in the beginning about the options for critical theory) just mention that a politicized version of dialectic and negativity would have less of a normative grip than I want it to have.

5. ETHICAL FUNCTIONALISM: THE TALE OF THE TWO VERSIONS (FREDERICK NEUHOUSER)

Let me get now to the philosophically most demanding issue: the deep-seated normative grammar of forms of life, as Frederick Neuhouser has raised it. Fred is absolutely right to point out that not only the ontological side of my account but also the very possibility of evaluating and criticizing forms of life depends heavily on how to comprehend their normativity and, more specifically, how to understand my thesis that forms of life are dependent on ethical-functional norms and modes of justification.

He is also correct in holding that my conception of forms of life as "normatively constituted entities" is an ontological claim that can be translated into a Hegelian framework as the claim that forms of life are instances of objective spirit—that is, of ethical life, or *Sittlichkeit*. (It is precisely the specific understanding of normativity involved that makes mine a Hegelian instead of a Wittgensteinian use of the term.)

This implies that "normativity" here has to be understood in a broad way, referring to the Hegelian distinction between "spirit" and "nature." Normativity then is not restricted to morality, the narrower set of norms that determine what we intersubjectively "owe to each other"; it is rather a general term implying that human or cultural forms of life are shaped and created according to rules that human beings have set into place and agreed upon (even if only implicitly). It is, in other words, the realm of (however distorted and however deficient) freedom that we are talking about with reflexivity and self-consciousness as a crucial criterion in place.

This is, as Fred puts it, a holistic and comprehensive conception. Forms of life are not merely *informed* by norms; they are *made out of* norms, structured by norms; norms as they are embodied in social practices are part of the social fabric. Forms of life consist, according to this understanding, of historically instituted norms that are embedded in the practices of everyday life. This makes it easier to explain how norms can structure our lives both explicitly and implicitly. The normativity of a social order then reflects the fact that we are involved in a set of practices that rely on normatively laden interpretations.

I find Frederick Neuhouser's Hegelian "translation" of these claims clarifying and helpful, and I agree with him that the notion of the ethical-functional justification is of crucial importance for my account of forms of life and the possibility of immanently criticizing them. However, it is far from clear how to conceive of the way normative and functional moments intertwine here.

What I disagree with nevertheless is his story about the "official" and the "unofficial" (hidden) version of my approach and his critique of the official version. While he is right that more needs to be done in order to give a satisfying account of the relation between normativity and the functional aspects involved in social practices, I want to argue that the "unofficial version" that Fred seeks to discover is in fact the official one—and that the real difference between our positions lies in varying understandings of materialism or, as it may be, the naturalism involved. These are difficult questions, of course, and I am far from thinking that I have solved all the normative and ontological questions that I raise in my book. It is the notion of the normativity of forms of life that needs to be elaborated in the first place and that I attempted to elaborate in the third chapter of my book. Precisely what kinds of norms are at stake here? On which kinds of norms are the legitimacy claims that a form of life (as a normative or spiritual entity) comes up with based?

(Note that this is not a first-person normative perspective. I am not arguing that a specific kind of norm should be in place here; I am still on the social-ontological level, asking in which sense and by what kind of norms forms of life are structured or even made out of practices and norms. Note also that I here assume that forms of life establish claims to validity or at least to adequacy. This is not a position that can be taken for granted, and I spend quite some time in order to make this plausible.)

My assumption is that the key to understanding the specific normativity of forms of life is to be found precisely in the simultaneously descriptive and normative character of the judgments that comes to light here. I have to admit that my argument here is rather complicated and possibly misleading since it evolves in three steps.

In the first round, I figure out what kind of norms make up the normative infrastructure of a form of life. How can the "soft," informal, and habitual nature of forms of life be reconciled with the prescriptive character of norms?

I build here on Georg Henrik von Wright's distinction among rules, prescriptions, and directives with the subcategory of *customs*, which are located in an interesting intersection between rules and descriptions. These customs, which I then translate into "sittliche Normen" (norms of ethical life), are the norms we are looking for, I argue, since forms of life are not directed by prescriptions but emerge so that they can be implicitly embraced, and it makes sense to call them "anonymous norms," since it seems to be the whole community including its past members who are the norm givers in this case. At the same time they cannot be what von Wright refers to as rules—if the paradigm case for rules are the rules of a game. Norms that make up and structure a form of life are, according to my thesis, somehow "anchored" in the world as against rules, which are typically self-justifying. I use Joseph Raz here in order to make my point: the norms that structure forms of life are nonautonomous. In contrast to rules, which are typically self-referential, creating "reasons for their own validity," the norms that structure forms of life (norms of ethical life) are connected with what Raz calls "wider human concerns." This is another way of saying that they have an "objective reference" (*Sachbezug*) that relates them to the world and can prove them wrong or inadequate.

It is here already that I explore a line of reasoning that, according to Fred, is part of the "unofficial story": that practices have an aim or a telos and that it is with respect to this aim that we can judge them as adequate or inadequate. This is a very important aspect since it is only then (according to my account) that we can work out criteria for a normative critique of these practices or the respective forms of life. This connectedness to "wider human concerns" and the objective reference also lays the ground for what I want to recover from a materialist understanding of forms of life.

If I have already (even if tentatively) introduced the theses that norms of ethical life (as those that constitute forms of life) are characterized by some kind of aim or telos in this first round, I haven't given an answer at this point about the kind of telos in play.

The next round now asks, on which basis are these norms of ethical life justified? What claims to justification are involved in forms of life, and what kind of justifications would someone bring up if we were to ask her why she leads a certain kind of life, thereby obeying a specific set of norms of ethical life? (Again, remember that this is a social-theoretical investigation at this point, not a first-person normative perspective.)

It is at this point that I develop the distinction between conventionalist, ethical, and functional justification.

Now the first point Fred accuses me of is that I reject conventionalist justifications altogether while he wants to save some room for them:

> I believe, however, that it is a mistake to reject conventionalist justification altogether and that Jaeggi herself is dimly aware of this, since the position she goes on to develop allows some space for conventionalist justification, understood in a specific way. Essentially her rejection of conventionalist justification goes wrong by confusing two very different senses of "convention": one in which the conventional is equivalent to the merely arbitrary and another in which the conventional is that which has been determined by actual human agreement—as in Rousseau's claim that *convention*, the coming together of human wills, is the source of right within society.[9] Rejecting conventionalist justification *tout court* is a mistake because norms that are conventional in the second sense I have distinguished can acquire a limited degree of legitimacy simply by having been agreed upon by those subjects affected by them.[10]

I don't reject conventional norms *tout court*. In fact, I argue that the fabric of the social is in part made up by conventions. My claim is only that "the deeper level," the raison d'être of a form of life, cannot be conventional if we want to defend the Hegelian claim that forms of life are instances of ethical life. Of course, here I speak of conventions in Fred's first sense, as defined by their arbitrariness. Their content is contingent, and the relevant agreement is a joint stipulation, without its content being grounded in anything beyond this stipulation.

This is related to the argument made earlier about the importance of "points of references" ("Weltund Sachbezüge") for norms of ethical life: with conventions, nothing really is at stake. Conventions are rules that we agree upon. They easily could be otherwise without that affecting the "wider human concerns" I introduced with Raz. Conventions are "up to us," and in each case there are conceivable alternatives that are equally good or workable.

We can barely speak of justifications here since the typical answer to our question "Why are you doing this?" would be, "We just agreed upon it." (My example here is driving on the right- or left-hand side of the road. While it certainly matters whether or not we are introducing some rule at all, it doesn't matter whether we agree on driving on the left or the right side. This is purely conventional.)

Fred now defends a second version of "conventional" that one can find in Rousseau and claims that I confuse the two meanings of the terms. But I don't actually ever refer to this second meaning. Are the first and the second meaning even instances of the same phenomenon?

If I were to give an account of Fred's second meaning here, I would say that in specific circumstances (for example, when it comes to democratic decision-making), the fact that we have agreed upon something serves as some kind of a *second-order justification*. In these cases, notwithstanding the content we have agreed upon and the reasons we might have for agreeing or not agreeing on a certain matter, it is the fact that we have all come together that gives democratic legitimacy to a certain outcome. But we should carefully note the difference here. If in this case someone asks, "Why do you obey the law?" and you say, "Because this is what we all have (democratically) agreed upon," the deeper meaning of this justification is not conventional itself. In this case we are following a rule we have all agreed upon because this is what a democratic procedure demands. It is the nature of democracy to enter into this process of reasoning and to conform to the outcome of the decision thereby made. But neither is this itself a conventional justification nor are the (first order) reasons that are exchanged within the deliberative process of a conventional kind. Now as Fred himself holds, the more important part of my argument is my claim that forms of life are structured or made out of functional-ethical norms (or, more accurately, that norms of ethical life, "sittliche Normen," are norms whose justification is ethical-functional).

Here he seems to agree with my general thesis. But he would prefer another account of what the ethical-functional refers to.

The interesting question here is, of course, how to understand the hyphen, the way in which functional and ethical dimensions are connected and inform each other. As Fred rightly notes, the distinction is only analytical. In real life (in real *social* life), the ethical and the normative dimensions are always intertwined. I am serious about the strict character of this intertwinement. This is why with respect to social formations, in my view, we can't even find instances of pure functionality.

Therefore, if in explaining "functions" I refer to biological functions, this is no mere coincidence; it is due to the fact that with respect to social formations and practices, it wouldn't be possible to come up with an example where the functional is not already entrenched in the ethical dimension. There is no purely functionally definable moment at which the question concerning the success of a nexus of practices could be aimed, but this is always already ethically colored. Social formations function, when they function, always in ethically qualified ways. (Fred, while in general agreement, seems to be a bit less strict here, allowing for a looser relationship—but I will get back to this later.) The other way around, ethical norms do not float free as a kind of "value heaven" above social practices, but as conditions of normatively predefined success, they are "embedded" in the practices that constitute the forms of life.

Now the dramaturgic setup of my argument is the following: if in justifying a certain practice and norm (a practice that is constituted by a certain norm) we were to use a functional-ethical justification, it would go like this: this norm is justified since it is functional for a certain practice. But such a justification is obviously redundant. It is functional only in an internal sense, which makes it into the kind of argument I discussed earlier with respect to the rules of a game where (in some respect) it doesn't even make sense to ask for justification since following certain rules in chess is just what playing the game is about. This is why Fred suggests that there is confusion at work. Such norms, he says, should be conceived of as "constitutive," not as functional. And he might have a point here, even if I am reluctant to use the concept "constitutive" (apart from general considerations about the distinction between constitutive and regulatory rules) since my whole point is that forms of life are *not* instituted by constitutive norms. Instead, I work out how this would be deficient as a functional justification, pointing to the fact that as functional norms, they are incomplete unless we add more—a further telos and point of reference of the practice in play. (My main opponent here is someone who would give an account of practice norms in terms of rules.)

This was a confusing way to set up my argument, but what I meant to say is that this kind of ethical-functional justification is deficient exactly because it fails to explicate and justify the point of reference to the function. Hence a functional justification seems to depend on a further specification of the purpose that it does not provide itself. Whether a particular norm is functional or dysfunctional depends, as I said earlier, on the purpose or objective that guides the corresponding practice and on the set of practices it is connected with.

A function is a function, therefore, only with respect to a goal to be realized within a larger context. This is why at this point, we have to transcend the internal mode of justification.

Forms of life (the practices and norms of forms of life)—this is the thesis—are justified on an ethical-functional basis. But in order for this to work, we must transcend the internal and self-referential perspective that we have been stuck in (and that a normatively weaker account would remain within).

This context transcendence is an important part of the official plot—the one that actually develops the teleological story Fred is asking for while trying to give it a less biological twist than Fred has in mind.

On the second level of my argument (developed in the third chapter), I deal with the nature of the internal normativity of forms of life and the criteria of its fulfillment or nonfulfillment, and this concerns the requirements that forms of life make on themselves and that are objectively posited with them. So if we take it that the point of being a medical doctor is to heal patients, this refers to a broader idea, related to a form of life, about the human body, healing, and so on. In order to make an ethical-functional argument work here, we need to relate this to the encompassing set of practices, to the claims inherent in a whole form of life, and to the way the different practices within a form of life interact (as Fred himself seems to suggest). But then we need a point of reference. The next step—the point of transcendence from the internal to the context transcending normativity—asks whether there is an overarching normative point of reference for the success or failure of forms of life as forms of life and hence whether there is something that is good about them and not only good for them.

Over against positions that would simply say that forms of life as such cannot provide any reasons for how they are constituted or for how they came into existence and thus conceive of them as self-contained reference systems that simply "are what and as they are," I am searching for a point of reference located outside this internal system of references (therefore context transcending while still being internal to the form of life in question). This seems to be exactly what Fred suggests: a functional (as well as an ethical-functional) argument has to take into account an aim or goal with respect to which a certain practice and the norm governing the practice is functional or dysfunctional. We can't justify forms of life in an ethical-functional mode unless we refer to these aims—which is to say, unless we come up with a point of reference outside of the internal circle of justification that I started with.

I distinguish here between internal and external criteria of excellence. If the internal criteria guide a specific context of practices—a specific form of life—this context as such is still not legitimized. The next claim now gets us back to the problem of the functional as opposed to the constitutive role: only as soon as this broader context of a form of life can be said to be adequate (to use a weaker term than "justified") will the ethical-functional norm function in a way that is more than constitutive (which then would be functional only in a self-referential sense).

But what then can "justify" the broader context of a form of life?

(Frederick Neuhouser might have been a bit too impatient with this rather tedious line of argumentation.) For this problem I come up with a solution no earlier than in chapter 4 of *Critique of Forms of Life*, where I argue that forms of life can be understood as (different) ways of solving problems that arise for us in historically and culturally specific and normatively predefined forms. Understood in this way as problem-solving instances, their success or failure is measured by their ability to solve these problems that arise for (and with) them. The success or adequacy of their practices and norms is then the point of reference for their ethical-functional justification.

But however annoying the architecture of the book here might be (I apologize for this!), this is, as I would insist, part of my official story—not a hidden unofficial story. To conceive of forms of life as problem-solving entities means to provide them with a structure within which it makes sense to attribute ethical-functional aspects while at the same time avoiding a full-blown teleological framework. Fred's suggestions concerning further qualifications here are more than welcome and fit well within my overall framework.

Note, however, that I have so far only outlined the structure but not given any content to it. (Problem solving is only the structure; social or biological reproduction, for example, is more than that.) But even though the disagreement between us seems to be partly based on a misunderstanding due to my overly complicated presentation of my position, there is one important respect in which we disagree. This concerns the aim (and the status of the aim) in question. Fred seems to take it for granted that the most plausible way to come up with an aim that makes functional-ethical arguments (or rather, the functional side of it) work is by referring to reproduction understood in a biological sense (and then supplemented by ethical considerations).

Fred here develops a Hegelian interpretation to understand how, when it comes to the realm of the social, ethical and functional justifications are always intertwined, and he points to a way to pursue the argument that he thinks I have neglected to the detriment of my account. In order to illustrate the argument in question and to make sense of Hegel's notion of the "living good," he refers to the family. The Neuhouser-Hegel account here is the following: the family has the function of biological reproduction on the one—that is, the functional—side. But reproduction here also has an ethical dimension: the family is responsible for socializing and educating individuals such that they are introduced into the realm of freedom. Fred agrees here with me that these elements are intertwined. He says,

> Clearly, child-rearing plays a vital biological function—in reproducing the species—although in a spiritual form of life, the family does not merely produce the bodies of the next generation; it also develops and nourishes the subjective resources children will need as adults in order to realize themselves as free, and it does so in such a way that participation in the family can itself be conceived of as a form of free activity. In this view, ethical and functional moments (where the latter is interpreted purely biologically) are always intertwined, even though it is

> possible to distinguish in thought two types of ends rational family life serves: the ends of life and the ends of freedom.

Fred now thinks that it is important to keep the first moment, the functional moment of biological reproduction, in play in order to preserve a materialist element in Hegel, the materialist aspect of "life" as an entity that has to be reproduced on more than the spiritual level, as one might say. And certainly this material dimension resonates well with the term "form of life." Fred suspects that I am in danger of losing this materialistic element by not providing a story about the ethical-functional along these lines while suggesting that a plausible version of the ethical-functional would be of the kind he spelled out with respect to Hegel.

This is where our real disagreement is located. Rather than providing an idea of the "content" of the telos of human life-forms (which is social reproduction), I stay with the formal account of "problem solving." This follows from my conviction that with respect to forms of life (human forms of life in the plural), it is not possible to identify an overall telos. Human forms of life, as fluid, historically variable, and modifiable formations, cannot be pinned down through functional conditions and essential features in a similar way to the form of life of giraffes or lions. Therefore I start in the middle of things: problems as they have evolved historically. I am looking for an account of functionality that is not restricted to this specific content but develops the argumentative pattern of a functional account that works for the realm of the social.

But more important, Fred identifies the "functional" with some biological notion and even thinks that this is the (only?) means to keep some materialism and the "life" part of Hegel's "living good" in play, whereas I would argue that I am including the material element in a different way. If I were to name our disagreement in a provocative manner, I would say that Fred one-sidedly tends to identify the functional (and the material element) with the biological, while my materialism (if I am successful in defending some) is some sort of historicized materialism. So what is really at stake here are two versions of materialism.

In order to make my point, it is important, first, not to separate the two dimensions, the ethical and the functional, from the very beginning and to understand the "intertwining" as strongly as possible. (It is telling that at some point, Fred speaks of the functional moment being "supplemented by ethical considerations.") Related to this is the second component: for me (and with my problem-solving approach), talk of "the functional" does not necessarily imply any reference to biological survival as such.

Let me explain. To conceive of the functional and the ethical as strictly intertwined with respect to the family indicates that the family does not have a *double* function that happens to come together in most cases. It means that in order to reproduce *as a family*, we have to do it in the mode of freedom (while the understanding of what this freedom consists in has changed over the centuries). We are faced here with what Marx called "enlarged reproduction." The reproduction of cultural forms of life is always already enlarged reproduction in that it is the reproduction of a form, a *Gestalt*, that human life has given itself. Human beings don't reproduce mere life; they always reproduce specific instances: historically instantiated and normatively embedded forms of human life. The conditions for doing this are historically changing. Thus the material element we are dealing with (the needs as well as the means to satisfy them, as Marx famously said) has been transformed by a history in which various ways of socially and culturally organizing social reproduction have occurred.

This materialistic account is not biological but historical and cultural. But it is still materialistic since the element of material necessity or material constraints comes into the picture such that every cultural form of life somehow "evolves around" the problems posed by its material circumstances. Conceiving of this in a historicized manner and forms of life as historically imbued instances of problem solving means that we can't get hold of them as referring to "pure needs" or "mere survival" but only through their historically specific form. And this specific form not only is another layer that would be on top of needs and biological functions (conceived of as an anthropological constant) but also affects what we see and experience as a problem all the way down. As Marx (and later Adorno) writes, "Hunger is hunger, but the hunger gratified by cooked meat eaten with a knife and fork is a different hunger from that which bolts down raw meat with the aid of hand, nail and tooth."[11] We live in a man-made environment that has shaped our material needs and the resources to resolve them all the way down. So the Hegelian notion of "life" is still in place, but it is life in the context of a world (or objective spirit).

But referring to "cultural" forms of life should not suggest that we are in a realm of unrestricted freedom and malleability. Cultural forms of life are in some respect still "given," not entirely made by us. As forms that human beings gave to their collective lives, they are not without constraints. As Marx has observed in *The Eighteenth Brumaire of Louis Napoleon*, human beings make their own history, "but they do not make it under self-selected circumstances."[12]

Now what does this imply for the connection between the ethical and the functional?

It is because forms of life (the practices that make up our forms of life) are historical and cultural in the sense I spelled out that neither purely functional problems nor purely functional solutions arise with respect to them. The historicity and malleability of what is at stake imply that there is an opening for ethical considerations. We can do otherwise here; we do what we do because we assume that it is *good* to do it this way, that this is the right way of doing things (organizing families either in an exogenous or an endogenous way; building the institution of family or marriage around the idea of love; conceiving of work as the most important means for social integration). I am not suggesting that these considerations are always explicit, but if it comes to defending this or the other social practice and form of life, I take it we would say that neither this is the way we do it (which would come down to what I understand as a conventional justification) nor this is what works/functions best, but we would say (and this is my understanding of the ethical-functional nexus) that this is a good way of functioning.

Here the ethical and the functional are not only intertwined empirically, since families always serve both the (biological) functional and the ethical moment, as it would be according to Neuhouser/Hegel. There is no way to separate out these aspects. The functional, so to say, always comes in an already ethical mode; it is ethically infused, constructed or structured in a way that is ethical all the way down. There is no way we can biologically reproduce without doing this in a specific culturally and ethically determined way.

This has one important consequence, which points to another sense in which my approach intends to be a form of materialism while trying to eliminate the reductionism that is often paired with it. If the functional is ethical, the ethical is also functional, an effect of the functionality of a certain practice / set of norms. What in the last instance points to a materialistic idea of morality may be a departure from Hegel and a move on to Marx. But as I see it, even in Hegel, these moments can be found.

The point is, norms have functions and a material aspect, such that their very shape and content is as it is because it serves these functions. This is so even in a weak version of dependency and evolutionary functions: they have emerged for a variety of reasons, but they couldn't have been sustained without somehow addressing and serving the practical problems in question that come up with the reproduction of a social group (or society). But then, this is the beginning of another long debate that I hope to get Fred engaged in at some point.

6. DEMOCRACY AND ALIENATION (JOHN CHRISTMAN)

I completely agree that John Christman and I have been up to similar questions along parallel paths in many respects, and I am delighted that we finally were able to enter a conversation about these issues. Most of all I think that the concept of relational autonomy that John has worked out prominently over the years comes very close to what I reconstructed as nonalienated mode of self-determination. Moreover he has certainly identified aporias—or, I hope, difficulties rather than dead ends—with regard to the normative stance of a nonalienated life that trouble us both.

The first aporia deals with the criteria that allow us to define the nonalienated self and in turn to uncover alienation. This is a most important issue of course if we want to use alienation as a standard for critique. My objective throughout my book on alienation is to argue for a *qualified subjectivism* here—that is, to develop criteria that are neither purely subjective nor purely objective. Whether someone is "alienated from herself"—from her own wishes, desires, and activities—should not be judged from an external point of view or some essentialist notion of the good life, real needs, or meaningful activity. After all, I conceive of alienation as an obstacle to freedom, not, as paternalist versions of alienation theory would have it, as an obstacle to realize the objective good or to realize human nature. At the same time, the diagnosis "alienation," if it is supposed to be meaningful, can't be based on the subjective experience and assessment of the subjects involved alone. The qualified subjectivism that I defend here seeks to argue for a middle path (between Scylla and Charybdis?): instead of coming up with substantive goals that a nonalienated person should have met, I propose to turn the attention toward the *process* of will formation and the process of becoming identified with something and someone itself. Inspired by Ernst Tugendhat's attempt to formalize the good, the analysis of phenomena of alienation focuses on *how* relating to oneself and the world is carried out rather than on *what* an act of willing strives to achieve. The concept of appropriation then refers to a way of establishing relations to oneself and to the world, a way of dealing with oneself and the world and of having oneself and the world at one's command. Alienation, as a disturbance in this relation, concerns the way these acts of relating to oneself and the world are carried out—that is, whether processes of appropriation fail or are impeded. Alienation can then be understood as an impairment of acts of appropriation (or as a deficient praxis of appropriation).

Now John Christman fears that this formal account is not solid enough to establish the criteria we are looking for. On first sight, it might look like I have only shifted the matter in question. What are the standards then for a process of appropriation to be deficient?

Pinpointing a narrative conception of the self as the source for a definition of the nonalienated self, John reconstructs my approach as follows: "Proper, genuine, and authentic appropriation is defined as that which results in an ongoing self-understanding that meets narrative or hermeneutic standards of intelligibility." But then, and I share this qualm with John, we have to come up with standards for an adequate narrative since "it is not exactly clear what it requires, for virtually any sequence of experiences and actions can be woven into a story." I totally agree: there is always, for example, the possibility of a completely coherent but still paranoid or illusionary narrative. Coherence as such can't be a good criterion for an adequate narrative. As John writes, "Some orienting framework must be in place and operating to determine when an appropriation sequence (in Jaeggi's sense) is intelligible as the person's own and not artificially constructed or externally imposed." We might only have a minor difference here. But as opposed to Christman, I think that some narratives actually "don't work." They don't work on their own terms; that is, it is possible to identify faults and flaws in the very formation of these narratives without having to refer to an (external) orienting framework. Here I think we should try to overcome the false alternative between a purely internal and a purely external perspective—that is, between granting all the interpretational sovereignty to the narrator and, the other extreme, judging her from an external view and the respective framework.

In fact this is an operation most common in everyday life. We distrust the guy who tells us with a grim look how much he enjoyed our talk, and we suspect that something strange is going on when someone starts to blush and tremble but pretends to be indifferent when he approaches us. It is the same hermeneutics of suspicion that we use when judging the coherence of a narrative. What we do then is to look at discrepancies and contradictions—incoherences in a superficially coherent plot. Very often these incoherences come to fore because there are different registers involved (bodily reaction versus official statement). But sometimes we have to ask further in order to illuminate the disruptions within the plot. And sometimes this won't be in the open unless demanding (or in this case, even professional) practices—like the one that the psychoanalyst is engaged in to find out about the latent dream content—are in place. These practices then not only point to a disruption or contradiction; they help to bring it about.

It is not by coincidence that I mentioned "blockages of experience" or "denials" earlier. If we want to refrain from what I called external criteria, we might be stuck with negative criteria. An adequate narrative then is the one that is not marked by learning blockages and denials. The criterion, in turn, is that it "somehow works," that we get along with ourselves without a certain kind of practical disruption. This might be less than the self-transparency and self-control demanded in some ideas of autonomy. (But again, here I am in agreement with John's search for a less rigid version of autonomy.) With respect to John's insightful discussion of Steven in *The Remains of the Day*, this means that there is no way of finding out whether he has been alienated (and nonautonomous) during the time of his unquestioned service then to inquire precisely into the conditions of his will formation and the way he has been practically involved in what he was doing.

So again, yes, any sequence of experiences and actions can be woven into some kind of story. But not every story will be an adequate one unless it is (1) coherent with respect not only to some sequence but to the sequence of action that is relevant for the bigger plot and (2) somehow coherent with respect to the outside world. That is how the paranoiac narrative comes to the light. Still, there is no way to get out of a certain kind of regress or the appearance of circularity here. What if significant parts of the outside world comply with a paranoiac narrative? At which point will a neurotic narrative crack open? There is no Archimedean point available from which to decide. But still, I am claiming that the practical reflective equilibrium that we undergo here (weighing up between the various perspectives and evidences) leads to a virtuous, not a vicious, circle.

My general take here is that the aporias that John mentions are aporias in the strong sense only if you start with an all-too-demanding and foundationalist idea of normativity and justification—an aspiration, whatever one might say in favor of it, that is much stronger, or at least of a different kind from what I have in mind by establishing alienation as a normative standard.

A second point should be mentioned in order to trace the differences between John's and my positions. When I introduce "appropriation" ("Aneignung") as the opposite of alienation (as that what alienation obstructs), this is not completely captured by the criterion of an intelligible narrative and a coherent self-understanding. It is a less cognitivistic notion from the very beginning, even if I am aware that Christman enriches his picture by referring to habits and prereflective moments as well. But even more important, it has an "inbuild" reference to the outside world that from the very beginning is meant to overcome the narrow focus on authenticity. Not being alienated in my approach is not only different from a "traditional" notion of autonomy; it is also different from being "true to oneself" or leading an authentic life. I would distinguish here between autonomy, authenticity, and nonalienated self-determination or self-realization. While Korsgaard has done an impressive job in complementing an all-too-rigid and all-too-decontextualized Kantian notion of autonomy as self-legislation with a sophisticated account of identity, I would still—as I said rather roughly at this point—claim that my (krypto-)Hegelian account of alienation arrives at a slightly different understanding. The first is the role of identification with the world: it is the Hegelian pattern of "being oneself in the other" that I evoke here by claiming that one needs to identify with something in the world and with one's deeds that make a difference in the world in order not to be alienated.

The theory of alienation conceives of relations to oneself and the world as equally primordial. Therefore, an impairment of the relation to self—not having oneself at one's command—must always also be understood as an impairment of one's relation to the world. What is at issue is both the appropriation of one's own personal history and the appropriation of one's own activities in Marx's sense—what is of concern is always an appropriation of the world and at the same time an appropriation of the (variously defined) given preconditions of one's own actions.

The leading idea here is that one is vulnerable in one's relation(s) to the world since identity consists in identifying with something and someone. This idea seems to be very close to what motivates the concept of relational autonomy. We are autonomous (or, as it is, nonalienated) in and through our relations to the world, which then also means that we are dependent and independent at the same time. Self-determination, nonalienation, and autonomy then mean to work through and have a certain stance toward this dependency and the web of relations that ties us with the world and the others.

This is not far from John's suggestion that alienation is an obstacle to agency—but it should enrich our understanding of what agency is, besides being open for reasons. It is on this ground now that I want to address John Christman's second aporia, the "critical stance we want to maintain regarding that condition in the contemporary world." What then is problematic about alienation? What is the normative point in criticizing alienation, "what exactly is the *harm* or *loss* that alienation represents," as John asks? And the other way around, is leading a nonalienated life a good thing in itself?

I have two provisional answers here. First, I don't think that leading a nonalienated life can be equated with leading a good or a happy life, nor can it be put on a level with being just or morally exemplary. A state of nonalienation does not make us happy or just in itself, and it certainly does not provide us with happiness. If alienation is an obstacle to freedom (and autonomy, broadly understood), the concept of alienation investigates not only what prevents us from living well but, more important, what prevents us from posing the question of how we want to live in an appropriate way. In other words, what is at stake are the very preconditions for living "less wrongly" or living a good life but not the good or just life itself. In this sense, the pathology of alienation is somehow a second-order pathology that encompasses the other pathologies that John Christman mentions when he asks how to distinguish alienation from "general lack of flourishing, or experience of anomie or malaise, or simply pain and suffering." This is how alienation "cuts deeper" (as John nicely puts it). But this also means that an alienation diagnosis doesn't come up with substantial requirements, demands, and proposals for living our (collective) lives.

This fits with John Christman's suggestion "to tie alienation to agency and agency to reason-giving, something required for deliberative democratic practices," even if, as I said, we differ in our account of agency.

I totally agree with John that democracy is an issue here. I would even go further: the solved riddle of alienation is democracy—and the other way around, the solved riddle of democracy is preventing alienation. By which I mean, if alienation critique does not come up with substantial suggestions, its second-order quality is exactly directed at ways to inquire into the conditions of leading our lives that one might translate into an encompassing understanding of "democracy as a form of life."

Furthermore, if the promise of freedom and autonomy is deeply linked to the self-understanding of modernity, then one of its standards of evaluation is how it allows us to foreground the dimensions of alienation that prevent us from leading a free and autonomous life. In this way, we can see how the critique of alienation can be seen as an immanent critique of modernity itself.

I seem to be more troubled though than John is about the normative basis on which to establish this criterion. I am not ready to take "democracy" as rock bottom—as simply "a fact of modern life" that would then provide us with normative criteria. Thus I would suggest to go one step further. If we take self-determination as the core issue, and if we spell out how collective self-determination is the precondition for individual self-determination, we actually can give reasons for the advantages of a democratic form of life. But still, in comparison to the universalistic content of a theory that takes a view of human nature as its starting point, the scope of alienation critique, as I reconstruct it, is limited to a specific shared form of life; its reach does not extend beyond its immediate context.

In order then to make a claim for this exact form of life and in order to argue for the value of freedom, democracy, and modernity itself, we need more: an inquiry into these forms of life and their respective merit itself. This then was my starting point for my book on the critique of forms of life.

NOTES

1. See for this David S. Owen, *Between Reason and History: Habermas and the Idea of Progress* (Albany: SUNY Press, 2002), 16.
2. Cited after Linda Zerrili, *A Democratic Theory of Judgement* (Chicago: Chicago University Press, 2016), 165–66.
3. Karl Marx, *Marx to Arnold Ruge. September 1843*; Karl Marx, "Letters from *Deutsch-Französische Jahrbücher*," in *Marx-Engels Collected Works: Volume 3: Marx and Engels, 1843–1844* (New York: International Publishers, 1976), 166.
4. Max Horkheimer, "Traditional and Critical Theory," in *Critical Theory: Selected Essays* (New York: Continuum, 1975), 215.
5. G. W. F. Hegel, *The Philosophy of History* (Kitchener: Batoche Books, 2001), 45.
6. Karl Marx, *Critique of Hegel's Philosophy of Right* (Cambridge: Cambridge University Press, 1970), introduction.

7. On such a crisis-oriented understanding of immanent critique, see also my book *Critique of Forms of Life* (Cambridge: Harvard University Press, forthcoming), chap. 6.
8. Rahel Jaeggi, *Kritik von Lebensformen* (Frankfurt am Main: Suhrkamp Verlag, 2014), 202–3.
9. Jean-Jacques Rousseau, *The "Social Contract" and Other Later Political Writings*, trans. Victor Gourevitch (Cambridge: Cambridge University Press, 1997), I.4.1.
10. For an account of the version of this view subscribed to by Rousseau, see Frederick Neuhouser, *Rousseau's Theodicy of Self-Love: Evil, Rationality, and the Drive for Recognition* (Oxford: Oxford University Press, 2008), 209–12.
11. Karl Marx, *Grundrisse: Foundations of the Critique of Political Economy* (rough draft), trans. Martin Nicolaus (London: Penguin, 1993), 92.
12. Karl Marx, "Der achtzehnte Brumaire des Louis Bonaparte," in *Marx-Engels-Werke*, Band 8 (Berlin: Dietz Verlag, 1972), 115. My translation.

CONTRIBUTORS

AMY ALLEN is liberal arts professor of philosophy and women's, gender, and sexuality studies and head of the Philosophy Department at Penn State. She is the author of three books: *The Power of Feminist Theory: Domination, Resistance, Solidarity* (1999); *The Politics of Our Selves: Power, Autonomy, and Gender in Contemporary Critical Theory* (2008); and *The End of Progress: Decolonizing the Normative Foundations of Critical Theory* (2016). Her current research focuses on the relationship between psychoanalysis and critical social theory.

ROBIN CELIKATES is associate professor of political and social philosophy at the University of Amsterdam, where he directs the research project Transformations of Civil Disobedience. He is also a program leader at the Amsterdam Center for Globalization Studies and an associate member of the Institute for Social Research in Frankfurt am Main. His publications include *Critique as Social Practice* (2009; English translation 2017); *Sozialphilosophie* (2017; coauthored with Rahel Jaeggi); and the three edited volumes *Global Cultures of Contestation* (2017; coedited with Jeroen de Kloet, Esther Peeren, and Thomas Poell), *Transformations of Democracy: Crisis, Protest, and Legitimation* (2015; coedited with Regina Kreide and Tilo Wesche), and *The Irregularization of Migration in Contemporary Europe: Detention, Deportation, Drowning* (2015; coedited with Joost de Bloois and Yolande Jansen).

JOHN CHRISTMAN is professor of philosophy, political science, and women's studies at Penn State. He is the author of various works in social and political philosophy, including *The Politics of Persons: Individual Autonomy and Socio-Historical Selves* and *The Myth of Property: Toward an Egalitarian Theory of Ownership* (2009). He is also the editor of *The Inner Citadel: Essays on Individual Autonomy* (2014) and (with Joel Anderson) *Autonomy and the Challenges to Liberalism: New Essays* (2005).

RAHEL JAEGGI is professor of practical philosophy with emphasis on social philosophy and philosophy of law at the Humboldt University in Berlin. She has received her MA at the Free University in Berlin, Germany, and her PhD at Goethe University in Frankfurt, Germany, and has taught at Goethe University from 1998 to 2009. In 2002/2003 she was visiting assistant professor at Yale University. From September to October 2012, she was visiting professor at Fudan University, Shanghai, and most recently was the 2015–16 Theodor Heuss Professor in the Philosophy Department at the New School for Social Research. Her areas of specialization are social philosophy, political philosophy, ethics, philosophical anthropology, and social ontology.

DANIEL LOICK is currently visiting professor of critical social theory at Goethe University in Frankfurt. After receiving his PhD in 2010, he was junior faculty member of the Philosophy Department at Goethe University, postdoctoral fellow at Harvard University, visiting professor at Humboldt University in Berlin, and Theodor Heuss Lecturer at the New School for Social Research in New York. His main research interests are in political, legal, and social philosophy, especially critical theory and poststructuralism. Among his publications are four books, *Kritik der Souveränität* (2012, English translation forthcoming as *A Critique of Sovereignty*); *Der Missbrauch des Eigentums* (2016); *Anarchismus zur Einführung* (2017); and most recently *Juridismus: Konturen einer kritischen Theorie des Rechts* (2017).

EDUARDO MENDIETA is professor of philosophy and associate director of the Rock Ethics Institute at Penn State University. He is the author of *The Adventures of Transcendental Philosophy* (2002) and *Global Fragments: Globalizations, Latinamericanisms, and Critical Theory* (2007). He is also coeditor with Jonathan VanAntwerpen of *The Power of Religion in the Public Sphere* (2011), and with Craig Calhoun and Jonathan VanAntwerpen of *Habermas and Religion* (2013), and with Stuart Elden of *Reading Kant's Geography* (2011). He has translated Apel, Dussel, and Habermas and has edited works by all these authors. He recently finished a book titled *The Philosophical Animal*, which will be published by SUNY Press in 2018, and is at work on his *On*

Philosophy and War. His most recent essay is on Richard Rorty and is titled "Richard Rorty and Post-Post-Truth."

FREDERICK NEUHOUSER is professor of philosophy at Barnard College, Columbia University (New York), specializing in German idealism and social and political philosophy. He is the author of four books: *Rousseau's Critique of Inequality* (2014), *Rousseau's Theodicy of Self-Love* (2008), *Foundations of Hegel's Social Theory* (2000), and *Fichte's Theory of Subjectivity* (1990). Much of his recent work has focused on the topics of recognition and amour propre, but he is currently working on a project on social ontology and social pathology in eighteenth-, nineteenth-, and twentieth-century thought. Other interests include psychoanalysis and film, especially the work of Krzysztof Kieślowski.

MAX PENSKY is professor of philosophy at Binghamton University, where he also codirects Binghamton's Institute for Genocide and Mass Atrocity Prevention. He has published widely in contemporary political philosophy and particularly in critical theory as well as in theories of transitional justice and the philosophy of international law. His books include *The Ends of Solidarity: Discourse Theory in Ethics and Politics* (2008), *Globalizing Critical Theory* (2005), and *The Actuality of Adorno: Critical Essays on Adorno and the Postmodern* (1997).

ROCÍO ZAMBRANA is associate professor of philosophy at the University of Oregon. Her work examines conceptions of critique in Kant and German idealism (especially Hegel), Marx and Frankfurt school of critical theory, and decolonial thought. She is the author of *Hegel's Theory of Intelligibility* (2015) as well as articles on Hegel, Kant, and critical theory. She is currently writing a book titled *Neoliberal Coloniality, Critique, Resistance*.

INDEX